INVENTING
MODERN
ADOLESCENCE

The Rutgers Series in Childhood Studies

The Rutgers Series in Childhood Studies is dedicated to increasing our understanding of children and childhoods, past and present, throughout the world. Children's voices and experiences are central. Authors come from a variety of fields, including anthropology, criminal justice, history, literature, psychology, religion, and sociology. The books in this series are intended for students, scholars, practitioners, and those who formulate policies which affect children's everyday lives and futures.

Edited by Myra Bluebond-Langner, Distinguished Professor of Anthropology, Rutgers University, Camden, and founding director of the Rutgers University Center for Children and Childhood Studies

Advisory Board
Joan Jacobs Brumberg, Cornell University
Perri Klass, New York University
Jill Korbin, Case Western Reserve University
Bambi Schiefflin, New York University
Enid Schildkraut, American Museum of Natural History and Museum for African Art

INVENTING MODERN ADOLESCENCE

The Children of Immigrants in

Turn-of-the-Century America

SARAH E. CHINN

RUTGERS UNIVERSITY PRESS

New Brunswick, New Jersey, and London

Library of Congress Cataloging-in-Publication Data

Chinn, Sarah E.

Inventing modern adolescence : the children of immigrants in turn-of-the-century
America / Sarah E. Chinn.

    p. cm.—(The Rutgers series in childhood studies)

  Includes bibliographical references and index.

  ISBN 978-0-8135-4309-3 (hardcover : alk. paper)—ISBN 978-0-8135-4310-9 (pbk. : alk. paper)

  1. Children of immigrants—United States—History—20TH century. 2. Conflict of
generations—United States—History—20TH century. 3. Adolescence—United States—
History—20TH century. I. Title.

  HQ792.U5C45 2008

  305.23086´9120973—dc22

2007044898

A British Cataloging-in-Publication record for this book is available from the British Library.

Visit our Web site: http://rutgerspress.rutgers.edu

Manufactured in the United States of America

For Kris

Contents

Acknowledgments

I began this book very quickly and finished it very slowly. The initial speed was thanks first to a summer grant from PSC-CUNY that kick-started the whole thing, and more extensively to a fellowship from the Andrew W. Mellon Foundation that gave me a year to sit in an office provided by the Center for the Humanities at the CUNY Graduate Center and research and write every day. David Nasaw and Aoibheann Sweeney deserve endless thanks for deciding that this book deserved that gift of time, space, and energy. Amy Chazkel was moral support, intellectual spur, and a great friend throughout that year and still, as well as a font of information about Brazilian swimsuit fashions. Thanks must also go to the participants in the "Divided Loyalties" seminar that was supported by the same Mellon money for their generous and canny readings of my work.

The CUNY Faculty Publication Fellowship Program provided additional course relief to complete the book, and my colleagues in the program, led by the redoubtable Brijraj Singh, were expert readers and advisors.

Sophie Bell, Joseph Entin, Hildegard Hoeller, Lori Jirousek-Falls, Anna Mae Duane, Jon Hartmann, and Jeff Allred are the best readers I could hope to have. Their support through the writing and rewriting of this book has been a privilege and there are few pages here that have not benefited from their close and careful attention.

Robin Bernstein was the kind of reader every scholar dreams of. Her deep understanding of what this book was about and the myriad ways in which it could be improved were invaluable to me in the final stages of revision.

Although my experience with editors at Rutgers University Press felt much like the 1990s sitcom heroine Murphy Brown's with assistants—it seemed that no sooner had one arrived than he or she decamped to greener pastures—the press never missed a beat, or a deadline. Particular thanks go to Melanie Halkias, my editor at the beginning of the project, Kendra Boileau, who accompanied me through the process of readers' reports and revisions, and especially to Adi Hovav, who has carried this book through to the home stretch. Thanks, too, to Marilyn Campbell for chasing down miscreant copy editors and never once losing her cool.

It is a truism of academia that our institutional lives—teaching, advising, administration—get in the way of our "real" work of research and writing. Certainly it's hard to maintain both kinds of labor, but I can't imagine a scholarly life without my colleagues and students at Hunter College. I adore teaching at Hunter, and many of the ideas that found expression in these pages I first tentatively tried out on my undergraduate and MA students. Hunter students' passion for learning, their intelligence, their smarts, their uncertainties provided much of the inspiration for me to think about the history of young working-class people like them.

I couldn't ask for a more supportive work environment than I have found in Hunter's English Department. Senior colleagues, particularly Richard Barickman, Harriet Luria, Charles Persky, Trudy Smoke, Sylvia Tomasch, and Barbara Webb showed me how a truly collegial department can and should be run, how to keep principled disagreement separate from personal respect. I am proud to call Cristina Alfar, Jeff Allred, Rebecca Connor, Candice Jenkins, Lynne Greenberg, Jan Heller Levi, Donna Masini, and Mark Miller not just colleagues but friends, whose insights and wisdom have made the past six years such an adventure. Thom Taylor is a god among men, and all good things should come to him.

My co-collectivists at *Radical Teacher*, particularly Sophie Bell, Michael Bennett, Jackie Brady, Liz Clark, Linda Dittmar, Joseph Entin, Louis Kampf, Paul Lauter, Dick Ohmann, Susan O'Malley, Liz Powell (taken from us much too soon), Erica Rand, Bob Rosen, Saul Slapikoff, and Leonard Vogt, have kept my wits sharp and my politics honed. It's an honor to be one of their number.

The fact that Sophie Bell's and Joseph Entin's names appear several times in these few pages testifies to their centrality to me as colleagues, coconspirators, and friends. I cannot overstate the fondness and respect that I feel for them, to the extent that I have trouble remembering what my personal and intellectual life was like before we discovered each other. Sheri Holman is the writer friend every academic should have; in fact, she's the friend every person should have. Sarah Kelen listens even when I don't have much interesting to say, which is more often than I would like. My parents, Carol and Geoffrey Chinn, have supported me in innumerable ways.

This book took me longer than I'd anticipated, for a variety of reasons, personal and professional. What slowed me down the most was what has infinitely enriched my life: my children, Gabriel and Lia. While my hopes for them are unlimited, I know that I will be satisfied as a parent if they grow up to be as fun-loving, as shit-kicking, as revolutionary as the young people I chronicle here.

And Kris Franklin, to whom this book is dedicated, exists for me outside time. She has been my companion, my fellow explorer, my beloved partner for more than half my life, and there is no part of this book that she has not inspired in one way or another. I only hope that it comes close to embodying her best qualities: strength of character, sharpness of intellect, commitment, compassion, and love.

Parts of chapter 3, "'Irreverence and the American Spirit': Immigrant Parents, American Adolescents, and the Invention of the Generation Gap," appeared as "'To Reveal the Humble Immigrant Parents to their Own Children': Immigrant Women, Their American Daughters, and the Hull-House Labor Museum" in *Our Sisters' Keepers: Nineteenth-Century Benevolence Literature by American Women*, Jill Bergman and Debra Bernardi, eds. (Tuscaloosa: University of Alabama Press, 2005).

INVENTING
MODERN
ADOLESCENCE

Introduction

"I DON'T UNDERSTAND WHAT'S
COME OVER THE CHILDREN OF
THIS GENERATION"

The 1980s, the years of my own adolescence, were the decade of the films of John Hughes and his muse, Molly Ringwald. The most celebrated movie in his oeuvre, *The Breakfast Club* (1985), featured five teenagers, each of whom fit a specific adolescent stereotype: the jock, the bad boy, the nerd, the weirdo, the popular girl. Forced together for an all-morning detention, the five argued, got high, formed new alliances, and, finally, came to understand that despite their superficial differences they had one crucial thing in common: they were all teenagers in an unjust adult world.

Coming from a teen culture in England in which this was *not* the common wisdom, and in which clothing styles, racial identity, social class, political affiliations, and taste in music all combined to construct a variety of specific (and often mutually exclusive) youth identities, I found exotic the message that differences in style were ultimately meaningless.[1] Although a mainstream urban youth culture was definitely in abeyance in the mid-1980s in the United States, on hiatus from the fierce energies and fashion innovations of punk and funk and before hip-hop and its attendant styles reached beyond black and Latino neighborhoods, Hughes's movies represented an adolescent culture bubbling away in suburban and small town high schools, gently rocked by the conflicts between jocks and nerds, popular kids and hermits, bad boys and yearbook editors.[2]

In retrospect, the manageable suburban adolescents represented in popular culture during the 1980s were the exception rather than the rule when it comes to the way teenagers have been imagined in the United States. However, there was no question that they *were* teenagers, that is to say, members of a defined, knowable age cohort who had in common, if nothing else, their identities as adolescents. The 1990s returned the image of adolescence to its previous incarnations—threatening, exciting, wild, unpredictable, sexually powerful, and uncompromisingly urban—with the twin phenomena of postpunk rock and hardcore rap, movies like Larry Clark's *Kids*, and new fashions in clothing and body styles that sufficiently outraged parents and the mainstream media. Ironically, this combative relationship between the adult power structure and teenagers seemed both comfortable and convenient for all involved: older people could rest assured in their sense of superiority and confidence that this new resistance at worst opened up new market possibilities, and young people could occupy various postures of rebellion and independence through combinations of different commodities. Adolescent stroppiness has always been, after all, inextricable from the marketplace, from the short dresses and shorter haircuts of the flappers to the leather jackets of Marlon Brando and James Dean, the foppish glamour of the Rolling Stones, the antifashion of hippies and punks and (later) Seattle-birthed rockers, and the violence-infused glamour of gangsta rappers.

Although the insight that youth rebellion is more often than not intertwined with the pressures of consumer capitalism is hardly earthshaking (which is not necessarily to say that the market wholly co-opts or defangs the power of the protest), it did lead me to become interested in where these assumptions about adolescence as a time of *épater les adultes* came from.[3] I knew from my work in nineteenth-century U.S. cultures and literatures that the equation of adolescence with social mutiny was a fairly new phenomenon: among the bourgeoisie of the antebellum period and into the late nineteenth century, harmony between children and parents of all ages was a moral imperative. In texts in which there was generational conflict, the source was most often identified as a larger dysfunction outside the family that disrupted the family more generally.[4]

By the mid-1920s, however, this assumption of sympathy between parents and their adolescent children had become increasingly moth-eaten. It is an indication of the cliché that conflict between teenagers and their parents had become that Sinclair Lewis's 1922 satirical novel *Babbitt* took for granted that the Babbitts would complain about their distance from their son Ted, despite the comparatively good-natured relationship within the family. After a family dinner and an enthusiastic conversation between Babbitt and Ted about the virtues of correspondence courses, the young man takes off to give his friends a lift to their chorus rehearsal (could his choice of leisure activity be any less threatening?). Once Ted has left, Myra Babbitt laments: "Ted never tells me anything any more. I don't understand what's come over the children of this generation. I used to have to tell Papa and Mama everything, but seems like the children to-day have just slipped away from all control" (Lewis 75).

For Babbitt, this is a recent development. His daughter, Verona, a few years older than Ted, seems much less mysterious to him. During a party that Ted hosts for his high school senior class, Babbitt recalls a high school party held by Verona, eight years earlier, in which "the children had been featureless gabies," pliable and undistinctive. Ted's friends were quite different, not children but "men and women of the world, very supercilious men and women. . . . Babbitt had heard stories of what the Athletic Club called 'goings-on' at young parties; of girls 'parking' their corsets in the dressing-room, of 'cuddling' and 'petting,' and a presumable increase in what was known as Immorality." While this is not markedly different from the teenage affection a young George Babbitt bestowed upon his soon-to-be wife Myra Thompson, to him it feels quite separate. These young people "seemed bold to him, and cold" (Lewis, 185). For his part, Ted Babbitt condemns his father in the most damning terms he can imagine: "He doesn't know there's any fun going on anywhere" (187). (Ironically, Babbitt himself says the same thing about Verona, with her New Woman seriousness and her interest in self-improvement.)

What happened to American adolescence in the decades around the turn of the nineteenth century that made George and Myra Babbitt, the most phlegmatic of parents, assume that they have to worry about, and be held in contempt by, their teenage son? Most studies of adolescence place the development of this new identity in the 1920s and 1930s, with the flaming youth, the flappers, and the sexual freedom that cinemas and automobiles afforded young people of the middle classes.[5] Moreover, the number of young people attending high school increased precipitously at the beginning of the twentieth century. Joseph Kett has argued that the popularization of high school attendance among the upper working and middle classes that reached a peak in the 1910s was a powerful factor in redefining adolescence as a time and high schools as the place for socializing young people into the culture as a whole, "preparing [them] for membership in social and economic groups," reinforcing their membership in an age cohort while strengthening their class affiliations (236). Many of the rituals of adolescence, and the nostalgic myths to which adults look back, have grown out of the mass experience of a high school education and the feelings of age-group solidarity that developed from that experience (a solidarity that *The Breakfast Club* more than half a century later clearly invokes).

Many historians of adolescence have demonstrated that despite their group consciousness and apparent daring, the young people of the first two decades of the twentieth century were remarkably passive in relation to their parents (and, in fact, all adults)—much more passive, in fact, than was expected of prepubescent boys. Ted Babbitt himself is hardly a rebel, his most pressing social engagements being at school, church, chorus, and the local ice cream parlor. But it is telling that a twenty-first-century reader would be surprised by the lack of conflict between the Babbitts and their adolescent son, particularly since he manifests all the other signs of what we now understand as teenagerhood: the creation of a separate culture defined by fashion, commercial recreation, sexual experimentation, and membership in an age cohort. What is the history of this assumption of antagonism between adolescents and their parents?

I got my first clue to answering this question when I taught a course on the New Woman in U.S. culture from the 1880s to the 1940s. At the beginning of the course, we read Jane Addams's 1912 memoir and social history *Twenty Years at Hull-House*, and one story in the text leaped out at me. In her work at Hull-House, Addams became increasingly worried about the disintegrating relationships between immigrants and their U.S.-born adolescent children. Fully Americanized, usually working full-time in factories or department stores, with access to some disposable income and an impressive array of leisure activities on which to spend it, these young people developed a sense of superiority and even contempt toward their "greenhorn" parents that disturbed Addams. In response to the growing distance between parents and children, particularly mothers and daughters, Addams came up with the Labor Museum, a space in which immigrants could exhibit their native crafts. Addams's plan was not to display primitive folkways to a sophisticated bourgeois audience; rather, she hoped that the museum would show the teenage children of these immigrants how similar their factory work was to the traditional crafts in which their parents were steeped, and thereby reunite families through the dignity of work.

This episode in *Twenty Years at Hull-House* struck me with unusual force. As I began my research, I saw that at the turn of the century and into the 1920s, the teenage children of immigrants occasioned an impressive amount of hand wringing among reformers, sociologists, journalists, creative writers, educators, policy makers, and intellectuals of all persuasions. Moreover, the terms in which they discussed these adolescents were remarkably similar to the ways in which teenagers were agonized over for the century that followed. Concerns that writers at the end of the nineteenth and in the early twentieth centuries explicitly linked to the young people of immigrant communities—the explosion of commercial sites of leisure (amusement parks, dance halls, theaters, and beer gardens, for example), a loosening of controls on premarital sexuality, rebellion against parents and other authority figures—became the defining characteristics for teen culture more generally as the twentieth century progressed.

In fact, I came to recognize that the children born to the millions of immigrants who arrived in the United States between 1880 and 1920 and who lived in densely populated urban areas were the first "teenagers," as we understand the term today (although the word "teenager" itself did not come into use until several decades later). Rather than locating the beginning of a teenage identity in the 1930s, as Grace Palladino does in her book *Teenagers* (1996), or in the 1910s and 1920s, as Joseph Kett did in his groundbreaking *Rites of Passage* (1977), we can look further back, into the late nineteenth century, to see the foundations of U.S. culture's creation of the category of adolescence. United with each other, and often against their parents, by their familiarity with the

English language and their experiences as city kids, the immigrant young people constructed an identity—most commonly referred to as "youth" by contemporary commentators—that was cemented by participation in commercialized leisure, popular culture, and a kind of bricoleur Americanism that combined elements of their cultures of origin and what they saw as defining characteristics of "being American."

A combination of forces unites these young people: their class; their relationship to shifting labor markets; their involvement in and usually enthusiastic engagement with the semi-public, semi-private scenes of commercial amusement; their separation symbolically if not wholly from their parents, which freed them, at least in part, from adult supervision; their surprisingly self-conscious membership in an ethnically diverse, generationally specific, mixed gender cohort; their insistence on themselves as Americans. As *Inventing Modern Adolescence* shows, working-class youths carved out an identity that was sui generis, a new kind of American identity that then traveled beyond the geographic boundaries in which it was formed.

I also contend that dominant assumptions about immigrants and the worlds they made for themselves and their children in the cities of the turn of the century provided the framework for later beliefs about teenagers. The need to control the teenage children of immigrants—their seemingly insatiable appetite for fun, their sexual desires, their unprecedented spending power—set the stage for future conflicts between adolescents and adult authority that reappeared time and time again in social science literature, in novels, in films, and in the American imagination, and that did not appear in mainstream representations of adolescence until several decades later, emerging out of networks between immigrants and urban bohemians, filtered through the children of these first adolescents, and coming to fruition in the years after the Second World War, when white ethnics were almost wholly integrated into U.S. society.

What liberal and conservative social critics of the American fin-de-siècle had in common was a belief that adolescents had an innate desire for pleasure and recreation, but that the commercialization of recreation had transformed a healthy and generative need into a corrupted search for cheap thrills. Debates that raged over appropriate recreation for working-class youth, particularly young women, stemmed from a variety of sources. These concerns melded stereotypes about southern and eastern European immigrants with the meanings implicit in the emerging category of the adolescent, forming a new American sense of self that outlived its connections to immigrant identity and took on its own character. While these early discussions of adolescents conflated their urban immigrant circumstances with their age identity, within a few decades the language used about this particular group of young people migrated to the larger class of adolescents, particularly (and ironically) the bourgeois Anglo teenagers who were previously defined in opposition to these working-class kids.

This book, then, is about how adolescence, or, rather, *the adolescent*, emerged at the end of the nineteenth and beginning of the twentieth centuries as a new object of theory and prescription, an identity separate from childhood on the one hand and adulthood on the other, and how that identity formed in immigrant communities in the major cities of the U.S. Northeast and Midwest.[6] American studies has long been interested in how specific elements of U.S. identities are formed and find their way into the mainstream of the culture. As Michael Omi and Howard Winant have argued in relation to race (with a methodology that can certainly be extended to other categories of identity), American identity formation is a "sociohistorical process by which racial categories are created, inhabited, transformed, and destroyed. . . . It is a process of historically situated projects in which human bodies and social structures are represented and organized" (55). For Omi and Winant, the status of "race" is less interesting than the process of what they call "racialization"—the ways in which racial identity accrues, shifts, folds in on itself, and undergoes changes that are historically contingent but, in the aftermath, feel inevitable.

Age categories work in very much the same way. While the concept of adolescence has been part of the public American imagination for only a little more than a century, and the figure of the teenager for just over half that time, young people and adults today see as transparent and eternal the assumption that adolescents have "the right to choose their own friends and run their own social lives, based on teenage notions of propriety and style, not on adult rules of appropriate conduct," and we connect that belief directly to the experience of being an adolescent (Palladino 8). Nonetheless, that sense of self is hardly inevitable or necessary: it grew out of a specific set of historical, material, and cultural conditions that combined to make possible the quasi-independent identity of adolescence. There is a growing field of study around what Joe Austin and Michael Nevin Willard have called "age formation," that is to say, an examination of "the changes in the way 'youth' is historically constructed and understood as a social identity, . . . the discourses and meanings that are applied to young people and their lives" (4).

In light of this work, I have found myself exploring how discourses that later characterized adolescence were mapped onto the children of immigrants in large cities at the turn of the nineteenth into the twentieth century. The conventional definition of teenagers as not just as people over twelve and under twenty, but rather as young people suffused with the "determination to establish separate identities and to demonstrate their independence, one way or another, from their parents' world [that] often brands teenagers as potential troublemakers in the public mind," seems to dovetail perfectly with the kinds of fears immigrants, reformers, and anti-immigrant activists had about this huge new group of adolescents (Palladino xiv). At the same time, like all social formations, adolescence did not remain stable and unchanging. Like other social categories, adolescence "is marked historically by complex processes of continuity, rupture, and transformation" (Austin and Willard 3).

Mauricio Mazón's description of the adolescents who came of age during the Second World War functions as an excellent definition for the group that in 1941 was first labeled "teenagers": this group was "more independent economically than any preceding generation of American youth. They made their tastes felt in matters of clothing, movies, music, and language, and their younger siblings copied them" (7).[7] In his landmark study of (mostly male) adolescence, *Rites of Passage*, Joseph F. Kett traced the development of people who by dint of their age fell into the category of adolescence, and the identities of "adolescent" and "teenager" that crystallized around those people in the middle decades of the twentieth century. For Kett, the "pattern of age segregation" that characterizes contemporary adolescence is one of the most striking hallmarks of teenage identity and a singular development of the last century (3). In large part, Kett argues, the rise of the adolescent is intimately linked to the industrialization and urbanization of the United States, as young people became increasingly economically powerful, and as consumer choices became more available to them. These changes are reflected in the nostalgia among urban elites for "the rural past as a time when young people were firmly in their place, subordinated by the wise exercise of authority and bound tightly by affective relationships to family and community" (Kett 60).[8]

This nostalgia, in large part fictional, was nothing new. As Paul Boyer has shown, most reformers in the nineteenth century held onto the "conviction— explicit or implicit—that the city, although obviously different from the village in its external, physical aspects, should nevertheless replicate the moral order of the village" (viii). Moreover, reformers yearning for an agrarian past (which, ironically, was the background of many of the city dwellers they were trying to reform) ignored the realities of rural life, since in fantasizing that "communal warmth and subordination had been characteristics of the past, they missed all the elements of tension and conflict between age groups and ignored the footloose ways of antebellum youth" (Kett 61).

At the same time, these footloose ways were most usually attributed to "boys," a category that extended from prepubescence into the years before marriage. Boys were firmly distinguished from "men": a man "was expected to be a distinguished figure—sober and purposeful—while the boy possessed a sense of play that was utterly unacceptable in a man" (Rotundo 7). The end of boyhood did not signal the beginning of adolescence but movement *toward* manhood, a limbo period in which a young man "took his first steps toward marriage, a life's work, and a home of his own" (Rotundo 54). Even with the invention of "boyology," as Kenneth Kidd has shown, the definition of "adolescence" was inseparable from that of "boyhood," which stretched well into the teens, as far as organizations like 4-H or the YMCA were concerned. The concept of "youth," which began in a boy's teens and extended up to marriage or comfortable bachelorhood, was not adolescence as we know it now, but a kind of apprentice manhood, in which the "savage boy" was trained up into an assertive man.

Until their entrance into adulthood, though, young people were encouraged to lie low and deal as little as possible with the outside world. For much of the nineteenth century, Americans were eager to follow Rousseau's recommendation that young people maintain a childlike innocence for as long as possible. Although puberty as a period of biological development was seen as a time of great change and tumult, the cultural response was to calm the storms as much as possible and encourage self-restraint, obedience to authority, and, in the years after 1840, to regulate young people's environments and activities to "guarantee the right moral development for children and youth" (Kett 116).

Even if this kind of "moral development" was equally desirable for the working-class immigrants who increasingly peopled the United States and thronged the cities, it was certainly much less possible. The overcrowding of immigrant tenements, the need to send children out into the workforce, and the often more communal patterns of child rearing presented a significant challenge to bourgeois assumptions about the nurture and training of adolescents.[9] While the divisions between middle- and working-class social expectations had always been problematic to all parties (the complaints of the Tract Visitors of the mid–nineteenth century well attest to this), this new adolescence developed in a space that was created in large part not just by class but also by the predominance of immigrants in large urban areas, to the extent that the metropolitan working class was often indistinguishable from the group constituted by immigrants and their children.[10]

As I show in the chapters that follow, demographic, cultural, and legal changes brought into being the adolescence we recognize today. The campaign against child labor, especially successful in large urban areas, extended childhood into the early teen years, cordoning off the years after fourteen (and, in some areas, sixteen) for paid work. With children largely excluded from the labor market, and the marriage age climbing into the midtwenties, a new group of young people, old enough to work but not yet of an age to marry, dominated urban workplaces. In the early days of this new identity, formed around the coconstituting phenomena of teenage labor and commercial leisure, adolescence began later than we now imagine it, usually around fourteen, and could last into the early twenties.

Chapter 1 explores the changing demographic and discursive patterns of the late nineteenth century that made space for this new identity. The immense upswing in southern and eastern European immigration, mostly Catholic and Jewish, reshaped the urban working classes in major cities throughout the United States, particularly on the East Coast and in the Midwest. At the same time, psychologists and social reformers were taking an increased interest in adolescence as an age category. These two phenomena were filtered through a belief on the part of young working-class people that participation in leisure, mixed-sex socializing, and freedom of movement were nothing less than their due as single wage earners in brightly lit cities. The new adolescents socialized in age-segregated cohorts, saw leisure as inextricable from youth, and recreated urban space and working-class pleasures in their own image.

I discuss the work of psychologist G. Stanley Hall, whose 1904 magnum opus *Adolescence* both rejected growing concern about this new kind of young person and provided templates for analyzing adolescent development.

Chapter 2 traces one origin of that sense of self—the campaign against and phasing out of child labor in favor of adolescent workers. The increasing legal and customary exclusion of children from paid labor contributed to the belief in childhood as a time of play, intellectual and physical development, and nurturance of all kinds, a definition that for the first time was extended to children of the working classes and the poor. As a result, the workplace became a site of socializing and socialization for the adolescent children of immigrants.

Tracing the development in the late nineteenth and early twentieth century of conventions for photographically representing children, I show how Lewis W. Hine, the in-house photographer for the National Child Labor Committee (NCLC), borrowed from these conventions to construct an image of the child worker for the Progressive Era. These children were trapped by the claustrophobic spaces of city tenements, dwarfed by immense machinery in textile mills and coal pits, handier with an oyster knife or a berry-picking pail than with a doll or a ball. Drawing upon the muckraking of Jacob Riis, the stark industrial images of Timothy O'Sullivan, the sensitive portraiture of Gertrude Käsebier and Edward Steichen, and the compositional virtuosity of Alfred Stieglitz, Hine constructed a photographic language that was highly connotative, speaking beyond the immediate message of the images or the captions he wrote to accompany them.

Hine's lesser-known pictures of young workingwomen and workingmen, taken between 1890 and 1930, represent adolescent labor as energetic, efficient, and modern, the opposite of child labor. While much of the work these young people performed is similar to that done by the children in his NCLC photographs, his representation of the work could not be more different. In contrast to the claustrophobia of the tenement parlor table and the overwhelming size of machines on the factory floor, adolescent workplaces are, in these pictures, well ordered, clean, and spacious.

In Hine's photographs, as well as in their own self-representation, these young women and men integrated themselves into the economic life of their immigrant communities, creating an identity for themselves within the commercial world. Implicitly, then, the movement against child labor promoted the movement of adolescents into the workplace, the site in which they gained access to the conditions that made their identification as a group possible: spending money, freedom from familial control, and heterosociality.

Chapter 3 examines the language of the generation gap, a stereotypical complaint against American teenagers, and traces its origins to the divisions between immigrant parents and their American-born or -raised children. The change in power relations between immigrants who had trouble adjusting to the New World and their children who quickly assimilated the English language and American customs is a staple of the immigrant narrative. But this division was exacerbated by the financial power adolescent children of immigrants wielded, encapsulated by the phrase "I am earning my living and can do as I please." The majority of the chapter is taken up by an analysis of Jane Addams's Labor Museum and the ways in which Addams attempted to reconcile immigrant parents and their children. Addams imagined the Labor Museum as a living history of handicrafts, tracing their development from the most basic techniques to their transformation by mechanization.

The chapter concludes with a discussion of the conflicts between older and younger generations around that perennial source of trouble, sex, and a close reading of the letters of Maimie Pinzer, a former prostitute, to her patron. Like many of the commentators on immigrant youth, Pinzer saw her conflict with her mother as rooted in generational differences. Similarly, many reformers in the early twentieth century saw the recasting of sexual mores not simply as a matter of Americanization, but as a symptom of the breakdown of sympathy between immigrant parents and their adolescent children. While many parents tried keep a close grip on their children (especially their daughters), and the force of gossip and of the police attempted to keep young tenement dwellers in line, the power of the adolescent cultures these young people created often overwhelmed the efforts of even the most vigilant parents.

In Chapter 4, I analyze the importance dancing had for young working-class people at the turn of the nineteenth into the twentieth century, and the intensity of reaction from the political, social, and cultural establishment (newspapers, state and municipal legislatures, reformers, schools, and intellectual elites). Dance halls were crucial to the construction of an adolescent urban culture at the turn of the nineteenth into the twentieth century. They provided a public space away from the eyes of parents and their allies where young people could experiment with new social and sexual arrangements, where gender relations could be reorganized. Moreover, since they were commercial rather than strictly communal institutions, dance halls popularized the idea of leisure as inextricable from capitalism, a trend that, as many social historians have noted, characterized the end of the nineteenth century and that suffused working-class adolescence in major cities. Through analyses of Abraham Cahan's 1892 novella *Yekl*, short stories and poems from immigrant periodicals, and articles from the mainstream press, I discuss the enormous role dancing and dance halls played in forming modern adolescence.

In the final chapter I examine how these patterns of adolescent identity found their way into the mainstream. A major channel was the interaction between workingmen and workingwomen and the bohemians who frequented immigrant neighborhoods, particularly in New York and Chicago, in the years before World War I. I focus on three historical figures who were involved in this cross-pollination: the bohemian and antiwar writer Randolph S. Bourne, anarchist leader Emma Goldman, and anthropologist Margaret Mead.

While none of these people met, their stories overlap considerably, and young, American-born, working-class men and women stand at the center of their intersections. Goldman moved comfortably between Jewish immigrant cafes and bohemian salons, between the picket line and Provincetown. Bourne bridged the gap between uptown and downtown, bringing together politically progressive Columbia University academics, Greenwich Village bohemians, and Lower East Side anarchists. Finally, Margaret Mead's *Coming of Age in Samoa* was a book strongly shaped by changing ideas about adolescence in the United States—particularly interesting because of Mead's own connection to bohemians and radicals in New York in the 1910s and 1920s.

Much of this book focuses on adolescent girls and women. This emphasis has several sources: first, the majority of ink spilled about adolescent children of immigrants concerned young women. The sexual freedom that seemed part and parcel of this new identity was particularly threatening for those who saw themselves as the protectors of young women: reformers, antiprostitution activists, vice commissions, and, of course, parents and immigrant community leaders. Second, although these young women were hardly the first children of immigrants to enter the urban workplace, they were participating in a new kind of labor that was both gender specific and heterosocial. Third, as I show throughout this book, adolescence was constituted in large part by the existence of commercialized mass culture: department stores, dance halls, amusement parks, movies, and the like. These phenomena afforded young women a way to imagine themselves outside the boundaries of work and family—as Nan Enstad points out, "French heels" (that is, high-heeled shoes), cheaply made but glamorous, a sign of American "ladyhood" but bought only by working-class women, were "one of their first purchases" (2). While these shoes, like the dance halls, afforded as much discomfort as they did pleasure, and while that pleasure was often fleeting compared to the difficulties of their everyday lives, they were a symbol of the new identity working-class adolescent girls and women were constructing for themselves, an identity that horrified many of their parents and the reformers and social workers who studied and tried to help them.

Nonetheless, this book is not concerned only with young women. The young men who squired them at dances, formed social clubs with each other, and brought into being a confident, adventurous adolescent masculinity that combined a leftist political orientation with an enthusiastic engagement with popular culture created a legacy of adolescent identity that persists to this day. Most importantly, young women *and* men identified with and sought out each other *as* young, *as* American, as much as if not more than they connected with gender and ethnic peers.

I don't want to romanticize these young people, although I do think they were astonishingly brave just to live the lives they did, etching new ways of being onto the surface of American culture. But I do hope—through listening to what the children of immigrants said about themselves as well as what others said about them in literary texts, photographs, and social critique—to provide a different set of tools for thinking about not just adolescence, but the power of working-class and immigrant social practices. As much as America changed these children of immigrants, they changed America, creating an identity, adolescence, that we now cannot imagine living without.

1   *"Youth Must Have Its Fling"*

THE BEGINNINGS OF
MODERN ADOLESCENCE

How did adolescence begin? And who were the new adolescents? In this chapter I argue that a combination of demographic shifts in the working class, a rethinking of adolescence by social scientists and reformers, and the growth of commercial leisure brought about a new identity. In part this new cohort was the result of simple numbers—thanks to the immigration boom of the late nineteenth and early twentieth centuries, there were more young people in cities than ever before. Moreover, working-class identity became, in large part, inextricable from immigrant identity, as new Americans far outnumbered their U.S.-born working peers. Young people of diverse origins met in the workplace and on the streets, and together sculpted a new kind of American self.

Although demographic and statistical analyses hardly tell the whole story, they can be useful to clarify how closely the urban working class became identified with immigrant communities, and how the huge numbers of immigrants at the turn of the century brought into being proportionally the largest-ever generation of adolescents in U.S. history. The development of a new kind of adolescence depended upon the existence of a large, densely populated, and self-consciously "different" (from their parents and from the Anglo-American cultural consensus) group of young people. We can begin to understand the parameters of this group by a brief look at the demographic information available from censuses of the period.

The U.S. government has been collecting census data since the beginnings of the nation, but only at the end of the nineteenth century did the census take into account more than crude differences in age, national origin, and parentage status. In early censuses, only two age groups existed for free white males, for example: over and under sixteen.[1] By 1890, by contrast, the population was measured in age increments of five years across race and sex (Taeuber and Taeuber, 26). Nonetheless, even limited categorization can give us some sense of the division of the U.S. population by age. In the first years of the Republic, half the white population was under sixteen, due in equal part to high birthrates and short life expectancy. By 1850, this proportion had dropped to two-fifths, although Americans over sixty still constituted a tiny fraction of the population: only one in twenty-five. Over the following thirty years, the birthrate continued to drop and life expectancy to lengthen, until 1880, when just over a third of the population was under fifteen, a figure that remained fairly steady for the next four decades (Taueber and Taueber 26–29).

At the same time, the raw numbers hide a more significant figure. The immense increases in overall U.S. population during those same years—by almost 13 million between 1880 and 1890, an additional 13 million between 1890 and 1900, and a formidable 16 million between 1900 and 1910—camouflage the equally large increases in the number of young people.[2] Between the mid-1920s, when immigration was severely curtailed by law, and the mid-1960s, when limits on immigration were loosened considerably, censuses reflected a much more stable set of variables. Now, population changes were largely due to births, emigrations, and deaths, and demographic categories could be compared more easily than in the turbulent decades at the turn of the nineteenth into the twentieth century.

So percentage numbers of different age-groups cannot quite give us an accurate sense of the boom in the children of foreign-born parents at the end of the nineteenth century, or of how many of the young people between the ages of twelve and twenty were born to immigrant parents. In addition, we have to factor in how many of those adolescents were growing up in major cities, rather than on farms or in small towns, to which the burgeoning culture of adolescence did not come until the 1920s and even the 1930s. One way might be to compare this increase with a more familiar baby boom—that of the post–World War II era. In 1890 alone, children under five, who would be in their teen years in the middle of the first decade of the twentieth century, constituted over 14 percent of the population; compare this with just under 11 percent of the population in 1950, children who would have been between eighteen and twenty-three in 1968, the symbolic apex of the youth explosion in the United States. These numbers are even farther apart when we take into account, first, the thousands of single men and women who settled in the United States in the late 1880s, who inflated the proportion of adults in the population compared to children and adolescents, and, second, the much later age of marriage and childbirth at the end of the nineteenth century than in the two decades after the Second World War.[3]

Folded into these numbers are the proportions of children of immigrants in the nation as a whole and in urban areas in particular. From 1890 to 1930 approximately one quarter of all American sixteen-year-olds were of foreign-born parentage (Taeuber and Taeuber 82). Broken down by region, the numbers are even more dramatic—along the Northeast and mid-Atlantic coast in 1910, between one-third and one-half of all children five to fourteen years old were born to foreign parents, and a third of young people from fifteen to nineteen years old had parents of "foreign white stock" (Taeuber and Taeuber 86). A final variable is the number of Americans living in large cities, which grew considerably during this period, in large part due to the influx of millions of immigrants to urban centers throughout the country, and particularly to the Northeastern and Midwestern cities. In 1840, only 11 percent of the U.S. population were city dwellers; by 1900 that number had almost quadrupled, to 40 percent (Miller 106).

Niles Carpenter's 1924 study, *Immigrants and Their Children,* which was commissioned and published by the U.S. government, and much of which was based on data from the censuses of the preceding decades, synthesized many of these statistics. Even taking into account the massive northern European immigration of the middle of the nineteenth century, in which millions of German, Irish, English, and Scandinavian nationals came to the United States, the proportion of American-born children of foreign-born parents was significantly higher in the early years of the twentieth century than at any other time. Between 1890 and 1920, the number of children born to immigrants grew from 11.5 million to almost 19 million, about half of them under the age of fifteen (Taeuber and Taeuber 81); from 1900 to 1920, American-born children of immigrants represented between 14 and 15 percent of the population, a considerable increase from 1870, when they were just under 11 percent, and even from 1890, when the children of immigrants made up 12.8 percent of the population (Carpenter 6). The numbers are even more significant when we take race into account: in the first twenty years of the twentieth century, U.S.-born children of immigrants represented almost a quarter of the entire white population of the United States (Carpenter 6). Almost 70 percent of those children lived in urban areas, and they constituted almost 29 percent of the urban population, compared with only 13.6 percent of rural people (Carpenter 22).

More importantly for the purposes of this book, the larger the city, the higher the proportion of immigrants and their children: in major cities of over half a million people, "foreign white stock" made up two-thirds of the population (Carpenter 123). By the beginning of the twentieth century, the urban working class was overwhelmingly foreign born or the children of foreign-born parents; indeed, it is tempting to use the terms "working class" and "immigrant" almost interchangeably when talking about working people. The coincidence between city-dwelling and immigrant status grew dramatically in the first two decades of the century. In 1920, the majority of the population of the city of New York were either immigrants (35.4 percent) or their children (41 percent);[4] in Chicago, American-born children of immigrants represented 42.2 percent of the city's people, compared with 23.8 percent of the population who were children of native-born Chicagoans. (Of course, these statistics do not reflect which of those American parents were themselves children of the ongoing wave of immigration that began in the 1880s.)

Small wonder that politicians, reformers, educators, and other members of the social and intellectual elites of the cities most affected by these massive demographic changes were taken aback by the variety and intensity of immigrant settlement in urban America. Evangelical missionary Vivia H. Divers was astounded by her first view of "the Black Hole," a half-mile square of Chicago bounded by Van Buren and State Streets at one end of the neighborhood, and Twelfth Street and the Chicago River at the other. Not only was she shocked by the number and concentration of saloons and brothels on the streets, but also she was amazed by the diversity of the Black Hole's population: a "mixed multitude" of "[Anglo-]Americans, Africans, Italians, Spanish, French, Germans, Swedes, Jews, Arabians, and Syrians" (15–16).

G. Stanley Hall and the New Adolescence

As disturbing as the increasing numbers of immigrants entering the cities were, even more alarming were the geometrically larger numbers of their children, who filled the streets, schools, factories, sweatshops, and department stores. "Youth," as Austin and Willard argue, "becomes a metaphor for perceived social change and its projected consequences, and as such it is an enduring locus for displaced social anxieties" (1). Stanley Hall, already a famous (one might even say notorious) psychologist by the end of the nineteenth century, detailed these anxieties in his two-volume study, Adolescence—a text Joseph F. Kett calls, not inaccurately, "a feverish, recondite, and at times incomprehensible book; the flawed achievement of an eccentric genius" (6), which combined a variety of social fears about urbanization, the degeneration of America's ethnic makeup, and the enormous power the body had on intellectual and social functioning. Hall's earlier work on the development of young boys had shaken much of the educational establishment in the 1890s. His theory of recapitulation—that the development of the individual restaged human evolution from "savagery" to "civilization"—had caused major waves in psychological and educational circles, particularly his recommendation that young boys (that is to say, young white middle-class boys) be encouraged to express violence and intense competition in order to work through their "savage" stage and mature into responsible, "manly" men.[5]

By the time Hall had finished his study of adolescence in the early twentieth century, theories of recapitulation were out of fashion. While vestiges of this viewpoint lingered in Adolescence—Hall claimed that "the child revels in savagery" (1:x), and "the adolescent is neo-atavistic" (1:xi)—he adapted his evolutionary approach to changing times.[6] Rather than arguing that adolescents restaged crucial moments in human evolution, Hall sounded the alarm that teenagers were growing up too fast. "Never," Hall claimed, "is the body so imperiously dominant and so insistently in evidence," and the danger was that young people might unwittingly give in to their bodies' imperious demands. Adolescents were in thrall to their physical and emotional impulses, adrift in a period of life that was "pre-eminently the age of sense, and hence prone to sensuousness not only in taste and sex . . . but in the domain of each of the sense species" (2:38). Thrust out of childhood too soon by "our urbanized hothouse life, that tends to ripen everything before its time" (1:xi), the adolescent, with his or her delicate physical and emotional balance, was a disaster waiting to happen.

Hall's invocation of the urban environment is key here. Just as "urban" or "inner city" are today often code words for black and Latino ("urban programming" as a euphemism for television shows designed for black audiences, for example), at the turn into the twentieth century, "urbanization" meant immigrants.[7] Hall's work on adolescence managed to capture and articulate the fantasies of social scientists and the Anglo-American middle and ruling classes about the growing population of (as they saw them) rowdy, potentially dangerous teenagers filling city streets. "Increasing urban life," he wrote,

> with its temptations, prematurities, sedentary occupations, and passive stimuli just when an active objective life is most needed, early emancipation and a lessening sense for both duty and discipline, the haste to know and do all befitting man's estate before its time, the mad rush for wealth and the reckless fashions set by its gilded youth—all these lack some of the regulations they still have in older lands with more conservative traditions. (xv–xvi)

This passage thematizes the mixture of nostalgia for a more controlled era in which young people knew their place, and the desire for progress on terms determined by established authorities, not by the nouveau riche possessed by "the mad rush for wealth" or young workers who care only about "reckless fashions." Gail Bederman has analyzed in detail Hall's obsession with control, self-mastery, and the conservation of "vital forces," which Hall and his contemporaries imagined as a finite resource easily sapped by excessive sexuality, physical stresses, and the immense psychological pressures of modern life. This fixation carries over into *Adolescence*. The danger of adolescence is that it is "the age of wasteful ways, awkwardness, mannerisms, tensions that are a constant leakage of vital energy, perhaps semi-imperative acts, contortions, quaint movements, more elaborated than in childhood and often highly unaesthetic and disagreeable motor co-ordinations" (Hall 1:165).

Hall recognized that industrialization, although a significant result of the "progress of civilization" (to cite Bederman's term) his era lionized, posed a serious risk to young people. First of all, this progress made work itself less attractive to young people. As Thorstein Veblen had observed in *The Theory of the Leisure Class* five years earlier, civilization brought with it a "pervading sense of the indignity of the slightest manual labor" (42), and teenagers, with their "wasteful ways" were most liable to reject meaningful work in favor of trivial, energy-sapping pleasures. Moreover, these unaesthetic contortions and losses of vital energy were part and parcel of the sweatshop, factory, and department-store work adolescent children of immigrants participated in for hours each day. Industry, Hall argued, "is no longer under hygienic conditions, and instead of being out of doors, in the country, or of highly diversified kinds, it is now specialized, monotonous, in closed spaces, bad air, and perhaps poor light, especially in cities" (1:166).

Hall was particularly worried about adolescent boys, whose journey to manhood was fraught with dangers: "overcivilization," overstrain, nervous exhaustion. The values of late-nineteenth- and early-twentieth-century masculinity limned a narrow and demanding outline of ideal manhood: "courage, strength, endurance, duty, principled sacrifice," and complete obedience to authority (Rotundo 234). Adult men had to develop a fierce competitive sense, while integrating that "primitive" energy into fealty to the calcifying social hierarchies of corporate capitalism. Hall may have seen the "tender-minded boy with a gentle, reflective nature" as "an evolutionary mistake," but he was still unsure how those "tougher, more assertive" boys who were evolution's triumph could be transformed into masculine but loyal men (Rotundo 267). *Adolescence* was, in large part, an extended attempt to answer that question.

Much of Hall's book is an overview of scientific studies of the physical development of adolescents, locating their differences from children on the one hand and adults on the other in their rapidly changing bodies. Despite, or perhaps because of, his focus on the "new wave of vitality . . . new interests, instincts, and tendencies; increased appetite and curiosity" available to teenagers to the extent that adolescence constitutes "a physiological second birth," Hall spends much of the book discussing the possible obstacles to normal adolescent development (308). Modern life itself, the source of so many advances, presented the greatest danger for teenagers of all types, from the sheltered, educated New England girl, whom many gynecologists feared was "pallid, nervous, weak, lethargic, and enfeebled" (Brumberg, 21), to her factory-working counterpart in the cities.

Like his eugenicist peers, Hall was deeply alarmed by the promiscuous mixing of ethnic groups among the tenements of the country's major cities. Indeed, "the mixture of distinct ethnic stocks . . . increases the ferments of adolescence by multiplying the factors of heredity and so increasing its instability, [so] that we no longer wonder that many in these most vulnerable years make more or less complete shipwrecks at every stage of these hothouse demands, which in the entire life of our race are so recent" (322).

Hall's anxiety is clearly on exhibition here, from his invocation of the febrility of adolescence to the confused mixing of metaphors. But his characterization of adolescent boys and girls as vital yet vulnerable, resilient yet subject to the "shipwrecks" of the "hothouse demands" of a rapidly changing era, was echoed by many of his more progressive contemporaries. Reformers such as Belle Israels (later Moskowitz) in New York and Louise de Koven Bowen in Chicago organized their efforts around the needs of teenage immigrant girls. Bowen's 1911 study of "department store girls" expressed many of the same concerns as Hall, although with the welfare of the girls, rather than "the race," in mind: "It is evident that the long day of twelve or more hours cripples the human system, dwarfs the mind, gives no time for culture and recreation and shortens life" (n.p.). The average age of the young women working in department stores was nineteen, and almost all were American-born daughters of immigrant parents. Department-store girls were poorly paid, "constantly surrounded by the articles which are so dear to the feminine heart," but often unable to afford most of them (n.p.).[8]

Despite their ideological and/or methodological differences, Hall, Bowen, Israels, and Addams shared the belief that industrialization had compromised the adolescent need for activity. The absence of healthy outlets, they feared, could easily lead to criminality among boys and prostitution among girls. Not all these fears were unrealistic. The largest proportion of urban prostitutes were U.S.-born daughters of immigrants (Rosen 139); in 1900 over one-third of all girls in the New York State Reformatory were daughters of Jewish immigrants, mostly imprisoned for prostitution and petty theft (Perry, *Belle Moskowitz* 22). More often, prostitution was informal and part of a quid pro quo, with young women exchanging sexual favors for a night on the town or a day at the beach with their dates.

Nonetheless, given the explosion of mostly commercial recreations for young people, social commentators felt that they had to respond to the phenomenon. Addams saw recreation among youth as at the least a necessity, a steam valve for young people "overborne by their own undirected and misguided energies," and ideally a social good, since "one generation after another has depended upon its young to equip it with gaiety and enthusiasm, to persuade it that living is a pleasure" (*Spirit of Youth* 51, 3–4). Working-class women's desire for "frivolous" finery was a way to make that gaiety and enthusiasm visible; as Addams argued, "through the huge hat, with its wilderness of bedraggled feathers, the girl announces to the world that she is here. She demands attention to the fact of her existence, she states that she is ready to live, to take her place in the world" (*Spirit of Youth* 8).

Most of all, these new adolescents wanted to show off, be entertained, amuse themselves. In a word, they wanted to have fun.

Perhaps no quality of adolescence has more defined American teenagers than this desire for fun. When the concept of teenagehood came to full fruition in the 1940s, being "fun-loving" was one of the most important constituents of teenage identity (Palladino xv).[9] The current concept of fun itself—the evanescent, ephemeral pleasure of the moment, an adventure that requires no forethought and entails no regret—was in large part invented, and certainly perfected, by young people at the end of the nineteenth century.[10] After the mid-nineteenth-century pressures on young Americans of all classes to practice self-denial and self-restraint, the fin-de-siècle focus on recreation and amusement was a significant shift. Reformers, politicians, and social scientists all agreed, in G. Stanley Hall's words, that for young people "to have a good time is felt to be an inalienable right. The joys of life are never felt with so keen a relish; youth lives for pleasure, whether of an epicurean or an esthetic type" (2:77).

This definition of fun is different from the concept of play, which also enjoyed a new legitimacy at the end of the nineteenth century. Associated with the playground movement and various progressive educational theories like the Montessori and Waldorf methods, play was imagined as the purview of children as work was of adults (I discuss this in more detail in chapter 2). Playgrounds were useful, as far as Progressive reformers were concerned. Not only were they "the greatest antidote to such human frailties as result from cramped quarters, deoxygenized air and social isolation," but also they were sites in which children could develop into physically fit, socially responsible citizens, all under the eyes of caring and vigilant adults (Jerome 133).

Play was envisaged as inextricable from the effective functioning of the working-class family. The participants in a National Play Convention held in Pittsburgh in May 1909 issued a statement arguing that "when the family splits up for its recreation, there is danger. When young people take their places apart by themselves without a wholesome influence of family life, there is danger," both to the child and to the family (Jerome 132). Play that was "wholesome," safe, and mediated by the whole family represented an important resource for ameliorating the difficulties of urban life, in the eyes of Progressive Era reformers.

Fun, on the other hand, had no redeeming qualities. Particularly in the form of commercialized leisure, it allowed young people spaces in which they could separate from their families. It usually took place in crowded environments—dance halls, movie theaters, beach resorts—that were the opposite of the imaginative, activity-filled ideal of the playground. Rather than intensifying and extending childhood, as play could do, fun eased the transition from childhood to puberty and finally to adolescence. Finally, while play was always free, and enlisted a variety of material objects that could be transformed by imagination and activity, fun was thought of as predominantly manufactured, commercial, and consumerist—the playground versus the dance hall, Central Park versus Coney Island.

The variety, intensity, and availability of fun on offer to the children of immigrants in urban areas were unprecedented. While some urban institutions, most notably the saloon, had characterized men's leisure time in cities for a century, practices of pleasure emerged at the end of the nineteenth century that were new in several ways: they were mixed sex (very different from the almost all male saloon), class specific (unlike the "promiscuous" crowds that filled mid-nineteenth-century theaters), and age limited.[11] The organized social life of their immigrant parents focused on fraternal organizations and lodges, education, and politics, but young people were more interested in "amusement" and fun.

More importantly, as Kathy Peiss has shown, as leisure became increasingly commercialized it became concomitantly more available to women and their male companions: "Loosening the ties between leisure, mutual aid, and male culture, commercialized recreation fostered a youth-oriented, mixed-sex world of pleasure, where female participation was profitable and encouraged" (6). Where women's leisure time had previously been linked to the rhythms of marriage, housekeeping, and child care, organized around neighborly visits and religious life, and located on the boundaries between the home and the street, the new experience of leisure operated in public spaces that depended less upon social and family ties and more upon the availability of disposable income.

For Ruth True, a social reformer and author of *The Neglected Girl*, a 1914 survey of prepubescent and teenage girls in Manhattan's "Middle West Side" between Forty-second and Fifty-seventh streets, which later came to be known as Hell's Kitchen, fun was the prime motivator for the young women she was studying. The teenage immigrant daughter's search for meaning and a sense of self in a rapidly changing environment was "translated very lightly and gaily into the demand for 'a good time' and a keen interest in the other sex. . . . The city bristles with the chances she longs for—'to have fun and see the fellows'" (58). For the multiethnic young women in True's study, fun was by definition heterosocial and heterosexual.

The desire for fun was itself viewed with distaste and even horror by many middle-class observers. While G. Stanley Hall acknowledged that "youth loves intense states of mind and is passionately fond of excitement," he was hardly thrilled by this inevitability and saw his job as helping young people navigate the shoals of these intense states to the safe port of adulthood (1:73). Advice writer Ruth Ashmore traced one girl's downfall to her taste for amusement: "as most of the girls do, she wanted pleasure, she wanted pretty clothes, and she loved fun." Needless to say, this could end only in disaster. Led astray by handsome but unscrupulous admirers, the unnamed girl lost touch with her virtuous roots, going to the theater more often than she could afford, racking up debts, and eventually sliding into notoriety as a kept woman. Previously an underpaid but pure shopgirl, our fallen woman "never comes into the store now; she has plenty of fine clothes," courtesy of her latest paramour, but she has lost her most precious commodity: her virtue (Ashmore, 28).[12]

Adolescent Leisure and Pleasures

Concerns about the teenage children of immigrants usually followed one of three routes: their distance from and disaffection toward their parents; their increased spending power and intense engagement with commercialism of all kinds, for entertainment, commodities, and self-presentation; or the inability of adult authorities, whether parents, teachers, educators, or reformers, to control their movements, actions, or desires, especially in relation to the heterosocial and heterosexual focus of urban adolescent culture.

These worries were often expressed with equal vehemence by the immigrant parents of these young people. As we will see in chapter 4, commercial places of entertainment, the most popular of which were dance halls, were a cause of great concern to the older generation. Young people absorbed, often from dime novels and movies, ideas about love, romance, and heterosexual relationships that were at odds with the courting and marriage patterns of their home cultures. In urban orthodox Jewish communities, for example, religious and cultural authorities "became increasingly alarmed—and vocal"— about young people's abandonment of the mechanisms of *shidduch,* or the arranged marriage, choosing instead to initiate and pursue their own courtships (Joselit 18).

Moreover, new technologies of entertainment like the nickelodeon or the five-cent movie palace presented unanticipated challenges to the guardians of adolescent morality and safety. As Jane Addams pointed out, presciently anticipating popular culture studies scholars of recent years, the melodramas and crime pictures on offer at the movies filled a gap for young working-class people that the more established arts often provided for their bourgeois counterparts:

> "Going to the show" for thousands of young people in every industrial city is the only possible road to the realms of mystery and romance; the theatre is the only place where they can satisfy that craving for a conception of life higher than that which the actual world offers them. In a very real sense the drama and the drama alone performs for them the office of art as is clearly revealed in their blundering demand stated in many forms for "a play unlike life." The theater becomes to them a "veritable house of dreams" infinitely more real than the noisy streets and the crowded factories. (*Spirit of Youth* 75–76)

Much like the dime novels their post–Civil War counterparts devoured, movies provided a rewarding fantasy life for young working-class people at the end of the nineteenth century. But there was a major difference—dime novels were, as Michael Denning has shown, a shared resource, often passed from hand to hand or discussed on shop floors and on lunch breaks, while reading is usually a solitary experience. The movies, on the other hand, are communal, providing a fertile environment for adolescent bonding and sexual experimentation. Reform organizations like the Juvenile Protection Agency in Chicago were well aware of this feature of cinemas, and in their report on the five-cent theaters recommended that young people under nineteen not be allowed in unaccompanied by an adult (Lindstrom 100).

In *Young Working Girls,* their study of adolescent women in the workplace, National Federation of Settlements organizers Robert A. Woods and Albert J. Kennedy set out to analyze the social issues raised by the phenomenon of thousands of young women going out to work to support themselves and their families. Their findings go a long way to defining the anxieties reformers and immigrant parents had about adolescents in the urban workplace. As with so many reform texts, *Young Working Girls* describes the terrain by suggesting ways to reshape it, arguing: "Everything possible should be done to ennoble the relations between the sexes; to purify the tradition concerning romance through the spread of the great novels; to eliminate cheap kissing games, cheap plays, and low dances; to create a love of fine things in the home, in literature, and in life generally" (98).

The adolescent children of working-class immigrants were almost invariably earners. As I argue in chapter 2, one reason that adolescence gained meaning in the final decades of the nineteenth and first decades of the twentieth centuries was the impassioned organizing against child labor that led to the formation of the National Child Labor Committee in 1904 and the photographs the committee commissioned Lewis Hine to take of working children around the country between 1908 and 1921.[13] Although federal legislation regulating child labor did not survive a constitutional challenge until the 1938 Fair Labor Standards Act, many municipalities and states began outlawing and regulating various kinds of work by children starting at the end of the nineteenth century.[14] Certainly children remained in the workforce in significant numbers, particularly in rural areas, until the beginning of the Second World War, but the advances in union organizing in various industries, the institution of compulsory education, and the exclusion of children under sixteen from the permanent workforce created a new category of worker: the adolescent, not yet an adult but legally empowered to leave school and earn a wage.

Given the sharp increases in living expenses in major cities as immigrants crowded in, adolescent children represented a significant source of family income. In the first decade of 1900 in New York, fewer than half of working-class families depended upon the father for their sole financial support (Peiss 12). The novels of immigrant life that became increasingly popular in the early decades of the twentieth century—among them, Anzia Yezierska's *Bread Givers,* Abraham Cahan's *The Rise of David Levinsky,* and Willa Cather's *O Pioneers!*—invariably featured representations of adolescent children at work to help cover basic family living expenses.

Kathy Peiss's groundbreaking work on young women's leisure activities in New York at the end of the nineteenth century underscores many of the arguments I want to make here. As she points out, four-fifths of wage-earning women in New York in 1900 were single, and one-third were between the ages of sixteen and twenty. Moreover, nearly two-thirds of all women in New York between the ages of sixteen and twenty worked for wages (34). Although many young women handed over much or even all of their pay to their parents, many others had access to at least some of their income. Unfettered by children of their own and old enough to desire the pleasures the city had to offer, young women broke away from the leisure activities of their immigrant mothers: visiting with friends and female family members, sharing child care, gossiping with neighbors (Peiss 22). A burgeoning adolescent culture organized around leisure and sexuality suffused urban life, marking out a new terrain "distinct from familial traditions and the customary practices of their ethnic groups, signifying a new identity as wage earners through language, clothing, and social rituals" (Peiss 47).

This identity, I would argue, formed at the intersection of adolescent and new American identities in a culture in which adolescence was gelling into a meaningful identity category. While I am indebted to Peiss's work on immigrant leisure practices, part of my project here is to fill in a significant gap in her analysis. First, in organizing her study around "working women," Peiss does not differentiate between the young, unmarried women who are the major focus of her book and older women who found themselves in the workplace. Although she does not acknowledge it, Peiss is in fact writing about adolescent women—wage-earning, unmarried, unburdened by children of their own—who identified themselves as part of an age cohort as much as an ethnicity.

More importantly, a central concern of this book is with the *imaginative* lives of the children of immigrants, and with how their imagination found its way into literary texts or squeezed its way into the reports of social reformers and judging parents. As someone trained in the study of literature, I am always fascinated by what is not (or cannot be) said outright, by the ways in which cultural change is represented in literary expression. While much of the literature I examine here could certainly be considered minor—unpublished memoirs, light verse, and amateur short stories, as well as the reports of various commissions, advice manuals, jeremiads, and travel writing—it opens up whole panoramas of urban life that a more strictly historically oriented analysis cannot.

Unlike the more rigidly gender-segregated lives their parents led, working-class adolescent girls, the majority of them the children of new immigrants, were creating a heterosocial world for themselves through the flamboyant hats they wore, the dance halls they frequented, and their trips to amusement parks and vaudeville, an environment in which, as Peiss herself argues, "commercialized recreation fostered a youth-oriented, mixed-sex world of pleasure, where female participation was profitable and encouraged" (6).

Or, rather, encouraged by some. On the one hand, as Laura Hapke points out, the lives of young workingwomen were fascinating to their bourgeois contemporaries, and from the 1890s on, "staid publishing houses with a wide middle-class readership brought out numerous tenement tales with sweatshop and box-factory workers, shop girls and cloak models, genteel daughters of failed businessmen reduced to department store work, even former dance hall girls who manage saloons and female stevedores who take men's names" (4). At the same time, however, among reformers and philanthropists, enthusiasm for the ways in which young women were shaping and responding to work and leisure was muted, to say the least.

Contributing to this ambivalence were the ways young working-class daughters of immigrants took on styles of self-presentation that struck observers as inappropriate for virtuous young women. In constructing fashions for themselves, immigrant girls "adopted many of the manners associated in the public's mind with prostitution—wearing makeup, smoking cigarettes, going out at night alone, and engaging in sex outside of marriage—yet they clearly disassociated themselves from prostitutes" (Odem, *Delinquent Daughters* 53).

Young women and men used fashion to construct an image of conspicuous consumption, glamour, and affluence, whether those things were within their financial reach or not. Photographs of adolescent union members from urban sweatshops and factories invariably show young women and men dressed in the height of fashion, melding radicalism with style. The *Ladies' Garment Worker,* the Yiddish/English journal of the International Ladies' Garment Workers Union, occasionally published profiles of union activists, and the young women featured are impressively chic. One, Beckie Fisher, described as "a Russian-Jewish girl—one of the most active pickets in the [1911] Cleveland strike," looks like a glamorous actress—her hair piled up with a sparkling hairband surrounding it, an elegant black dress, one elbow resting on a high side table with her chin propped in her hand, and the other hand demurely in her lap ("Beckie Fisher" 12) (fig. 1).

Miss Fisher's self-assured appearance and her simultaneous embrace of radical politics and fine clothes mark her as a new American adolescent par excellence. Despite her youth, she has managed to fashion her own identity through both dress and action. As I will show in the chapters that follow, one thing that immigrant parents and Anglo-American reformers could agree on was that these young people were too independent from parental influence. On the one hand, as I have argued, many commentators believed, as G. Stanley Hall put it, "that youth must have its fling"—but within tightly controlled

Figure 1 "Beckie Fisher: A Russian-Jewish Girl." Beckie's glamour clearly hasn't damaged her as a committed participant in the Cleveland strike. *Ladies' Garment Worker* 2.10 (1911): 12.

boundaries, under "careful supervision and wise direction" of adults (89).[15] Working-class children of immigrants worked as hard as they could to resist exactly the kind of surveillance that Hall suggests is an intrinsic part of the proper cultivation of adolescents. While their bourgeois counterparts may have been sneaking off in cars and necking in dark corners, in the final analysis working-class offspring acknowledged the authority of their parents over them, rooted in large part in their financial dependency upon them. Joseph Kett persuasively argues that one "common thread running through youth organizations in colleges, high schools, and churches in the late nineteenth century was adult leadership" (another, he shows, was "passivity" [211]). More strikingly, although the "architects of adolescence" in the beginning of the twentieth century "announced their intention to understand and to sympathize with the problems of adolescents," more often their efforts resulted in a variety of new ways to keep an eye on and regulate the behavior of young people (Kett 238).

Another group of male adolescents, young middle-class men coming to the city to work, entered a series of all-male spaces at work and at play.

As Anthony Rotundo has shown, "the people closest to [a young man of the middle classes] were likely to be his own age and sex. The offices, counting-houses, and classrooms where a middle-class youth spent his days were sex-segregated. The boardinghouses and dormitories where he lived away from home were all-male environments, and the literary clubs, debating societies, and fraternities where he spent his spare hours were not open to females" (86). The only women these male adolescents came into contact with were either prostitutes or the wives and daughters of their employers and older colleagues, hardly candidates for easy socializing.

By contrast, urban working-class adolescents had not just the financial power to evade their parents' eyes, and the commercial spaces in which to follow their own social lives, but spent most of their time in mixed-sex environments, from work to the settlement houses to picture shows to dance halls. Moreover, working-class adolescents of both sexes shared a sense of themselves as part of a heterosocial "peer society" mediated by mass culture on the one hand and their alienation from the middle classes on the other, two crucial elements of teenage identity even now (Cohen 144). While the ruling classes were worrying that modern young men "had become so dangerously civilized that their relationship with their own primal needs was now dangerously disrupted," working-class youth were experimenting with leisure and pleasure practices that scandalized those same elites (Rotundo 232).

The qualities that experts on adolescence valued in young people—conformity, anti-intellectualism, physical culture—and the suburbs and small towns that were seen as the laboratories for these characteristics were rejected both implicitly and explicitly by the teenage children of immigrants. The stereotypical teenagers of today are closer to these working-class kids than to the bourgeois teenagers who were, by virtue of class and location, their closer counterparts. But for all that teenagers might be marked by conformity to their own codes, they actively resist being seen as "just like everybody else."

By contrast, despite the brouhaha about the "flaming youth" and, as Babbitt puts it, "Immorality," time and time again, middle-class youth in the 1920s rejected the countercultural ideas that were turning the cities upside down. While their working-class immigrant peers were flirting with anarchism, bohemianism, and socialism, marching on picket lines, and breaking away from their families, one opinion poll of middle-class teenagers after another "consistently failed to turn up any real evidence of intergenerational discord" or political radicalism, hallmarks of later teenage culture (Kett 262).

This is not to say that the children of immigrants were the only influence on twentieth-century white adolescence. The powerful intersections between African American cultural and musical practices were immensely important for teenagers, particularly in the years after the Second World War. It's hard to imagine the youth culture of the past fifty years in the absence of the rich, complex, and often exploitive relationships between black political, social, and artistic styles and white youth experience. And of course, the ragtime and "tough" dancing that migrated from immigrant neighborhoods and alternately thrilled and scandalized the Anglo bourgeoisie in the second decade of the twentieth century found its roots in the black strongholds of New Orleans's Storyville and San Francisco's Barbary Coast.

At the same time, in the years in which the kind of social attitudes that came to characterize adolescence were forming in urban centers like Chicago, New York, and San Francisco, black populations were comparatively small. While black migration to northern and mid/western cities was ongoing in the late nineteenth and early twentieth centuries, motivated by the agricultural disaster of the boll weevil and the social blights of Jim Crow and racist violence, the movement of African American people to cities was a steady but slow stream compared to the torrent of black migrants that was released at the end of the 1910s and lasted until the 1940s.[16]

The ambivalent romance that white America had for black culture was not defined by age group or limited to adolescents until the years after the Second World War. The classic novels of the Harlem Renaissance—Nella Larsen's *Passing*, Wallace Thurman's *The Blacker the Berry* and *Infants of the Spring*, among others—represent white travels into black worlds as the bailiwick of intellectuals and bourgeois "slummers," not the adventures of rebellious teenagers flouting their parents' respectability.[17]

Ultimately, *Inventing Modern Adolescence* argues against the standard narratives of Americanization popularized by immigrant writers themselves (Mary Antin, Anzia Yezierska, Leonard Covello, and others) that the children of immigrants were wholly transformed by their experiences in the United States. As some scholars have recently argued, the relationship between the children of immigrants and the culture they negotiated their way into was much more dynamic and interdependent.[18] As my discussion makes clear, rather than a unidirectional process of Americanization, the concept of adolescence was mutually constructed and constructing, implicated in what, for lack of a better term, we might think of as "immigrantization," in which urban immigrant understandings of adolescence deeply affected the larger culture, usually without explicit comment from the mainstream. The enormous but unheralded changes in the meanings of adolescence in the dominant culture echoed the movement of now-adult children of immigrants out of urban centers and into American suburbs. Indeed, as I show in the following pages, the story of the shifts in the concept of adolescence itself suggests an alternative narrative of immigrant acculturation and assimilation, one in which immigrants themselves impressed their own images on the New World, and new Americans spoke the language of America through their own mouths.

2   *Picturing Labor*

LEWIS W. HINE, THE CHILD LABOR
MOVEMENT, AND THE MEANINGS
OF ADOLESCENT WORK

One of Progressive documentary photographer Lewis W. Hine's most famous pictures is his so-called Italian Madonna (1905), a triumph of composition and style (fig. 2). Part of his series on immigrants at Ellis Island, the picture is almost luminous, encapsulating a mother's tender affection for her child, and the child's love for and dependence upon its mother. The photograph is deeply affecting: the mother and child dominate the picture in sharp focus, the child gazing up at the mother as the mother casts her eyes down at her child, creating a closed circuit of love and devotion. The woman's hands are slightly out of focus; her left hand is holding the child's arm, with her wedding ring showing. The mother's intricately brocaded bodice and ornamented necklace and pendant stand in distinct contrast to the embroidered white gown on the child. In fact, Hine's use of contrasts is particularly striking in this picture. The child's pale, open face is sharply contrasted with her dark flowered headscarf, the dark mass of the mother's sheltering body with her child's light, almost ethereal form.

Many published versions of this image are cropped so that the mother and daughter take up almost all the frame. However, Hine's initial framing expanded the scene beyond the mother-daughter dyad, as the uncropped image makes clear.[1] Directly behind the two seated figures is a holding cell occupied by several standing male figures. The cell is bounded by a metal diagonal grid, whose clarity shifts from slightly out of focus on the right to very blurry on the left. Behind the metal fencing to the right, looking directly at us, is a boy, perhaps eight or nine years old, in a jacket and cap. Behind him to the left is an older man, in his fifties or so, wearing a hat with a white square on it (possibly an immigration tag). More difficult to distinguish but still visible are several figures to the left of the older man: a quite blurred younger man, a very blurred man behind him, and to the far left another boy whose face is turned away and who wears a light hat.

This print tells a series of interconnecting but conflicting stories. On the one hand, the composition of the photograph clearly speaks to the convention of the Madonna and Child painting. The semicircle of men in the holding

Figure 2 Lewis W. Hine, "Italian Madonna" (1905). Photography Collection, Miriam and Ira D. Wallach Division of Art, Prints, and Photographs, New York Public Library, Astor, Lenox and Tilden Foundations.

area forms an arc around the mother and child, as though they are adoring angels or various saints arrayed in worship.[2] Much like the Madonna and Child paintings of the Renaissance, the photograph wants to both suspend and invoke time, just as the early modern paintings created an eternal and allegorical present in which the Christ child could coexist iconographically with various saints and bishops in the space of the painting, people who could never have occupied the same time and place as the historical Jesus. Hine's Italian Madonna is simultaneously outside time, the eternal mother, and rooted in moment and locale. Hine originally entitled the picture "Mother and Child—Italian—Ellis Island—1905," constructing a set of signifiers by which the viewer could fix the subjects of the photograph along the matrices of time, place, national origin, and intention. On the other hand, this is not any mother and child—it is a woman waiting to gain entrance into the United States, a woman from a rural culture (indicated by her dress and her rough hands) who in moments will be absorbed by one of the most urban environments in the world. Moreover, in his explanatory caption Hine uses this picture less as an occasion to comment on the meaning of the mother and child than to point to the situation of the men and boys who look in on her: "This beautiful mother and child sit outside the detention cell. Sometimes 1700 immigrants were crowded into a room which was built to accommodate 600."

This moment is frozen in time, but it is human, not allegorical, time. We see that the mother and child are not wholly removed from their surroundings (and not only because of Hine's comment). Even as our eyes are drawn to the mother and child, we register the men and boys in our peripheral vision. What is the look on the young boy's face? Challenging? Curious? The older man seems to be staring blankly, as though dazed by his new surroundings and the sight of the camera itself. The mother and child create a charged circle of connection, but just behind the fence is a whole other world, of material realities.

This contrast between the idealized image of mother and child and the larger historical context is a perfect introduction to the photographs of Lewis W. Hine, particularly the pictures he took for the National Child Labor Committee (NCLC) in the first and second decades of the twentieth century. Hine's child labor photographs called upon many of the tropes of child portraiture of the previous century, while their context (in mines, canneries, sweatshops, textile mills) pointed to the bitter dichotomies between ideal childhood and the lives of working children. Drawing upon the rhetoric of the movement against child labor on the one hand, and conventions of the representation of children and the use of photography on the other, Hine created a powerful and highly effective narrative about the role of children in an industrial society. Moreover, by photographing children all over the United States, Hine helped forge a definition of the American child as outside the world of work.

The Italian Madonna prefigures this work in several ways. The hopeful and loving gaze the child casts upon her mother is quite different from the wary but defiant look lobbed at the photographer/viewer by the young boy behind her. Rather than the timeless story of religious iconography, the various figures in this photograph could narrate quite a different trajectory: from the innocence of babyhood to the trials of an immigrant childhood to the blurred despair of a lifetime of poverty. The mother and her child are in front of the caged detention cell, but soon enough they will be on the other side of the fence, and even the most protective mother will not be able to shield her child from the overcrowded pressures of immigrant life and the immense demands it places on young children. America's promise for this child is as yet incomplete, the threat of years of premature work in direct opposition to what an American childhood should be.

But what of the young man at the far left of the picture, who has turned his back to the camera? All the other figures in the photograph face the viewer, whether looking directly at the camera or absorbed in another person. Only he has turned away, his expression obscured not only by the lack of focus, but also by his own movements. His place in the various narratives one might apply to this picture is ambiguous—is he part of the picture? Is his turning away an act of resistance? Shyness? Bad timing? In many ways his ambivalent relationship to the camera and to the viewer encapsulates the place of the adolescent immigrant: neither completely of the immigrant story yet wholly transformed by it.

The dynamics created by the interrelation of these different figures in many ways express the arguments I will be making in this chapter about child labor, adolescent work, and the ways in which they were represented photographically and rhetorically (especially, but not exclusively, by Hine). The camera focuses on the central relationship between an immigrant mother and child, attempting to fit them into a preexisting tradition of representation. Meanwhile another child hovers in the background, hinting at the ways in which children really function within urban capitalism. Finally, partly engaged and partly detached, the figure of the adolescent looks outside the frame of the picture, perhaps to a different scene altogether. My focus in this chapter will be in large part the discourses around child labor at the end of the nineteenth and beginning of the twentieth centuries, particularly by the anti–child labor movement as mediated by the photographs of Lewis W. Hine.

Such a focus may seem like a digression from a study of the construction of adolescence during this period. However, as this chapter will show, the sharpening of the rhetoric of the child labor movement and the way it represented childhood, particularly *American* childhood, created a space for the redefinition of adolescents as workers (and, perhaps more importantly, as *earners*); it is a telling coincidence that the NCLC came into being in 1904, the same year that G. Stanley Hall's *Adolescence* was published. Certainly, teenage workers were not the central concern of reformers hoping to outlaw child labor. But out of these reform efforts, both directly and indirectly, developed a self-defined class of young single workingmen and workingwomen, hardly children (to the extent that child labor laws rarely extended past sixteen, and usually only to fourteen) but not yet limited by the adult entanglements of marriage and children of their own. Given how crucial their status as wage earners was to their forming a sense of themselves as a separate, identifiable group, defined as much by their spending power as by their age, adolescents were as compellingly influenced and shaped by the movement against child labor as children themselves were, even if as an unintended consequence.

That adolescence exists suspended between childhood and adulthood is a truism but worth exploring here. As Karen Sánchez-Eppler has brilliantly shown, a defining characteristic of modern American childhood is dependence (and, as a corollary, a defining characteristic of adulthood is to *have* dependents). Adolescence, then, is a state of at least partial independence, from both the need for parental resources and the demands of one's own dependents. Hine's photographs, by powerfully reinforcing the assumption that children should be provided for, that they should be the beneficiaries of wage labor, not actors within it, created a new representational space for adolescents as active, competent, and part of the world of commerce.

Lewis Hine's photographs of working children are justly famous for their documentary clarity and their emotional impact. They were widely distributed by the NCLC, who were well aware of their power. Indeed, Hine himself understood the rhetorical force of his pictures and the ambivalence many viewers felt in relation to the relentlessness of his vision. "Perhaps you are weary of child labor pictures," he told his readers in "Social Photography: How the Camera May Help in Social Uplift." "Well, so are the rest of us, but we propose to make you and the whole country so sick and tired of the whole business that when the time for action comes, child labor pictures will be records of the past" (Hine 112). Hine's invocation of his photographs as historical records *avant la lettre* is more revealing than he imagined. For the power of his pictures was to contrast the bourgeois ideal of the child as an ahistorical creature with the reality of the working child, whose very existence was determined by historical and economic realities.

Photographing Children at the End of the Nineteenth Century

Hine's representation of children came out of a series of conventions in both photography and child portraiture. As Anne Higonnet has argued, images of childhood created a new and important identity at the end of the eighteenth and beginning of the nineteenth centuries, that of the "Romantic child." For Higonnet, modernity brought with it new ways of representing childhood that "revolved around an innocent child body, a body defined by its difference

from adult bodies" (23). The Romantic child floated outside the usual signifiers of social identity: class, gender, and intellectual activity. As Higonnet
puts it, the Romantic child was "socially, sexually, and psychically innocent"
(24). In large part, this way of understanding childhood was a product of
industrialization, the growth of a sizeable and powerful bourgeoisie, and the
phantasmic division between domestic and public worlds.[3]

If, as Jane Tompkins has argued in *Sensational Designs*, middle-class white
American women in the mid-nineteenth century were represented as innocent children, the converse was also true: bourgeois children of both sexes
were feminized, represented as suspended from history, outside the sullying
influence of the marketplace, and divested of carnal bodies.[4] By the beginning of the twentieth century, bourgeois Americans imagined "properly
loved" children much as they thought of properly cared for women,
"belong[ing] in a domesticated, unproductive world of lessons, games, and
token money" (Zelizer, *Pricing* 11). Moreover, as Karen Sánchez-Eppler
argues, "the figure of the child demarcates the boundaries of personhood, a
limiting case for agency, voice, or enfranchisement. Hence for people who
are not male, or white, or American, or considered sufficiently sane or sufficiently rich, exclusion from civil rights has often been implemented through
analogies to the child" (xxiv).

As photography became a central mode of representation for the middle
classes, it reshaped the way many Americans recognized the narrative of
their lives. As many commentators on photography have pointed out, pictures bridge the deep gap between past and present, creating a sense of oneself as an actor, however small, in history.[5] This historical sense of self comes
in play when photos "are used to interpret the present in light of the past,
when they are presented and received as explanatory accounts of collective
reality," which is to say, almost always (Trachtenberg, *Reading American
Photographs* 6).

Photography's status in the mid- to late nineteenth century was powerfully linked to the belief that photographs were, in essence, truthful. The
very language of photography and the way it merged the metaphorical and
the material, with, as Alan Trachtenberg has observed "its subset of terms,
like *image* and *reflect, lens* and *shutter, light* and *shade* . . . , provided a way of
expressing ideas about how the world could be known—about truth and
falseness, appearance and reality, accuracy, exactitude, and impartiality"
("Photography" 17). Despite, or perhaps because of, the common practice of
touching up photographs with paint to invest them with more lifelike colors,
photography was called upon to speak a variety of truths, either the truth
of a specific moment, or a larger, more abstract truth, embodied in the
nineteenth-century practice of collecting cartes de visite and larger portraits
of famous Americans as a form of moral education (McCandless 49).

Photographs of children represented a certain tension between these two kinds of truth. On the one hand, photography could be used to make manifest the allegorical truths that childhood was believed throughout the bourgeois Anglo-American world to express. British photographer Julia Margaret Cameron's highly stylized photographs of children from the mid-nineteenth century, for example, are less portraits than "representations of an idea, the concept of idealized beauty and animate inner life" (Cox and Ford 64–65). Cameron's self-image as an artist rather than a technician allowed her to focus on what she believed to be the transcendent qualities of children, "paradigms of cherubic innocence and contentment" (68).

On the other hand, a photograph's ineluctable tie to the past placed children in history, in time. Looking at a photograph of a child almost necessarily brought with it an acknowledgment of the passage of time, the difference between the child of the picture and the living, growing, changing child, between the frozen moment of the shot and what Susan Sontag has called "time's relentless melt" (15). The rise of pictorialist photography, embodied by American artists like Alfred Stieglitz, Clarence White, and Gertrude Käsebier, involved a redeploying of many of these assumptions about children and childhood. Their emphasis on photography as fine art—something that, unlike the cheap studio portraiture and family snapshots that dominated the photography market, could not be defined simply by financial value—dovetailed perfectly with the Romantic belief in the "priceless child," an "uncorrupted, and therefore worthy witness to the natural sublime" outside the industrialized world of money and schedules, as well as of national ideals of spontaneity and individualism (Dimock, *Priceless Children* 11). Käsebier's "Happy Days" (1905), a pastoral scene of playing children, expresses many of these values (fig. 3). Four children of varying ages gather in a field, surrounded by flowers. The youngest two seem to be dancing or playing, perhaps Ring around the Rosie, bedecked by flowers. "Happy Days" is dramatically framed: the top of the picture cuts off the head of the oldest girl and much of the dancing younger girl, to place the youngest boy in the middle of the picture. This extreme framing creates a sense of an endless moment that extends beyond the frame of the picture, a never-ending summer so capacious that a photograph cannot contain it all, a world untouched by materiality. The children's play seems unrehearsed and free-form, a perfect example of the untrammeled self-expression characteristic of the American child.

Edward Steichen's "Mother and Child," from the same year, invokes many of the same feelings: a toddler reaches up toward his mother, whose head almost touches the branches of the tree under which she sits (fig. 4). The summer light is soft, perhaps late afternoon, and the bond between mother and child and between childhood and the natural world seems both inevitable and sublime.

Figure 3 Gertrude Käsebier, "Happy Days" (1902). An archetypal example of pictorialist representations of the Romantic child. Library of Congress Prints and Photographs Division.

The Representation of Childhood
in the Movement against Child Labor

Given the ways in which representations of children and childhood had developed over the course of nearly two centuries within the United States, the movement against child labor had a rich archive of sentiment from which to derive its rhetorical attacks on the industrialization of children's work.

Figure 4 Edward Steichen, "Mother and Child—Sunlight" (1905). Library of Congress Prints and Photographs Division.

Movement agitators took several tacks to weaken arguments in favor of child labor: the Deweyan belief that "play is children's work"; a reiteration of the equation of children with nature (or, more accurately, the pastoral mode expressed by Käsebier and Steichen); the more general Progressive antipathy to industrial and consumer capital that undergirded so many social reform movements of the time; a belief in childhood as a nationally specific phenomenon whose corruption could, in turn, destroy the nation; and, of course, the humanitarian empathy, or at least sympathy, invoked by the appalling conditions, long hours, and disabling physical strain most child labor imposed upon young workers.[6]

The working child was the polar opposite of the Romantic American child. Whereas the Romantic child was invaluable and outside the mundanities of history, race, gender, and class, the working child embodied the power of those forces. As Viviana A. Zelizer argues: "The price of a useful wage-earning child was directly counterposed to the moral value of an economically useless but emotionally priceless child" (57). The working child was defined by his or her price, however low—a construction of the market, a symptom of industrialization and the devouring maw of capitalism—"made to feel at an early age that his value is determined by what he can earn" (M. Adams 100). While the American child floated in a continuous idyllic present or lingered on the threshold of the material world to be shepherded into adulthood by nurturing parents, working children were products of economic and historical forces, moving through the world in industrial time.

Yet the enemy was not work itself, but the exploitative and meaningless nature of the work children were pushed into. Activists against child labor made explicit distinctions between the kinds of work children did in the early days of the Republic or on family farms or as a co-operative family endeavor and the work they did in the context of industrialization.[7] Indeed, a tenet of much anti–child labor activism was that, under very specific conditions, work could be salutary for children. Reformer Jessie P. Rich laid out the requirements for meaningful work for children that, in the negative, encapsulated all the objections the movement had against child labor: "children need work as they need food and . . . this work should be constructive. It should give opportunity for self-expression and should contribute in some way to the welfare of the family group. . . . It should teach the value and joy of labor, and to accomplish the best results, it must be performed under the guidance of father, mother, or some trusted person" (102).[8]

According to Rich's implicit logic, child labor was objectionable because it was about making money rather than about shaping young minds; it deadened the imagination and destroyed families; it fostered a disgust for work at a young age; and it was controlled by business interests for their own profits, not by parents for the good of children. This last argument was a particularly sore point for the NCLC and, as we shall see, for Lewis Hine. Often reformers argued that parents valued money over their own children and were willing to hand them over to unscrupulous padrones, factory bosses, newspaper dealers, and other unsavory adults. In large part, this antipathy to immigrant parents derived from Progressive distaste for children working for any kind of pay or being identified as economic actors in any way: for NCLC activists, "true parental love could only exist if the child was defined exclusively as an object of sentiment and not as an agent of production" (Zelizer 72).

At the same time, reformers worried that child labor destabilized parental authority. In a world in which money was power, children's earning capacities could erode the primacy of parents in working-class and immigrant families. Even worse, children's tender and malleable natures were not ready for the kind of economic and personal responsibility required by engagement in the workplace and, by extension, in the larger adult world. Not only could children become prematurely exposed to "vice and the haunts of vice," but they could also, in the words of Felix Adler, take on "a startling independence before the moral nature is fit to maintain independence" (24). By early adolescence, girls in particular could be corrupted, transformed into "women with a knowledge of evil that is pathetic in the extreme" (Chesser 85). Following the model of the Romantic American child, child labor reformers saw preadolescent children as existing outside the adult realms of sexuality, financial exchange, and responsibility for others.[9] Their place was at home or in school, preparing for adulthood, not participating in adult activities.[10]

The institution of child labor also called into question the flourishing of American society, particularly of white Anglo-Saxon America, even though the majority of child workers were from southern, eastern, and central Europe. Given how important the image of the American child was to the bourgeois U.S. self-image, it is not surprising that opponents of child labor made explicit links between the protection of American children and the righteousness and integrity (physical and moral) of the American nation. (Karen Sánchez-Eppler's work on the ambivalent figure of the newsboy in the mid-nineteenth century is an excellent example of this phenomenon.) Child labor activist Leonora Beck saw the struggle against the industrialization of children as "the movement to preserve Anglo-Saxon children, and the countries they stand for, from premature blight and decay" (17). Felix Adler set the bar even higher, asking his readers how they might find "our instincts of mercy, where is the motherliness of the women of this country, whither is the chivalry of our men that should seek a glory in protecting the defenseless and the weak?" Moreover, Adler argued, there was "a vast social interest at stake, the interest of American civilization" (18, 23).

Combining political Progressivism with the social evolutionary theories of Herbert Spencer, Adler argued that this civilization depended upon the availability of the correct conditions for children to develop into fully realized adults. As highly evolved organisms, human beings needed extensive time to prepare "to take up the struggle for existence" (Adler 23). Children's proper development was crucial to the health of the nation, and the appropriate activities—play, education, parental nurture—were essential to that development.

The inextricability of childhood and play, and the mutual exclusion of paid work and meaningful play, were themes that suffused anti–child labor literature. In his article "Children of the Coal Shadow," which first appeared in *McClure's* in 1903, Francis H. Nichols observed that "the children of the Coal Shadow have no child life. The little tots are sullen, the older children tight; they rarely play" (141). Features in the *Child Labor Bulletin* aimed at children focused on the absence of play from the lives of working children. In Lydia Hale Crane's playlet entitled "The Messenger Boy," which appeared in the *Bulletin* in 1914, young Ned envies the eponymous boy for his "uniform and seeming freedom" to play whenever he liked between errands.

Ned's father soon disabuses him of his fantasy, however, exclaiming: "Play-time! Messenger boys are not supposed to have play-time. All they have is *waiting* time. . . . And they *must go wherever* they are sent, no matter where it is, or even if they don't like it one little bit" (23, emphasis in original). The messenger boy concurs with Ned's father, expressing his longing to play and go to school, neither of which is possible with his work and his family's finan-cial needs. By the end of the play, Ned rues that he ever envied the poor boy.

For the NCLC, play was a precious commodity, something that once lost could never be regained. Like childhood, play was part of a delicate develop-mental balancing act that required careful attention and was an essential ele-ment of healthy growth, inseparable from the basic human needs for clean air, food, and water, as well as more intangible but no less important require-ments such as love and intellectual nurture. Pauline M. Newman, herself a former child worker and an organizer with the International Ladies' Garment Workers Union, implored her readers to empathize with working children who had no access to the basic elements of childhood, asking them to "think what it must mean to a child who never can play; who is deprived of sunshine and air, of love, and of life itself! And let us not forget that we only have one childhood!" ("Child Labor" 43).

Not just the child, but also childhood was priceless, irreplaceable. And "childhood" was increasingly defined along very specific lines: characterized by play, removed from the commercial world, supervised and directed by adults. Lewis Hine translated these assumptions about childhood, and the ways in which child labor contravened such assumptions, into a vast archive of photographs.[11] In his pictures for the NCLC, Hine framed Progressive beliefs about working children, using his lens to juxtapose representations of the working child with beliefs about the ideal American child. His aesthetic, which melded the conventions of child portraiture with the photography of outrage exemplified by Jacob Riis, played out the contrast between photog-raphy as art and photography as document. Most importantly, in deploring the impressment of children into historical time and material reality, Hine handed over the bourgeois institution of childhood to working-class and immigrant children. In his photographs, Hine transformed the Romantic child from ideal into norm, dissolving the class divide for the sake of a uni-versalizing identity.

With their commitment to redefining childhood in the United States, part of the NCLC's ideological work promoted by Hine's photography was to dis-articulate the phrases "working child" and "American child," and to trans-form them into opposites. When Hine looked forward to the day when "child labor pictures will be records of the past," he was also anticipating a process by which working children would be folded into the American polity through their status as nonproductive, nonuseful nonactors ("Social

Photography" 112). Certainly, children became less attractive as workers as new sets of immigrants streamed into the mostly but not exclusively urban workplace at the end of the nineteenth and beginning of the twentieth century, adults who may have demanded higher wages but were also significantly more productive (Zelizer 63). But the economic issues were less important than the ethical and ideological imperative: the American child did not work.

The Aesthetics of Lewis W. Hine's Child Labor Photographs

Lewis Hine's work is remarkable not because he invented documentary photography or was the first to imagine photography as an aesthetic, or as he called it, "interpretive," practice. Certainly, he was not the first person to photograph industrial scenes. On a government-sponsored survey of the Southwest, including the Nevada silver-mining industry, Clarence King brought famed Civil War photographer Timothy H. O'Sullivan, whose pictures appeared in King's 1870 report, *The Mining Industry*. And in the photographs he published later, O'Sullivan became a pioneer in representing industrial work in the United States.

Hine was also not alone in taking pictures of urban poverty. His best-known predecessor, Jacob Riis, had made something of a career of exposing the wretchedness of the slums through his pictures of New York's tenement districts in his 1890 exposé, *How the Other Half Lives*. Riis's use of magnesium-based flash powder had illuminated the cellars and attics, the saloons, police stations, and alleys of the Lower East Side. But Riis, despite his zeal to reform the tenements, raise the wages, and clean up the trash-filled streets of the urban poor, brought a different kind of sensibility to his discussion of working children. For Riis, the "street Arab" who sold newspapers, blacked boots, and ran errands was "as bright and sharp as the weasel, which, among all the predatory beasts, he most resembles." Calling upon the romanticization of street boys that stretched back at least to Horatio Alger, Riis praised the street Arab's "sturdy independence, love of freedom and absolute self-reliance" (153). While he praised the work of organizations like the Children's Aid Society in their attempts to rehabilitate street boys, his hope that "an era of better sense is dawning that shall witness a rescue work upon lines which, when the leaven has fairly had time to work, will put an end to the existence of the New York Street Arab" stands in its vagueness in sharp contrast to his concrete suggestions to demolish and redesign the tenement houses from which these boys escaped (163).

What is so original and affecting about Hine's photography (aside from the compelling nature of its subject matter) is the way in which he combined a variety of influences to create his own aesthetic. While he insisted upon the realism of his photographs and styled himself as "a working photographer performing a kind of cultural (and political) labor" (Trachtenberg, *Reading* 168), he also saw himself as a kind of auteur, a "specialist" capable of making an "intelligent interpretation" of social phenomena (qtd. in Stange 72–73). Drawing upon the muckraking of Riis, the stark industrial images of O'Sullivan, the sensitive portraiture of Käsebier and Steichen, and the compositional virtuosity of Stieglitz, Hine constructed a photographic language that was highly connotative, speaking beyond the immediate message of the images or the captions he wrote to accompany them.[12]

Hine's pictures of child workers also borrowed structurally from the narrative photography of the American West. Western photographers "thought of their medium as a narrative one, whose richest potential was realized not by one picture but through a string of images augmented with literary text. . . . They thought of themselves as storytellers" (Sandweiss, "Undecisive Moments" 99). The commentary that Hine wrote to accompany his photographs was not simply descriptive. Rather it told a story about each individual image and about the series of pictures as a whole, which was deepened and broadened with each additional picture and caption, like "a long quotation from appearance: the length here to be measured not by time but by a greater extension of meaning" (Stange 128).

Like Santa Fe photographer W. Henry Brown, who wrote extensive architectural, historical, and anthropological notes on the back of his pictures of Pueblo Indian villages, Hine created a multilayered set of visual and written texts. And as with Brown's series of pictures, "together, the images comprised a kind of guided tour [for Brown, of the Rio Grande Valley; for Hine, of the situation of child laborers state by state, industry by industry]; individually, they were imputed with a rich narrative historical significance that only a text could elucidate" (Sandweiss, "Undecisive Moments" 118). Indeed, we might even read Hine's NCLC pictures not as a collection of images separated by time, region, and industry, and connected only by the goal of social reform, but as a kind of extended photo-essay that, in the words of W.J.T. Mitchell, generates "tension between the claims of the ethical, the political, the aesthetic, and the rhetorical" (287). Through his child labor photographs, Hine both enacts and disrupts the allegorical figure of "the child," exposing the ways in which national growth had put thousands of children to work while still claiming childhood as a resource for the nation's moral center.

In his photographs of working children, Hine deployed a variety of techniques of composing, framing, and cropping the images to tell the story of child labor. As Maren Stange has shown, Hine exercised considerable control over the presentation and contextualization of his NCLC pictures—he was involved in selecting, cropping, captioning, and arranging the photographs for maximum effect (67–68). His use of camera position and surrounding architecture and landscape created what in a literary context would be called subtext, meanings hovering around, below, and beyond the denotative sense of the photograph. His reiteration of three major themes—children's play being foreclosed by their work, the diminutiveness of children in contrast to the hugeness of industrial machinery, and the corruption of family spaces and family life by the institution of child labor—forms an integrated narrative of a world in which human values have been severely compromised and the meaning of childhood perverted.

An excellent example of the ways in which Hine's aesthetic choices generate an array of subtextual meanings is his 1915 photograph "Bootblacks fill up spare time pitching pennies, New York City" (fig. 5).[13] This picture is atypical of much of his child labor photography in that it is neither a portrait nor an action shot of working children. Rather, it shows boys at play, participating in a rudimentary gambling game popular among urban children. The youngest looks about six years old, the oldest around ten, fairly typical for bootblacks, young boys who plied their trade on street corners of major cities. Hine's composition is electric: the photograph is a little off-kilter, so the pennies are in the foreground to the mid-left of the frame, and the line of

Figure 5 Lewis W. Hine, "Bootblacks fill up spare time pitching pennies, New York City" (1915). Photography Collection, Miriam and Ira D. Wallach Division of Art, Prints, and Photographs, New York Public Library, Astor, Lenox and Tilden Foundations.

boys seems to lean around to the right. They are in a mix of stances, crouching, leaning, and standing. The boys are for the most part absorbed in the game; those in the front row sit on their boxes, while an older boy stands on the far right, gazing down the street, probably on the lookout for police or truant officers (his box is still on his back; perhaps he is unable to let go of his work stance even for a moment). The boy who has just pitched his penny leans forward to see the result.

This picture represents boys at play, but theirs is not the play of the Romantic child. They are not engaged in healthful recreation but are "fill[ing] up spare time" between jobs. Their playtime is hemmed in by the rhythms of the work world. Compositionally, the photograph is a series of geometric shapes: circles, lines, squares, and rectangles. The camera is pitched low along with the boys who crouch or sit at ground level. In fact, the picture is framed to cut off the very top of the tallest boy's cap, creating a sense of compressed space. In marked contrast to the children in Käsebier's "Happy Days," whose play seems to exist in an idyll outside temporality, these boys are more like factory workers taking a short break before punching in again. Even at a lighthearted moment of play, the bootblacks are contained by the city, possessed by the conditions that send them to work. Moreover, their play itself is defined by the relations of capitalism—they're gambling with the pennies they've earned blacking boots.

The framing of the photograph mimics the lines of the bootblack's box, and there is a repetition of box shapes and straight lines throughout the picture. The posters on the baseboard of the shop window echo the lines of the windows above the boys' heads and the grating in the pavement below their feet; the boxes the boys carry restate the box of the photograph itself. Where Käsebier's tight framing created a sense of endlessness, Hine's generates a feeling of claustrophobia and restriction.

The perversion of play Hine documents in "Bootblacks fill up spare time" reappears in several other photographs that even more explicitly draw the contrast between childhood defined through play (which is to say, an appropriate American childhood) and defined by work. These photographs are all organized into opposing pairs, work versus play. One set appeared in the *Child Labor Bulletin* in 1912 under the title "Contrasts"; the other is a pair of photographs Hine himself put together with connected captions of "Rosie," a young girl who worked in an oyster shucking plant.

"Contrasts" comprises two sets of photographs, each organized around a different childhood activity. The first pair centers on dolls: "They Who Play with Dolls" (fig. 6) and "They Who Help Make Them" (fig. 7). In the first picture, captioned "All the maternal impulse and play instinct cherished and developed," two girls, about five and three years old and dressed in winter coats and wool hats, play with a doll in a wicker pram. The older girl proudly holds onto the handles, while the younger bends over the pram, arranging the doll's blankets. While these children are clearly standing on a city street, behind them are grass and trees, probably a park. The open space stretches out behind them, as the girls are absorbed in their play. The edge of the pram suggests an undulating line echoed by the soft edges of the grass behind the girls. The photograph also creates a gentle upward slope, from the supine doll leaning up slightly in the pram, to the white-hatted head of the younger girl, to the upright figure of the older girl, suggesting a progression of development from beloved infant to nurturing child to loving mother.

"They Who Help Make Them" shows two girls and their mother sitting around a tenement house parlor table assembling doll parts as their younger

Figure 6 Lewis W. Hine, "Contrasts: They Who Play with Dolls." Captioned by Hine: "All the maternal and play instinct cherished and developed." *Child Labor Bulletin* 1.2 (1912): 35.

brother looks on. Hine dates the picture as taken February 1, 1912, and describes the scene in a lengthy caption:

> Lena, 12, and deformed, and Nettie, 9, are helping make Dolls. They work after school and often until 10 P.M.
>
> After the arms and legs are stuffed, their task is to sew up the tops— 48 arms and legs for 5c.
>
> The father, a laborer, often idle, says that the only two who work steadily all day are the deformed child and Rosie, aged 14 and not in the picture, who has to stay out of school sometimes, because "her eyes are too sick." ("Contrasts" 36)

The photograph contrasts with the previous image in more than just content. Unlike the open and airy feeling of "They Who Play with Dolls,"

Figure 7 Lewis W. Hine, "Contrasts: They Who Help Make Them." Hine's "Contrasts" series sets in sharp relief the oppositions between the Romantic and the working child. *Child Labor Bulletin* 1.2 (1912): 37.

this picture is cramped and claustrophobic. Hine frames the photograph to emphasize the restrictiveness of tenement space, so that the mother's head is cut off by the top edge, and the edge of the table holding the doll parts extends beyond the frame of the picture, as though they go on and on into the space of the apartment. While the frame of "They Who Play with Dolls" is proportioned to the bodies of the girls and at the same time suggests an unseen but benign adult presence, the inclusion of the mother in "They Who Make Them" in the condensed composition of the photograph implies the helplessness of the adults who care for these children.

The next pair of photographs presents an even starker opposition. "They Who Pick Natural Flowers" (fig. 8) is an almost stereotypical Pictorialist image of the Romantic child in a pastoral setting. A little boy in knee breeches sits on a meadowy hill, his face turned away from the camera in partial profile, gazing happily down at a bunch of wildflowers that he holds in

Figure 8 Lewis W. Hine, "Contrasts: They Who Pick Natural Flowers." *Child Labor Bulletin* 1.2 (1912): 65.

his hands, embodying Florence Kelley and Alzina Stevens's declaration that "to be carefree is one of the prerogatives of childhood" (68). His body is relaxed and mimics the soft line of the hill, and the grass around him is dotted with flowers. This idyll is unmarked by time or place; the caption (whether written by Hine or by an editor of the *Bulletin*) invokes the imaginary connection between the health of the child and the health of the nation: "Joy in Play and Freedom./Of such is the making of a Nation" ("Contrasts" 64). This boy is embraced by nature and embraces it in return. He has an appreciation for beauty and for wildness, as we can see in the bouquet he has gathered from the hill. As in "They Who Play with Dolls," the child is unnamed and unidentified in terms of place or date; this scene is imagined as happening anywhere and everywhere that children are free.

The central figure in the contrast picture, "They Who Make Artificial Ones," is positioned quite similarly to the boy in "They Who Pick Natural Flowers" (fig. 9). Her face is also in profile, and she looks down at a collection of flowers in her hands. But she is staring not at an object of aesthetic pleasure, but at the petals of artificial flowers she and her mother and siblings are assembling. Rather than sitting in repose, she stands at a tenement table. According to Hine's caption she is the "youngest *actually skilled* worker found by the National Child Labor Committee. . . . She is three years old" ("Contrasts" 64, emphasis in original). Although the caption mentions three other siblings, aged nine, eleven, and fourteen, who also work on flowers, the picture does not identify them explicitly. Tucked behind the girl is an older sister, and we also see her mother. Another pair of hands protrudes into the frame on the far right, and the picture itself seems like a symphony of hands, in postures that resemble prayer, separating and gluing flower petals.

The contrast between these two pictures extends to the kinds of flowers invoked here. The Romantic child of "Those Who Pick" is gathering *natural* flowers; he seems an organic part of the pastoral scene, leaning into the slope of the hill. "Those who make" are making *artificial* flowers, feeding consumer capital's devouring hunger for fakeness and artifice. Unlike the little boy picking flowers, who rests comfortably on a grassy hill, the flower maker stands at the table, her body at stiff attention to the task at hand. While he basks in natural sunlight, she is forced to work by the artificial light of the kerosene lamp, well into the winter night.

As in "They Who Help Make Them," Hine identifies this scene by date—February 2, 1912—but in this picture he also includes the time, 8 P.M. Certainly he wants to emphasize the fact that a child barely out of babyhood is working well beyond a healthy bedtime. But there's a larger rhetorical purpose here. The pictures of children playing with dolls and picking flowers are without markers of time and place. They represent supposedly universal qualities: maternal impulse, play instinct, joy in play, and freedom. While

·Figure 9 Lewis W. Hine, "Contrasts: They Who Make Artificial Ones." For Hine, the artificial-flower industry's use of child labor epitomized the corruption of a natural childhood. *Child Labor Bulletin* 1:2 (1912): 67.

someone must have taken these pictures, the accompanying text does not attest to that material necessity. These pictures are supposed to speak for themselves, and the children represented within to transcend the specifics of geography, time, and mechanics.

By contrast, not only are Hine's photographs of working children carefully dated but also the dating—"Photo taken Feb. 1, 1912," or, even more specifically, "This photo was taken at 8 P.M., Feb. 2, 1912"—articulates child labor with, first, the evidentiary act of photography (that these children were, irrefutably, at a certain time in a certain place, performing these acts) and, second, the precision of time and date industrial capital imposes upon children, who should be free of such encumbrances. Even (or perhaps especially) within the supposedly protective sphere of the home, where children should be shielded from the exigencies of historical time, the hand of capitalism extends, disciplining adults and children alike in its attention to schedule and productivity.

The second set of photographs that deal with the relationship between work and play is more challenging to the viewer. Taken in early 1913 in Bluffton, South Carolina, these two pictures are of the same subject, Rosie, a seven-year-old who works in an oyster cannery. One is titled "Rosie Playing with Her Doll" (fig. 10) and the other, "Rosie at Work" (fig. 11). Hine clearly intended these photographs to be seen in tandem; in the New York Public Library collection, he paired them under the heading "Child labor means cheated childhood."

In both pictures Rosie is looking up at the camera, her eyes directly engaging the viewer. We see her whole body in "Rosie Playing with Her Doll," her arms cradling the toy, her head ducking down a little as she looks at the camera. The frame of the picture is almost coterminous with the lines of her body—her toes touch the bottom edge of the picture and the top edge is an inch or so above her head. The doll actually seems a bit out of place, awkward, as though Rosie is not quite sure what to do with it. Rosie's face is clean, as are her clothes, although they are pretty worn and torn in a couple of places. Her hair is arranged so that a nimbus of blond escapes out of her ponytail, ringing her face. She seems to be standing on a residential street, with a couple of houses in the distance behind her, but the dirt road implies a rural town. Her boots are very dusty, the toes almost completely worn away, and her shadow stretches out behind her, suggesting midafternoon. Despite the sparseness of her surroundings, Rosie's vitality leaps out at the viewer, her small body coiled with energy. Her smile is almost sly, as though she's sizing up the photographer as much as he is analyzing her.

"Rosie at Work" is taken much closer up. Rosie holds a large, muddy oyster in one hand and is splitting it with a large knife with the other, and the confidence and strength with which she mimes shucking the oyster is in marked contrast to the awkwardness with which she nestles her doll in the companion picture. Her hair is more tightly gathered to the top of her head, and her white frock is mostly covered with a mud-stained apron. She looks up at the camera, but quite solemnly—her face is much more open and smooth than in the doll picture, much more exposed. She looks more like a child here, more unformed, unlike the knowing, playful girl in the doll picture. In spite of the physical strength of Rosie's arms, especially the one holding the shucking knife, which is thrust forward toward the camera, her personality seems to have been leached out of her. Her face is beautiful but blank, and the viewer's eye is drawn instead toward the working hands and arms.

This child's labor, Hine is arguing, has turned Rosie's life upside down. More comfortable with a shucking knife in her hands than with a doll,

Figure 10 Lewis W. Hine, "Rosie Playing with Her Doll" (1913). Photography Collection, Miriam and Ira D. Wallach Division of Art, Prints, and Photographs, New York Public Library, Astor, Lenox and Tilden Foundations.

she has been transformed from a creature of play to a creature of work. The ambiguity of her expression and the lack of affect with which she holds her toy in "Rosie Playing with Her Doll" intensifies this point. Unlike the girls in "They Who Play with Dolls," Rosie does not reproduce the nurturing role of ideal mother, but instead reenacts the implicit attitude of her own neglectful mother who allows her seven-year-old daughter to work. "All the maternal

Figure 11 Lewis W. Hine, "Rosie at Work" (1913). Child labor has made Rosie more comfortable with a shucking knife than with a doll. Photography Collection, Miriam and Ira D. Wallach Division of Art, Prints, and Photographs, New York Public Library, Astor, Lenox and Tilden Foundations.

impulse and play instinct" are not "cherished and developed" in Rosie. Rather, these qualities have been suppressed by work.

Hine's argument that child labor disrupted the natural order of things also finds its expression in his photographs of children operating industrial equipment. In these pictures, he is particularly interested in the disproportion between the size of the children and the outsize machinery they are expected to work. His photographs of child labor in textile mills tell the story of children dwarfed by machinery, in thrall to it. He often draws attention to the size of the children he photographs, either calling them "little" or recording their height in inches. "A Little Cotton Spinner," taken in Lancaster, South Carolina, in late 1908 is an excellent example of this (fig. 12). While Hine's caption is brief—"She is one of many children of this age in the mill"— the image itself speaks volubly about the ways in which children are ill-suited for mill work. Hine's main interest in this picture is in line and proportion: how little the spinner is, how her small vertical body is almost overwhelmed by the horizontal lines of thread, wall, and floor. The line of bobbins seems endless—it repeats and repeats out of the frame of the foreground and recedes into the back. The vanishing point of the floorboards reinforces the expanse of the mill, as the girl's black-booted feet intersect with them at a

Figure 12 Lewis W. Hine, "A Little Cotton Mill Spinner" (1908). Hine's use of exaggerated differences in scale between child workers and their industrial environments reminds us that children don't belong in factories. Milstein Division of United States History, Local History, and Genealogy, New York Public Library, Astor, Lenox and Tilden Foundations.

sharp angle. The black pipe on the left and the high, whitewashed walls and windows emphasize the smallness of the girl, as do the wheels out of focus at the very top of the picture. The walls of the mill stretch up from the lower left edge of the frame and out of sight. Although there is another, almost obscured, female body behind the girl, visible only by the edge of her skirt, the girl is the central figure of the picture, emphasizing her aloneness, her abandonment by the adult world. The bobbins she is working on are in sharp focus, but everything else is blurry, as though to say it doesn't matter where along the row she is—the work is so anonymous and repetitive.

The repetitiveness of industrial labor is a powerful trope in two pictures of "back-roping boys" taken at the Chace cotton mill in Burlington, Vermont, in May 1909. Compositionally similar, both feature barefoot boys standing dwarfed by the machinery in the mule-spinning room of the mill, with its hundreds of bobbins and dozens of wheels. As in the picture of the girl spinner, Hine takes advantage of the long horizontal lines of the pipes and floorboards and the multiple verticals of bobbins and window frames to

Figure 13 Lewis W. Hine, "Edward Marcotte, a 'back-roping' boy, who has been here one year" (1909). New York Public Library Photography Collection.

create a vertiginous sense of a small child enveloped by huge machinery. The pictures are subtly different, however. In the first, which Hine captions "Edward Marcotte, a 'back-roping boy,' who has been here one year," the boy appears far away from the viewer (fig. 13); our eyes travel down seemingly endless rows of bobbins and wheels to reach him. The pipes on the left side of the picture intensify the feeling of extended space, and the two sets of horizontals hem the boy in, forming a narrow canyon that contains and constrains the standing Edward.

In the second picture, "A 'back-roping boy' in the mule-spinning room, Raoul . . . has been here two years," the boy stands closer to the camera and is less overwhelmed by the machinery that surrounds him (fig. 14).[14] But he is covered in scraps and loose threads, as though he has become part of the milling process. Pulling spun cotton from the bobbin, with fabric draped over his shoulder, he is almost indistinguishable from the machine and the threads, particularly with the white walls and folded curtains behind him. The pipes along the wall echo the horizontal pattern of the floorboards that extend to the small blurred window in the rear of the shot, an exit from the mill that Raoul himself seems cut off from.

Hine takes this sense of disproportion even further in another mill picture. One of his best known, taken in Loudon, Tennessee, in December 1910, it is captioned "This little girl is so small she has to stand on a box to reach her

Figure 14 Lewis W. Hine, "A 'back-roping' boy in the mule-spinning room, Raoul . . . has been here two years" (1909). Photography Collection, Miriam and Ira D. Wallach Division of Art, Prints, and Photographs, New York Public Library, Astor, Lenox and Tilden Foundations.

machine. She is regularly employed as a knitter in a hosiery mill in Tennessee. She does not know how long she has worked" (fig. 15). The photograph is shot from below, so that in clearest focus are the box, the girl's shoes, and the cascading piles of knitted goods at her feet. The picture gives the viewer a feeling of disorientation, a sense that everything is out of proportion—the girl takes up a large area of the picture but is clearly tiny in relation to the woman standing behind her and the machinery itself, not to mention the large folds of fabric below her. The box appears immense, jutting out toward us, and the girl leans so far into the machine that it looks as though it will swallow her up. Two women stand at their own machines with their backs to her, and another is partly obscured by her body and the box; they seem huge in comparison.

Hine also constructs the picture along an extended horizontal that separates the two rows of workers, at the end of which stand two blurred figures, possibly a man and a woman. Their identities are unknown: are they factory forepeople? Other workers? At any rate, mirroring the photographer and the viewers of this picture, they suggest an audience beyond the machines that stands in the distance and gazes upon the imbalances of size and work.

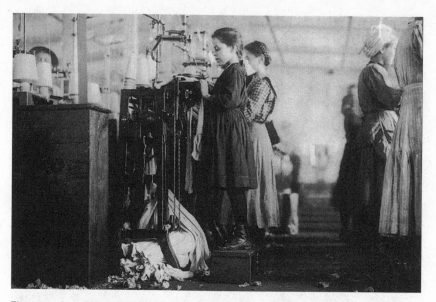

Figure 15 Lewis W. Hine, "Little Girl Age 7" (1910). This little girl is so small she has to stand on a box to reach her machine. Library of Congress Prints and Photographs Division.

A final example of Hine's use of inequalities of scale is one of the most dramatic and politically pointed (fig. 16). The caption to the 1912 photograph hardly hints at the power of the image: "A 7-year-old newsboy who tries to short change customers when he sells papers. Another boy says of him: 'He can rustle de poipers O.K.' Many youngsters like this are selling around the national capitol." In the picture, the little newsboy holds onto his papers, which are almost half his size. The street, nearly empty but for a parked car and a very few people on the pavement, stretches toward the horizon, and at the rear of the picture looms the Capitol building. The road is very wide, exceeding much of the frame of the picture, and the boy's head lines up almost vertically with the dome of the Capitol.

The message here is hardly subtle—Congress has resisted passing child labor laws even as young children work in its literal shadow. What saves the picture from preachiness, though, is the look on the newsboy's face. He looks out beyond the frame of the picture, as though searching for another customer. He's still hustling for opportunities. But there is a more profound point—submerged by commerce, he's oblivious of the political ramifications of his work, or the allegorical meanings of his image. Completely alone, outside the protective structures of modern society, he is a product of capital, not the Capitol. More important still, in the center of American national identity, this child represents a practice that denies him the ability to be a genuine American child.

Figure 16 Lewis W. Hine, "7-Year-Old Newsboy, Washington, D.C." (1911). The Capitol in the background sharpens Hine's critique of federal inaction around banning child labor. Library of Congress Prints and Photographs Division.

In all these pictures, the children are either literally or figuratively isolated. Whatever adults occupy the frame of the photograph with them are obscured by the body of the child or seem to ignore the children in their midst. While Hine makes it clear that these children are hardly unusual cases, either by photographing similar scenes with different children or recording in the caption the presence of other children at the same job, these photographs convey a sense of absolute isolation from both adults and the world of children.[15]

In his photographs of tenement house labor, though, Hine condemned not just the larger structures of capital that kept children separated from the right to play and develop, but the immigrant parents who he believed were either unable or refused to see the damage they were doing to their children. In these pictures, Hine emphasizes the ways in which pushing children into work not only harms the children themselves but also compromises the integrity of the family. The communal table, which should be a space of nourishment and love (particularly maternal love), is transformed into a place of work, stunting the development of expansive familial affection and nurturance.

Hine took dozens of photographs of tenement homework: families cracking nuts, assembling artificial flowers, pulling seams, and other labor-intensive, low-paying work. A 1908 photograph of a family making artificial

Figure 17 Lewis W. Hine, "Malatesta Family" (1908). The family includes "Frank, 14 years, John, 11, and Lizzie, 4," who "work with their parents at home making artificial flowers." Library of Congress Prints and Photographs Division.

flowers is typical of these pictures, although the family here seems a little better off financially than many of the tenement groups Hine documents (fig. 17). The picture is crisp and clean, and all the details are amazingly clear, down to the oilcloth on the table, the bow in the little girl's hair, and the scattered petals. The orderliness of the bundled flowers and the cleanliness of the scene are in conflict with the caption that reminds us how exploited this family is: "Frank, 14 years, John, 11, and Lizzie, 4, work with their parents at home making artificial flowers. The father helps because his health is too poor to do other work. The boys work from Saturday afternoon and evening until 10 or 11 P.M. Lizzie separates petals. They make regularly from ten to twelve gross a week for which they are paid 6¢ a gross." The shot is in medium close-up—despite the spareness of the room, the long line of the front of the table crowds the family into the background of the photo, as though they are being pushed back out of the space.

Most of Hine's photographs of child labor in the tenements follow similar lines to this one. The pictures are shot at close range, and the family members are grouped tightly around the table, which doubles as workspace. In many of these pictures, Hine reveals signs of the domesticity that contradicts the scene of working children: folded linens, wall decorations, and curtains, even in the most deprived homes. His picture of the Darelli or Tarelli family

Figure 18 Lewis W. Hine, "Darelli or Tarelli Family Making Artificial Flowers" (1912). Library of Congress Prints and Photographs Division.

(Hine gives both spellings of the name in his caption), also making artificial flowers, is angled to include the family's set of china arrayed on decorative shelves and an ornamented kettle on the stove (fig. 18). This photograph makes evident the deep disjunctures between the domestic desires of working immigrants and the ways in which they are abused by the city.

Hine's representation of tenement work was not always this sympathetic, either in the images or in the words accompanying them. His condemnation of food processing in tenement rooms—in this case the cracking and picking of nuts—veers uncomfortably close to opprobrium for the immigrant workers and their children themselves. The photograph of the Marengin family, on the "Lower West Side" of New York, evokes these contradictory emotions in him (fig. 19); in the Library of Congress collection, Hine's caption is lengthy and detailed, veering from sympathy to outrage and disgust:

> Mrs. Raphael Marengin, . . . St., first floor rear. Pepine, 10 yrs. old, cracking nuts with her teeth. The mother had just been doing the same. Carmine, 8 years old, has cross eyes, and with the boy about same age works too. Some of them work until 8 or 9 P.M. at times. Boy holding baby is foolish. Husband works on railroad part of the time. 10-year-old-girl cracking nuts with her teeth. The mother had just been doing the same. 8-year-old child has cross eyes and works, as well as the boy. New York City, 1911. Manufacture of food in tenement homes is now prohibited in New York State.

Figure 19 Lewis W. Hine, "Mrs. Raphael Marengin and Family" (1911). Library of
Congress Prints and Photographs Division.

At first glance, a viewer might mistake this for a family scene, with children gathered around the table, their heads bowed, like the artificial flower
makers,' perhaps in prayer. But the piles of nuts on the table, the concentration on the mother's face, and the dirt that covers everyone's clothes make
clear the true meaning of the scene. This is a cruel parody of family harmony—mother and children united through exploitation. Indeed, the
mother and her children seem aware and even ashamed of how appalling
their situation is, since they look away from the camera; the youngest boy
looks down at the floor, his face hidden by his cap. Only the baby seems eager
to be included in the group. Although Hine tells us that another brother is
holding the baby, the older boy is out of the frame of the photograph, and
the baby appears to be leaping from the edge of the picture, trying to propel
himself into the rest of the family.

Unusually, here Hine directs his outrage more at the family than at their
employers, the nut distributors. The first detail he provides about the scene is
that the little girl, Pepine, is cracking nuts with her mouth, and "the mother
had just been doing the same." After a short description of the family, he
repeats the same information almost word for word, explaining that food
production in tenements has now been prohibited. (In fact, in the New York
Public Library collection, Hine makes a causal connection between these
two facts: "Such conditions led to a prohibition of the manufacture of food

in tenement homes in New York State.") This disgust crops up several times in his captions to photographs of nut picking at home. In a similar picture in the Library of Congress collection, he points out that the children cracking nuts with their parents are "the dirtiest imaginable, . . . pawing over the nuts," and in almost all the nut-picking photographs he describes parents, children, the home, or all of them as "dirty."

Given his compassion for other working children, Hine's ambivalence here is striking. It is true that the tenements he photographed were remarkably dirty, but the filth of breaker boys in coal mines and of children working in fields and oyster plants does not seem to bother him, or, at least, he rarely comments upon it. Perhaps this scene is too reminiscent of what an ideal family group should be—parents and children gathered over food at a common table—but at the same time irreconcilable to it.[16] Child labor has degraded these families so completely that they have been rendered abject, thrust out from equal consideration with other victims of capitalism. While the institution of child labor draws the denizens of the home—women and children—into the public sphere, food processing in the tenements too thoroughly breaks down the division between the realms of domesticity and labor, as its articulation in the term "homework" suggests, allowing the temporality of industry to completely suffuse what should be the timeless space of the home. Food is no longer nourishment but work, not something a mother provides for her child but something on which mother and child work side by side. Cracking nuts between her teeth along with her mother, Pepine (however unknowingly) makes a mockery of the communion of the family meal, biting down on food she will never herself eat.

Hine's 1911 photograph of five-year-old Olga Schubert, who worked with her mother in a canning factory in Biloxi, Mississippi, encapsulates all these themes—the perversion of the family, the erasure of play, the diminution of children (fig. 20). If Mrs. Marengin's children are ambivalent about being photographed, Olga actively resists it. Her hands cover her face and she curls up her body in response to the camera. Hine comments that Olga had been at work since 5:00 AM, "was tired out and refused to be photographed." Olga's pose is in direct contrast with classic pictures like "Cherry Ripe" and "The Age of Innocence," in which Romantic children gaze directly, if a little coyly, at the viewer. There are similar signifiers—the little hands and arms, the smallness of the body—but Olga hides her face and her hands are rubbing her eyes.

As in many of his child labor pictures, Hine here is commenting on smallness, and Olga seems especially defenseless. Another girl sits to her left, somewhat out of focus, perhaps two or three years old. Hine does not identify her, but her placement raises any number of questions. She gazes with curiosity at the resistant Olga: might she be an even younger Schubert child?

Figure 20 Lewis W. Hine, "Olga Schubert, Age 5" (1911). "She was tired out and refused to be photographed," Hine comments. Library of Congress Prints and Photographs Division.

is she a younger sister, seeing in the tiny Olga her own fate in only a few years? Unlike Olga's tightly twisted pigtails, the other girl's hair is in loose curls around her head, perhaps representing a greater level of physical freedom, less bodily restraint. Their body language, too, is quite different. The younger girl leans forward, thumb in mouth, clearly curious about Olga and possibly about Hine himself. Olga has been robbed of any of the outward signifiers of childhood—no thumb sucking for her—and of the natural curiosity of childhood. She wants only to shut out the world, neither to look nor to be looked at. Whatever the actual relationship between these children, their closeness in age is belied by their very different economic roles. In a world without child labor, these two girls might be playing together. Instead, they are isolated from each other by the work Olga has been impressed into and that compresses her into a tight ball of fatigue.

Hine documents not just Olga's exhausted refusal to be photographed, but her mother's response to her resistance: "Oh, she's ugly." The word "ugly" and Mrs. Schubert's intent in using it here have a number of possible meanings. Olga's mother's comments in response to her daughter's refusal to be photographed might be based in what she believes are the aesthetics of photography—she could be saying, in essence, you're missing nothing by not getting a picture of her face; if the appropriate child subjects of photography are beautiful, she's not worth it.[17] Her belittling diagnosis of her daughter might be defensive or embarrassed, that is to say, minimizing her daughter's resistance in the face of what seems to her middle-class authority: a man in a suit with a camera. Alternatively, and this seems to me most plausible, "ugly" here could be part of a Southern vernacular, meaning, when applied to children, ill-tempered, difficult, willful.[18] Olga's "ugliness" is a kind of work stoppage, a refusal to have her identity as a child used by yet another adult, and at the same time a childish response based in individual exhaustion.

Ultimately, the pathos of this picture is terrific and, despite Olga's mother's declarations to the contrary, beautiful to look at; even as (or perhaps because) Olga resists being represented and hides her face, she carves out a statement of self. Hine wants to show how she has been totally erased by the experience of work, but in his desire to show her erasure, he too negates her desire just to be left alone, to be a tired child. He still takes her picture. In many ways this photograph is an "unpicture"—what we don't see tells us as much or more about child labor, parental complicity, and the power wielded by the camera than we would learn if we could look at Olga directly. Ironically, although this photograph encapsulates Hine's larger arguments against child labor, it also challenges his project, implicitly accusing him of using images of children for his own needs. These children are case studies, not participants, "empirical evidence and representative type[s]," in the words of George Dimock, not the subjects of personal portraits (15).[19] Despite the hard physical labor expected of the children, Hine represents them as first, foremost, and only victims rather than as economic actors, producers, manufacturers, and children trapped in an economic system not of their own making. Likewise, he is more inclined to indict their parents as (at best) complicit in the exploitation of child workers than to recognize that much of the time the parents and their children have more interests in common—which is to say survival—than the children have with Hine himself.[20]

Photographing working children was, ultimately, emotionally messy for Hine. It evoked deeply contradictory responses in him, which he transmitted to his viewers through both image and word. The intensity of emotion that he experienced about child labor—its conditions, its participants both child and adult—as well as about the cultural and ideological structures of the American child that he reproduced through his photography translated into pictures that were electrifying. It would not be an exaggeration to say that Hine created a visual vocabulary for Americans to use when looking at pictures of and talking about working children, just as he had tried to find new ways to represent incoming immigrants at Ellis Island.

Hine's influence in redefining the national role of children as nonworkers had another effect: the repositioning of adolescents as ideally suited for work, fitting into the rhythms and demands of the industrial workplace, and integrating personal and work lives effortlessly. As we'll see in the chapters that follow, this image of working adolescents was inextricably intertwined with the development of a highly sophisticated consumer culture and popular entertainment, but Hine's major interest in young working people was in the ways in which they could move easily between work and leisure identities. Unlike children, whose faces and bodies were stamped with the impress of long hours and paltry pay, the adolescents in Hine's pictures seem untroubled, even energized, by their work.

Hine did not explicitly (or perhaps even consciously) intend his pictures of working adolescents to be seen in direct contrast to his photographs of child laborers. Most of these images are classified as simply representing "men" and "women" at work. However, the people he photographs are overwhelmingly city-dwelling teenagers, and in his desire to imbue their work with dignity and even fun, he contributes significantly to the construction of the urban immigrant adolescent as both producer and consumer.

Visions of Adolescent Workers

The NCLC's campaign against child labor certainly succeeded. Although unable to get federal legislation to stick until the 1938 Fair Labor Laws, the campaign eroded the use of child labor throughout the industrial sector: between 1900 and 1930, the number of children ten to thirteen years old in nonagricultural work decreased from 186,358 to fewer than 30,000 (Zelizer 57).[21] As children were increasingly removed from the eligible labor pool by law and custom and by technological advances, and as the definition of "American child" was set in opposition to "child worker," the teenage children of immigrants, immersed in defining their own American identities, took on new significance in the workplace. For some child labor activists, teenage workers could fill the gap left by children taken out of the workforce and were preferable to them, since "everything done by children under sixteen years of age could quite as swiftly be done by young people between sixteen and eighteen years" (Kelley and Stevens 68). At sixteen, and sometimes fourteen, "children" became "young people," prepared for the world of work.

While boys still plied their trade selling newspapers, blacking boots, and carrying messages well into the 1920s, their older brothers increasingly replaced them in urban manufacture, especially as tenement homework was phased out. Young women, educated until the age of fourteen or even sixteen, entered a workplace that was as much a social center as a source of income, and they often resisted staying in school for personal as well as financial reasons. As one young daughter of immigrants put it: "I don't mind studyin' [until graduation at eighteen], but all my friends are goin' t'work, an' I don't want t'stay. . . . Graduate? Gee, stay two [more] years? Not for me— it's too slow" (True 42).

Teenage workers also manifested such impatience in their willingness to switch jobs at a moment's notice. In part this was due to the conditions of the work. Semi-skilled, tedious, and offering few to no fringe benefits, light manufacturing and service work in department stores, restaurants, and other businesses did not encourage loyalty when workers could easily transfer the skills they had to an analogous job elsewhere (True 45–46).

For adolescents, the work itself was hardly rewarding. Hilda Satt Polacheck recalled in a memoir how tedious her work was, sewing cuffs in a factory or typing up mail orders in an office. Hull-House offered her respite from the mind-numbing sameness of such work in the form of the Ariadne Club, which, "like the mythological daughter of Minos, who led Theseus out of the labyrinth by a thread . . . , led many of us out of a labyrinth of boredom" (Polacheck 94). Industrial work was physically demanding on adolescents, whether the repetitiveness of factory work or the strain of standing on one's feet for hours at a time in a department store, but those were not the only challenges teenage workers faced. Reformers worried on the one hand that adolescents were stultified by their work, but on the other that paid work "hastens the sense of physical and emotional maturity, which is in itself a source of danger," especially for adolescent girls (Woods and Kennedy 20–21). This combination of boredom and premature development also struck Jane Addams, who saw a causal link between the two: "it may be illuminating," she mused, "to trace the connection between the monotony and dullness of factory work and petty immoralities which are often the youth's protest against them" (*Spirit of Youth* 107).

In *Young Working Girls: A Summary of Evidence from Two Thousand Social Workers*, an extensive study of working adolescent girls published in 1913, Robert A. Woods and Albert J. Kennedy commented repeatedly on the mixed-sex nature of many workplaces, which created opportunities for young women to "become careless in their conduct, slack in manners and conversation, immodest in dress, and familiar to a degree that leaves them open to danger" (23). Even worse, department stores, which employed thousands of teenage girls across the country, normalized, or even heroized, commodity consumption; girls who worked in them had to "live in the highly developed atmosphere of temptation to expenditure with which every shop is charged" (Woods and Kennedy 26).[22]

In large part, whether one shares Woods and Kennedy's horror at what mixed-sex workplaces did to adolescents, they were right about the results. Just as in later years high school was "a sort of socializing agency" for middle-class Anglos (Kett 236), the workplace socialized young immigrant men and women into their identities as new Americans and, in turn, helped recreate what it meant to be an American worker and an American adolescent. Although many adolescent workers were engaged in trades that were

generally segregated by gender (women in millinery and men in cloak making, or women in department stores and men in telegraph offices), and
within the needle trades certain tasks were gender specific—sewing cuffs as
opposed to pressing finished garments—a large number of workplaces
employed both women and men. Hine's photograph in *Women at Work* of an
"old time sweatshop" taken in the early 1910s exemplifies the mixed-sex
workplace whose employees were mostly in their late teens and early twenties. Few of the workers pictured seem to be much out of their teens, and the
intimacy of the workplace, with women and men facing each other over
sewing machines at narrow tables, created a level of cross-sex sociability
unknown to most of the parents of these young people.

Hine's pictures of women workers taken in the late nineteenth and early
twentieth centuries often focus on the young, unmarried women who were
the primary labor source for light industry in major cities.[23] Although few of
the pictures have the kind of thorough captioning of the child labor photographs, the images themselves are rich with detail and, like Hine's pictures of
children, carefully composed and framed. Many of the pictures represent
trades in which women predominated—millinery and other needle trades,
plume binding, and textile production—although there are a number of pictures of women assembling artificial flowers. Hine was also interested in
photographing young workers socializing on the street during their lunch
breaks and after work, capturing the spontaneity whose loss he chronicled in
his child labor pictures.

While much of the work performed by the young women in Hine's
"Women at Work" series is similar to that done by the children in his NCLC
photographs, his representation of the work could not be more different. In
contrast to the claustrophobia of the tenement parlor table and the overwhelming size of machines on the factory floor, adolescent workplaces are,
in these pictures, well ordered, clean, and spacious. His series of photographs
of women working in millinery shops exemplifies this model. In one picture
of a young woman in her late teens or very early twenties, Hine captures his
subject's youth, beauty, and concentration on her work (fig. 21). The fabric of
the hat she is working on (a modified mob cap) is lush and full, and the young
woman is draped with the white ribbon she uses for trimming. She is smartly
dressed in a shirtwaist with a pin at her collar, clearly equal to the rich garment she is shaping. The scene has a calmness and confidence quite absent in
the child labor pictures and in Hine's later series of pictures of men at work,
which emphasize the massive and the heroic, rather than the smaller, more
communal scenes of women's work.

Hine's close framing of the picture allows the viewer to linger on every
curve and line of the girl's face, on the textures of fabric, hair, skin, ribbon,
and ornament. This young woman is pictured alone, but her solitariness is

Figure 21 Lewis W. Hine, "Worker in Factory of Robert M. Halpern" (1913). Here Hine captures his subject's youth, beauty, and unself-conscious connection to her work. Photography Collection, Miriam and Ira D. Wallach Division of Art, Prints, and Photographs, New York Public Library, Astor, Lenox and Tilden Foundations.

Figure 22 Lewis W. Hine, "Table in a Flower Factory" (191?). The neatness and order of this workshop contrast with the dark chaos of the tenement. Photography Collection, Miriam and Ira D. Wallach Division of Art, Prints, and Photographs, New York Public Library, Astor, Lenox and Tilden Foundations.

not the same as the isolation of the solo portraits of child workers. It is, rather, a sign of her independent identity as a worker and as a person—she defines the space she inhabits, not the other way around.

Similarly, two pictures of young women working in artificial-flower factories are significantly different from Hine's child labor representations of the same activity. The sharply dressed young women sit in orderly rows, contrasting with the mostly grimy kitchen tables around which families assembling flowers are seated in the tenement photographs (figs. 22 and 23). The dim closeness of the tenement is replaced by the bright high ceilings of the workshop, and the tight circle of mother and children by the even rows of young women at long tables. Many of the workers wear hair ornaments, brooches, or necklaces, signs of their disposable income or, as was equally common, popularity with the young men who might have bought these "cheap frivolities" for them (True 50). In one photograph, a young woman, though plainly dressed, sports a highly ornamented comb in her hair, indicating both her stylishness and her access to cash. Although this work was most likely tedious and a strain on the eyes, the young women in these pictures do not seem trapped by their workplace; some smile, and others lean toward each other in unconscious companionship.

Figure 23 Lewis W. Hine, "Making Foliage" (19??). Photography Collection, Miriam and Ira D. Wallach Division of Art, Prints, and Photographs, New York Public Library, Astor, Lenox and Tilden Foundations.

Hine's photographs of young women working in millinery shops exemplify the same kind of humor and connectedness. In one, the workers are almost all young women in white shirtwaists, sitting in rows at tables (fig. 24). Their hats and coats hang on hooks on the walls, and while the room is cluttered, the evenly spaced rows of workers suggest an orderliness typical of Hine's pictures of young women in light manufacturing. Although most of the women are white, one of the most prominent figures in the photograph is a young black woman wearing a cameo brooch and looking almost directly at the camera. In the row behind her Hine shows the smiling faces of three other young women, clearly in conversation with each other, effortlessly combining work and social lives. In fact, several of Hine's photographs of young workingwomen feature smiling or laughing workers, quite different from the quiet solemnity or angry resistance of the child workers he photographed for the NCLC.

Hine was also interested in the social life of these young women workers. While he did not follow them to their places of leisure—the dance halls, nickelodeons and outdoor resorts around which their socializing revolved—he did photograph them in their off-hours on the street. While these photographs have no captions and no specific purpose—they provide neither what Hine called the "negative documentation" of his exposés of industrial

Figure 24 Lewis W. Hine, "Crowded Workroom on Broadway" (19??). Most striking in this scene are the smiles on the women's faces. Photography Collection, Miriam and Ira D. Wallach Division of Art, Prints, and Photographs, New York Public Library, Astor, Lenox and Tilden Foundations.

Pittsburgh or of child labor, nor the "positive documentation" of proud, satisfied workers—they do represent an important part of young workers' lives, the times in which work functioned as a social center as much as a source of income.

One of these photographs, undated but probably from the early 1900s, given the fashions of the day, represents groups of young women spending time outside a building that houses several workshops (fig. 25): the plaques on the exterior wall—A. P. Babcock, Perfumer; Zuckerman & Joyce, Boys' Wash Suits; David Hurwitz, Waists and Costumes; and P. F. Collier and Son, Publishers—illustrate the wide variety of work young people participated in. All the young women have elaborate hats and a couple have fur stoles; a different shot of the same scene reveals one young woman with a fur muff and another, who looks barely sixteen, gazing out of the frame of the picture (fig. 26). The young women are talking and laughing. At right in the first picture, some young men appear, but their role is not clear: are they talking to each other, waiting for an opportunity to approach the young women, or both? A similar photograph from around the same time, but perhaps earlier, shows four young women standing in front of a tenement stoop just below a sign that reads "Woolens, Silks, Velvets, [illegible] Goods, Trimmings"; they

Figure 25 Lewis W. Hine, "Group of Women Workers Gathered outside the Dix Building, Where They Work on Millinery" (19??). Photography Collection, Miriam and Ira D. Wallach Division of Art, Prints, and Photographs, New York Public Library, Astor, Lenox and Tilden Foundations.

Figure 26 Lewis W. Hine, "Group of Women Workers Gathered outside the Dix Building" (19??). For these young women, work is an introduction to a freer social life, quite different from the imprisonment of child labor. Photography Collection, Miriam and Ira D. Wallach Division of Art, Prints, and Photographs, New York Public Library, Astor, Lenox and Tilden Foundations.

Figure 27 Lewis W. Hine, "Group of Women Workers Gathered on Sidewalk in Front of Several Millinery Establishments" (19??). Photography Collection, Miriam and Ira D. Wallach Division of Art, Prints, and Photographs, New York Public Library, Astor, Lenox and Tilden Foundations.

are beautifully dressed in poplin jackets and enormous hats covered with artificial flowers (fig. 27). Their faces are mostly obscured, except one in profile of a woman who seems to be about sixteen or seventeen. They constitute a social group of their own, defined by their age, their earning power, their fashionable dress, their unmarried status, and their urban American identities.

Although none of the young people in these pictures are shown working, they are marked as workers in several ways. First, their proximity to workplaces is telling: they stand in doorways or next to halls inscribed with the names of manufacturers and stores, evidently trying to extend the time they have before they must return inside. Second, their camaraderie with each other mirrors the scenes of conversation and laughter that Hine photographed in various sweatshops and factories. Finally, their fashionable clothes and hats, their youth, and their stylishness combine to create the image of the young workingman and workingwoman. But unlike the disapproving voices of the ILGWU and the Women's Trade Union League, which, as Nan Enstad points out, "routinely chastised working women for their ceaseless pursuit of fashion . . . and their 'affected' style," Hine's pictures

Figure 28 Lewis W. Hine, "A Young Flower Maker Going Out at Noon for Lunch" (19??). Photography Collection, Miriam and Ira D. Wallach Division of Art, Prints, and Photographs, New York Public Library, Astor, Lenox and Tilden Foundations.

seem affectionate, opening up to us the social and work worlds of immigrant teenagers and young adults.

Even more appealing is Hine's photograph of a young woman worker stealing a moment in a doorway with a young man who may be her boyfriend. He is wearing a uniform—the caption tells us he is the elevator boy—and he smiles in a jaunty manner (fig. 28). Her hair is a little disheveled (whether from work or from recent intimacies we can only guess) and she gazes warily at the camera, as though wondering whether Hine will tell her parents what she is up to. The picture has a winsome spontaneity, as though Hine had just interrupted a kiss before the young couple's parting. This picture captures the gendered divisions of sexuality that the children of immigrants dealt with daily: in the young man's confidence and his girlfriend's guardedness we can see the different stakes with which each has to contend, with both parents and peers. And yet, in this intimate scene Hine reveals the ways in which mixed-sex socializing in the urban workplace allowed young people new ways of connecting and gave them the space to develop a new and American identity as workers and as adolescents. Much like the dance halls that I discuss in chapter 4, neither wholly public nor wholly private, the workplace provided an arena for immigrant adolescents to experiment with

Figure 29 Lewis W. Hine, "Through the Threads" (1928). Work as aesthetic object. Photography Collection, Miriam and Ira D. Wallach Division of Art, Prints, and Photographs, New York Public Library, Astor, Lenox and Tilden Foundations.

and work through their relationship to gender and sexuality, and to construct identities that they understood as "American."

Hine's greatest focus, though, was on the work itself. Although he did not heroize women's industrial labor in the way he did men's in books such as *Men at Work*, he did produce a series of gorgeous photographs of women working looms at Shelton Looms in Connecticut in the 1920s and 1930s.[24] Framed so that the foci of the images are the hundreds of fine threads and the capable and sensitive hands of the loom worker, these pictures define young women's work as not just useful but beautiful, an achievement not only in industry but in aesthetics (fig. 29). Unlike the disproportion between child workers and the machinery they have to contend with, here worker and machine are in perfect proportion. Her hands are visible through the light scrim of threads, and the threads themselves are light and delicate. We are a long way from the overwhelming bobbins and looms, the children standing on boxes and dwarfed by the machines they work. Here, worker and machine are in harmony, each seen through the lens of the other.

The weavers, sewers, pressers, tailors, flower makers, milliners, and other young workers Hine photographed seem to be bursting with confidence.

Paid work, rather than destroying teenagers as it did children, and rather than erasing their national identity, seems in these photographs to have the opposite effect. As Woods and Kennedy observed in *Young Working Girls*, paid labor transformed the teenage daughter of immigrants: "Her personality expands with almost startling rapidity; and her opinion of herself as an independent and all-conquering being is reinforced by evident material accomplishment," both the production of consumer goods and the earning of the weekly pay envelope (34). Similarly, the confidence of the young men in Hine's photographs is very different from the bravado of the newsboys and breaker boys of the child labor pictures; even if they might be sharing living quarters with parents and younger siblings, or lodging with several other young men in a tenement family's parlor, in Hine's images they are well dressed and comfortably socializing with their female coworkers.

In these pictures, the young workers are hardly trapped by capitalism. Instead, they are smoothly interpolated into it, mastering the machines that produce the goods they themselves will go on to buy: shirtwaists, hats, suits, overcoats, collars, artificial flowers. Unlike little Rosie with her doll, more uncomfortable with the traditional accompaniments of childhood than she is with an oyster-shucking knife, Hine's teenage workers seem confident among the trappings of consumer capital that help define them as adolescents and as Americans. Work, and the money that work produced, made the accessories of the adolescent culture they were forming available to them: fashionable clothes, heterosociability, access to commercial entertainment, and comparative freedom of movement in public spaces.

In these photographs, Hine deconstructs the child/adult binary he so carefully engineered in his child labor series. Neither children nor adults, these young people occupy a cultural and economic space that in many ways they themselves have created. While it may not have been Hine's intention, these pictures document not just the changing industrial landscape, but the creation of a new kind of American identity: the adolescent.

As we shall see in the chapters that follow, a crucial element of the new American adolescence that these young people created was having money to spend. In large part the generation gap that came to define the new adolescence, and the commercial pleasures immigrant teenagers indulged in, as well as the ability for teenagers to function as cultural tastemakers for each other, issued from young people's twinned sense of financial and cultural independence. While middle-class and Anglo teenagers were still making their purchases under the supervision and within the purse strings of their parents, and imitating adult fashions, the children of immigrants were exercising their own consumer choices and creating their own styles. As high school attendance became the norm for all adolescents of all classes (even though among the poorest, staying in school until the age of eighteen is still not necessarily the rule), the image of the working-class teenager as the ideal young worker faded. But the fruits of immigrant adolescent employment— the assumption that teenagers should have money to spend and the freedom to spend it as they saw fit—was reproduced over and over in the American mainstream.[25]

3

"Irreverence and the American Spirit"

IMMIGRANT PARENTS, AMERICAN ADOLESCENTS, AND THE INVENTION OF THE GENERATION GAP

In 1899, Hilda Satt, the daughter of Jewish immigrants to Chicago, visited Jane Addams's famous settlement house Hull-House for the first time. Her father had recently died, and although her mother "faced life with the heroism of the true American pioneer" (Polacheck 44), she was barely scraping by. Hilda hoped that Hull-House, with its low-cost cafeteria, its activities for immigrant women, men, and children, and its focus on neighborhood outreach would be able to alleviate her family's dire financial and emotional situation. While the initial visit made some impression, it was Hilda's second trip to Jane Addams's settlement house that had the greatest effect on the girl.

Jane Addams took Hilda on a tour of Hull-House, starting off with one of the house's most innovative projects, the Labor Museum. The museum featured the traditional crafts of the immigrant communities that made up Hull-House's neighborhood and "showed the evolution of cotton, wool, silk and linen" (Polacheck 64). Next to the textiles were descriptions of how each crop was raised, spun, woven, and dyed. The spectators at the museum were a mixed crowd: immigrants and their children, well-heeled philanthropists, devotees of the then avant-garde Arts and Crafts movement. The museum was also fully interactive; when Hilda finished looking around, Mary Hill, the museum's coordinator, "asked me whether I would like to learn to weave something that was typically American . . . ; very soon I was weaving a small Navaho-style blanket" (Polacheck 64).

As Hilda soon learned, the Labor Museum was not simply a showplace for traditional handicrafts. It was also a money-making venture: Hull-House sold the products of the people who exhibited their skills in the museum and used the money to fund settlement house projects. However, as Hilda Satt, writing decades later as Hilda Satt Polacheck, pointed out, one of the museum's primary concerns went beyond consciousness- or fund-raising. She realized that "Miss Addams found that there was a definite feeling of superiority on the part of children of immigrants towards their parents" who participated in the museum's exhibits (65). Hilda saw that for these children, mostly in their teens, "the Labor Museum was an eye-opener. When they saw crowds of well-dressed Americans standing around admiring what Italian, Irish, German, and Scandinavian mothers could do, their disdain for their mothers vanished. . . . I am sure the Labor Museum reduced strained feelings on the part of immigrants and their children" (66).

Addams's discovery of this "feeling of superiority" was hardly a surprise to her. She designed the Labor Museum in order to counter it, a fact of which Polacheck, whose memoir *I Came a Stranger: The Story of A Hull-House Girl* was dedicated in "humble gratitude to the memory of JANE ADDAMS" (2), could hardly have been unaware. Jane Addams created the Labor Museum as a way to address a problem that obsessed her contemporaries: the attitudes of American-born children of late nineteenth-century immigrants toward their parents on the one hand, and toward the United States on the other—what was often thematized as the conflict between the "Old World" and the "New World."[1]

In this chapter I explore how both immigrants and native-born Americans dealt with the "problem" of American-born teenage children of immigrant parents, particularly the daughters of immigrant women, and how Addams and others represented that problem in their writing. These children provided a bridge between their parents and the culture of the United States, which was often undecipherable to the older generation, and also built between themselves and their parents a wall that popular American culture helped construct and maintain. I would argue, too, that the discourse of the separation between parents and children both was a product of and produced the modern subject position of "adolescent." Rather than an inevitable divide, the gap between generations served a specific purpose: it was a vehicle by which the adolescent children of immigrants could construct a new identity for themselves that drew on both their own communities and a larger sense of "America" for its raw material. The language of "Old World" and "New World," "greenhorn" and "American," made space for a new American identity that could stand in opposition to immigrant parents for its legitimacy, rather than to foreign parentage or even foreign birth. By enacting the generation gap, the children of immigrants dissolved the conflation of "American" and "Anglo-Saxon"—instead, to be American meant to be sophisticated, to be involved in industrial labor or commerce, to participate in commercial leisure and consumer spending, and to reject the "Old World."

For Jane Addams, the boundary between foreign-born parents and U.S.-born children seemed self-evident, and it was a barrier she wanted to overcome—she had, as she put it, "an overmastering desire to reveal the humble immigrant parents to their own children" (HH 171–172)—and she imagined that the Labor Museum would go some way toward achieving that goal.[2] But she was fighting a powerful cultural trend. Whatever the desires of the children themselves, the explicit task of Americanization taken on by the public schools often ignored and erased the home cultures of students, discouraging or outright forbidding the use of home languages and, as Leonard Covello has put it, teaching immigrants' children to be Americans "by learning how to be ashamed of our parents" (44). Even in the preteen years, working-class immigrants' children made clear distinctions between their home, street, and school lives. By the time they reached high school or entered the workplace, the language of separation from their cultures of origin was ingrained within them, and "experience had taught . . . us that the spreading chasm which separated us from our parents could never again be bridged and that what happened to us in the outside world belonged to us alone" (Covello 68). Second, the adolescent children of immigrants were in the vanguard of creating and adopting a new and in many ways unique working-class culture organized around paid labor and the leisure that their incomes made possible. This culture bore many of the hallmarks we still imagine are typical of American teenagers but that in the early years of the twentieth century marked a shift among young people from being identified as "immigrant" to claiming Americanness: a strong investment in mass culture, particularly music and performance; an open and often playful sexuality; a focus on fun as a self-sustaining reason for activity.

The idea that parents and their teenage children have little or nothing to say to each other is of fairly recent vintage. Carroll Smith-Rosenberg's now classic research into romantic friendships between women also revealed the close emotional ties between bourgeois American mothers and daughters in the middle of the nineteenth century, and, as Joseph Kett has shown, the adolescent sons of the middle classes cast into roles as clerks and accountants expressed deep homesickness.[3] The young working-class women who flocked to textile factories in the early years of industrialization were often heavily policed, but not because they were imagined as having radically different desires, tastes, and behavior from their parents'.[4] Nor was being at odds with one's parents understood as a typically American model of adolescent attitude, as it was by the beginning of the third decade of the twentieth century.

In the 1960s, this idea gained a name: the "generation gap." Although, of course, animosity between generations is not age or relationship specific and could exist just as easily between, for example, middle-aged adults and their elderly parents, or young children and their teachers, the term "generation gap" was coined to refer in particular to the seemingly unbridgeable abyss that stretched between baby-boom teenagers, whose numbers were swelling in the mid-1960s, and their mothers and fathers, who were approaching or in their forties. After a few early appearances in the first years of the 1960s, the term took off during the period of greatest conflict between American adolescents and their parents, roughly the years 1967 to 1969.[5]

Although the generation gap felt very new to the middle-aged parents whose children were transformed before their eyes, many of their own parents and grandparents in fact had established this pattern forty or so years earlier. Many of the elements of the conflict between parents and children in the 1960s echoed the wrangling between immigrants and their adolescent children in the first decades of the twentieth century: struggles over clothes, music, leisure, sex, and propriety were a staple of texts describing the relationships between immigrants and their American-born offspring in the peak years of southern and eastern European immigration at the turn of the nineteenth into the twentieth century. While adolescence as a phenomenon of modernity, and the bane of the older generation, did not enter the mainstream until the 1920s, the teenage children of immigrants had firmly established meaningful cultural distance between themselves and their parents in ways that alarmed many observers.[6] Much like their 1960s counterparts, in the early twentieth century "parents from Eastern and Southern Europe bickered and quarreled" with their adolescent children "over chaperonage, curfews, clothes, cosmetics, entertainment, and money" (Alexander 23).

In this chapter I explore the ways in which the generation gap became a standard way of talking about urban working-class immigrants and their children, and how the teenage children of immigrants both suffered and benefited from this emerging discourse. Certainly, the change in power relations between immigrants who had trouble adjusting to the New World and their children who quickly assimilated the English language and American customs is a staple of the immigrant narrative. By the beginning of the twentieth century, the story of alienation between immigrants and their American-raised children was so familiar that it appeared almost everywhere in descriptions of urban immigrant life. "There is no story more tragic in the annals of life in Chicago," lamented Myron Adams in 1905, "than the break between the American boy of foreign parentage and his tenement home" (102). Jane Addams recalled in 1910 "a play, written by an Italian playwright of our neighborhood [in Chicago], which depicted the insolent break between Americanized sons and old country parents so touchingly that it moved to tears all the older Italians in the audience" (HH 269). In her 1918 memoir, Rose Cohen recalled that at barely thirteen, she was given the task of assigning herself and her siblings Americanized names, since "of father and myself, I was the more Americanized" (152), and that her sister's "quickness in adopting American ways" led to her taking complete responsibility for preparing her younger siblings for the outside world: "She would wash and dress the children, curl their hair on her finger, 'American fashion,' and take them out onto the street" (150–151).

Mary Antin's The Promised Land, published in 1912, is an effective example of this archetype, and Antin mournfully narrates the story of "the sad process of disintegration of home life" that took place in her family. Her parents were inexperienced in the ways of the United States and "in their bewilderment and uncertainty they needs must trust us children to learn from such models as the tenements afforded" and "they must step down from their throne of parental authority and take the law from children's mouths; for they had no other means of finding out what was good American form." The result of this, for Antin, was the inevitable "laxity of domestic organization, that inversion of moral relations which makes for friction, and which sometimes ends in breaking up a family that was formerly united and happy" (213). The parents depend upon the children to interpret not just the language but also the culture, and the children have every incentive to translate to their own advantage.

The generational conflict was based on more than parental unwillingness or inability to adapt to new circumstances, however. After all, Rose Cohen's father quickly cut off his beard and adopted "American" dress after he arrived in New York, and Mary Antin's father was a freethinker back in his hometown of Polotzk. He discouraged his wife from bringing her wig with her to New York and "would have no bar to our social intercourse with the world around us, for only by freely sharing the life of our neighbors could we come into our full inheritance of American freedom and opportunity" (Antin 194). Nonetheless, Rose Cohen recalled that, when she was just thirteen, it was "pathetic to see how [her mother] looked up to me because I had already been here a year, and probably showed off a little" (150). For David Blaustein, a Jewish educator and advocate for immigrants, the "gulf between the parents and the children" was a result of the incomplete Americanization of the older generation. Immigrant parents allowed their children to get away with behavior that American parents would never permit, since the new arrivals "can not tell the true from the fake Americanism" (61), and the children were rarely inclined to disabuse them. As Sophonisba Breckenridge learned in her study of immigrant Chicago families of Polish, Italian, Jewish, and other backgrounds, adolescents persuaded their parents that they "should accept [their] dictum that everything [they] want to do is 'American' and that it is hopeless for [immigrant parents] to try to understand" (178).

Young people broke away from their immigrant parents less to join a preestablished instantiation of the American character than to construct their own in a delicate balance of ethnic specificity, adolescent solidarity, and national identity. Given that commentators on this phenomenon noted a similar occurrence among the children of immigrants of any number of national origins, it's clear that this identity, while often rooted in friendship groups and social scenes that usually remained ethnically fairly homogenous, established a kind of transethnic Americanism. That is, what one Mexican parent called "this terrible American freedom" was only partly American and only partly *Mexican* American (Odem, *Delinquent Daughters* 163); more accurately, it was a culture created by new American adolescents using similar tools to forge their own definitions of American identity that made distinctions less along ethnic lines than between "greenhorns" or "foreigners" (like, for example, their parents) and "Americans" (which is to say, themselves). Similarly, while Hutchins Hapgood observed Jewish adolescent boys rejecting the meeting places frequented by their fathers, "for the young bring irreverence and the American spirit" (17), he observed their trajectories: "away from the supper table to join his gang on the Bowery, where he is quick to pick up the latest slang; where his talent for caricature is developed often at the expense of his parents, his race, and all 'foreigners'" (26).

The desire of these American-born or American-raised boys to carve out their own identities is, in Hapgood's narrative, focused on the twin rhetorical tools of slang and mimicry, both of which construct a self through reshaping the origins of native and adopted languages. Slang, after all, most often takes familiar terms and deploys them with different meanings, distancing them from their source while still acknowledging their roots. Similarly, mimicry is a highly ambivalent form of performance embodying simultaneous contempt and affection. Slang became a marker of Americanization *within* the context of immigrant life: outside the world of immigrant neighborhoods, the same slang signified foreignness, just as the cultural practices of immigrant communities seemed distinctively American to newcomers but alien to Anglo-Americans.

In "The Jewish Girl in Chicago," Viola Paradise makes exactly this argument: "The very things which strike the native born as foreign seem to [an immigrant] as distinctly American: the pretentiousness of signs and advertisements, the gaudy crowded shop windows, the frequency of fruit stands and meat markets, her own countrymen in American clothes, women carrying great bundles of unfinished clothing on their heads—she sums it all up as 'America'" (701).

As almost every chronicle of immigrant life observes, language itself was an area of intense contestation between immigrants and their Americanized children in which parents often felt "at sea" about their teenage children's work and recreation (Breckenridge 179). Educators like David Blaustein and Antonio Mangano argued that children must be encouraged to hold onto the language of their parents not just for practical reasons of communication, but as a way to "respect and honor their parents" (Mangano 109). The inevitable feelings of "helplessness" of the Italian mother whose children "talk English in the home and even plan to disobey her before her eyes when she has no idea what they are saying" were, for Mangano and Blaustein, not simply due to the mother's inability to speak the language, but also must be laid at the feet of the children, who saw her native language as something "to be despised and cast aside" (Mangano 109–110).[7] American institutions exacerbated this division, as Leonard Novello described in his memoir *The Heart Is the Teacher*. A high school teacher of French and Spanish, it never crossed his mind to ask why the public schools did not offer Italian as a language option; instead he accepted that Italian was to be relegated to the tenements.

This compartmentalization of life experienced by the children of immigrants was represented as being in stark contrast to the integrated lives their parents lived in Europe, in which a family "worked together and played together with other family groups . . . ; the entire family participated" (Breckenridge 63). Although, as Elizabeth Ewen points out, immigrant community events like weddings, funerals, first communions, bar mitzvahs, and the like involved the entire family, the social intermixing of the generations often ended at the tenement door. The flourishing of an adolescent social world gave rise to a discourse of parental exclusion: in America, "the children have all manner of interests which the parents cannot comprehend," David Blaustein lamented, "and this leads to [the family's] being torn apart" (162).

Despite the complexities of the relationships between immigrants, their children, and the varieties of U.S. culture that these immigrants experienced, many contemporary social workers placed much of the blame for the generation gap on the parents. The distance between the generations could not be laid solely at the feet of these young people, since "it is only when parents neglect to make the child a partner in their plans that there is likely to be hard feeling" (Woods and Kennedy 47). In *Young Working Girls*, Woods and Kennedy warm to their criticism of the older generation: the social standards of immigrant mothers "[are] totally inept, and they find themselves incapable of supplying that advice which would meet the daughter's more modern experience and common sense" (47). These authors' vision of the immigrant family is of an institution on the edge of destruction, with the adolescent children spinning out of their parents' control. Unable to speak their children's language, both literally and metaphorically, most immigrant parents "are uncertain where their daughters spend their evenings," a sure recipe for familial disaster (61).

For Woods and Kennedy, the shame that adolescents feel for their greenhorn parents is as much due to the emotional tone deafness of the older generation as it is to the rebellious independence of the children or to their desire to carve out an American identity for themselves. If these young people believe that their mothers represent "all that is un-American" (51), they are, as far as Woods and Kennedy are concerned, not so far from the truth. Both parents "fail to understand the daughter's point of view," falling far short of the empathy and intimacy that characterizes their ideal family. Of course, Woods and Kennedy have a sure solution for this problem—the intervention of settlement houses. Clueless immigrant parents require "that kind of interpretation which is only possible through the acquaintances which the social worker provides" (79). In this narrative, Woods and Kennedy reorient the traditional story of new Americans depending upon their children to translate urban U.S. culture and the English language to them. For them, the parents and their children have become so foreign to each other that they all need interpretation to facilitate communication across the generational divide.

"I Am Earning My Own Living and Can Do as I Please"

Immigrants' children separated themselves from their parents through language, but an equally powerful tool was the pay envelope. A vast majority of urban adolescents with foreign-born parents worked (Antonio Mangano estimated upward of 90 percent), and their status as economic actors reshaped power within the family and eventually established the model of the adolescent as a financial force. Since, as we have seen in chapter 2, working outside the home implicitly carried with it a separation from childhood, these young people used their identity as workers to deepen the gap between themselves and their parents, not least because, wrote a contemporary observer, "they know far more about life than their fathers and especially their mothers. They are seized with the desire for complete freedom" (Mangano 201).

The ramifications of this new freedom were, not surprisingly, inflected by gender. Given the large-scale entrance of young women into the workforce, many reformers were especially concerned with the divide between young immigrant women and their parents. As Woods and Kennedy commented, "the vital and baffling nature of the problem of the adolescent girl of the tenement-house family and the city factory or department store has come to be so keenly felt among settlement workers" that it seemed a natural topic for the first comparative study undertaken by the National Federation of Settlements at the end of the 1910s (v). Similarly, in her analysis of young women living in the far western end of midtown (then called the Lower West Side, now Hell's Kitchen or Clinton), Ruth True found "the greatest strain" in immigrant households to be "between mother and daughter" (53).

For Woods and Kennedy, the alienation between the young working girl of immigrant parents and her home life was close to absolute, and the "outside world and the home may become almost antagonistic phases of her existence," with the larger world taking precedence in her loyalties and attention (36). Absorbing the lessons of dime novels and story papers, these young women linked financial and familial power in their relationships with their parents. Woods and Kennedy observed with dismay that an adolescent girl who has found her place in the work world "chafes under authority, becomes impatient with narrow conditions, seeks freedom from home responsibilities, demands more in amusement and clothing, becomes dictatorial toward younger brothers and sisters. She begins to enter into hitherto forbidden amusements, and justifies herself by the claim 'I am earning my own living and can do as I please'" (36–37). While the critic must beware the clear judgments and generalizations that Woods and Kennedy are making in their account of intergenerational relationships here, this narrative of financial independence (however limited) followed by struggles for personal freedom is a cornerstone of the construction of urban adolescence.

Even young people who were expected to hand over most or even all of their pay envelopes gained power in their homes. As Louise Montgomery, a reformer in Chicago, commented: "Those who faithfully hold to a difficult and uncongenial occupation, bringing home the entire wage to the family and submitting to an almost patriarchal control in other matters, will demand a freedom in the use of their evening hours before which the foreign parents are useless" (32). While they may not have controlled their own income, their status as earners granted them a modicum of control over their nonworking hours.

In large part this conflict (and, equally importantly, the *perception* of conflict) was due to the reorganization of gender that resulted from mixed-sex urban workplaces. As Kathy Peiss has argued, when young women entered the paid workforce, their experience of work and time was more like that of men, making clear distinctions between "work time" and "leisure time" that the homosocial world of their mothers blurred. Like their male counterparts, adolescent girls wanted more say in how to spend their money and, by association, their time. In the words of Nan Enstad: "Hats, dresses, and shoes were symbols of a generational struggle in which young women believed that, as workers, they deserved a portion of their pay for their own use, just as was customary for men" (9).

Typically, adolescent workers chose to spend their money on amusements and fashion, both of which their parents imagined to be uniquely American commodities. While reformers like Sophonisba Breckenridge acknowledged that it was "only natural that a young girl should want to look as well as possible" (173), they also recognized that the concept of clothing as commodity rather than necessity, luxury, or both was alien to many immigrant parents. Young women were willing to spend money on shoddy goods that looked glamorous, a very different attitude from the one their mostly rural and poor mothers had been trained to, having owned a few homemade clothes that were designed to last. Even immigrants from urban areas were unaccustomed to the plethora of commercial opportunities on offer in working-class neighborhoods in large American cities. As Breckenridge observed, it was not surprising that an immigrant woman "and her daughter should clash on the question of what to buy" in the way of clothing, when, "to her normal distress at buying goods of poor quality at any price there is added an outrage to her native thrift, because the price of these fashionable goods is actually greater than for goods of better quality" (173–174).

The irony of this conflict between generations was that while the children of immigrants succeeded in distancing themselves from their parents through dress and leisure activities, they were hardly paradigms of mainstream Americanness. Their immersion in mass culture, their inextricability from the workplace (whether they themselves worked or not), their adoption of extravagant fashion, even their often radical politics—all defined them as apart from the Anglo-America that they represented to their parents, and, as Lizabeth Cohen argues in her study of working-class Chicago between the two World Wars, the fact that they felt "alienated from their parents' world did not necessarily mean that they forsook it for a nonethnic, middle class one. . . . While trying to be American, they learned to be *Chicago* Italians, Jews, and Poles" (147, my emphasis).[8]

In major urban areas, the fashions that the children of immigrants adopted were heavily inflected by their own experiences, their own backgrounds, their own heterogeneous neighborhoods. Critics have often cited Mashah, the middle sister in Anzia Yezierska's *Bread Givers,* as the paradigm of feminine Americanization, with her hat ribbons and artificial flowers.[9] But what is most striking to me is how much her aspirations toward fashion and propriety are shaped by the adolescent culture of the Lower East Side of New York, not by the elite New Yorkers whose houses she cleans or by the bourgeois New Women who were represented in the American mainstream as the ideal adolescent.

When we first encounter Mashah, she has run into the tenement apartment she shares with her parents and three sisters and is busy pinning artificial roses on her hat. Modeling in front of the "cracked, fly-stained mirror [she] turned her head first on this side and then on the other side, laughing to herself with the pleasure of how grand her hat was. 'Like a lady from Fifth Avenue I look, and for only ten cents, from a pushcart on Hester Street' " (Yezierska 2). Given the extravagance of East Side fashions, though, and the profusion of artificial flowers, plumes, rosettes, and other adornments young workingwomen attached to their immense hats, it is unlikely that Mashah really resembles a doyenne of Fifth Avenue.[10] More likely, she resembles the other young women of her acquaintance who hang their best dress up in the front room of their apartment, who use fashion as a tool to negotiate "extremely difficult material and ideological constraints [to build] a new range of representations, symbols, activities, and spaces with which to create class, gender, and ethnic identities" (Enstad 6). Moreover, she uses her *own* money to pay for the paper flowers, skimps on lunch to adorn herself, misses sleep to attend concerts in the park, and window-shops while searching for work.

For Sara, the young narrator, Mashah's beauty and fashion are predicated on her individualism, the quality that more definitively separates her from her parents. Unlike her sister Bessie, the "burden bearer" who "carried the whole house on her back," Mashah makes a clear distinction between her needs and those of her family (Yezierska 35). She resembles the "neglected girl" in Ruth True's report, who "follows the lure of her desires with an imperious insistence which does not scruple to shirk the irksome claims of home" in search of a life "glittering with 'good times and fun'" (51). Almost a caricature of the beautiful blond, "Mashah took first her wages to make herself more beautiful and left the rest of us to worry for the bread and rent" (Yezierska 35). She insists on her own towel and toothbrush, and when her mother refuses, she waited until "the day for the wages came [and] quietly went to the Five and Ten Cent Store and bought, not only a toothbrush and a separate towel for herself, but even a separate piece of soap" (6). In many ways, Mashah is like the immigrant adolescent for whom, in Jane Addams's words, the desire for "frivolous" finery was a way to make the "gaiety and enthusiasm" of youth visible. As Addams argued: "Through the huge hat, with its wilderness of bedraggled feathers, the girl announces to the world that she is here. She demands attention to the fact of her existence, she states that she is ready to live, to take her place in the world" (*Spirit of Youth* 8). More censoriously, the antiprostitution Committee of Fifteen identified that same individualism with the working girl's temptation toward prostitution. Rejecting the communalism of their immigrant parents and the civic virtue of their bourgeois counterparts, the committee argued in *The Social Evil*, many young women slipped into prostitution because they were "impregnated with the view that individual happiness is the end of life, and their lives bring them no happiness, and promise them none" (11).

While Mashah may resemble a "doll" and a "lady from Fifth Avenue" in her own mind, her relationship with pianist Jacob Novak reveals that she is more a product of the tenements than of the larger America she aspires to. Unlike the working-class immigrants of Mashah's social circle, "Jacob looked like from rich people. It didn't shout from his clothes, the money they cost. . . . He did not wear a checked vest, nor on a red necktie a gold horseshoe pin. But it breathed from his quiet things, the solid richness from the rich who didn't have to show it off any more" (Yezierska 56). When Jacob's father comes to visit, "we saw it was the richest man that had ever been in our house" (58).

Mr. Novak exerts his power over Jacob and forbids him to see Mashah again, very much like Mashah's own father, Reb Smolinsky, who arranges the marriages of three out of four of his daughters. Yezierska's narrator, Sara, the youngest Smolinsky daughter, tells her father that her refusal to "slave for you till my braids grow gray . . .—till you find me another fish-peddler to sell me out in marriage [like her sister Bessie]" is based in her identity as an American: "Nobody can stop me! I'm not from the old country! I'm American!" Yet her independence distances her as much from established American Jews like the Novaks as it does from her "Old World" father. More importantly, it distinguishes her from her middle-class Anglo-American counterparts, who were very much under their parents' control.[11]

The independence that the teenage children of urban immigrants insisted upon, and often attained, was comparatively unknown to adolescents living in small cities, suburbs, and rural areas.[12]

Similarly, reformers concerned about the disintegration of the immigrant home did not extend that alarm to the families of native-born Americans. "The home" as a concept was, as David Blaustein insisted "an American institution" and Americanization was more than "the mere acquisition of language and the ability to ape the salient customs of the country"; it was the "preservation of the home," not its destruction (48). Jane Addams declared "the home to be the foundation of society," and while she cited a number of examples of "family affection" among immigrants, particularly from parents to children, she charged social workers with "do[ing] nothing to direct the force upon which the continuity of the home depends" (31).[13] Neither Blaustein nor Addams, often at odds in their reform philosophies, suggested that the Anglo-American home was in any danger, or that middle class parents should worry about the alienation of their teenage children's affections, nor did they argue that Anglo-American working-class families in New York or Chicago faced the same challenges as the families of the foreign born. The generation gap was an issue for working-class *immigrant* families, a phenomenon created by the distinctive American identities adolescent children of immigrants adopted and the almost ritual rejection of "the old country" those identities necessitated.

Generational Difference and Jane Addams's Hull-House Labor Museum

The perceived dissolution of the immigrant family was the social ill that Jane Addams created the Labor Museum to remedy. Addams's project to reconcile immigrant parents and their American-born children derived in part from a desire to restore dignity to the lives of the older people and to the cultures from which they came, but it also resulted from a need to reinstitute the model of parent-child power relations that had been so formative in her own childhood. Addams's mother died when she was a young child, and she admired her father with an almost violent passion.[14]

Concerned about the omnipresence of commerce in young women's lives, "all that is gaudy and sensual, by the flippant street music, the highly colored theater posters, the trashy love stories, the feathered hats, the cheap heroics of the revolvers displayed in the pawn-shop windows," Addams wanted to recreate the self-sustaining relationships between parents and children that for her were the bedrock of familial relationships (*Spirit of Youth* 27). She sustained a fantasy of country life as harmonious, in contradistinction to what she and her contemporaries saw as the conflict-ridden family life of the city. At the same time, unlike many other bourgeois reformers, Addams recognized the many examples of "family affection" and "family devotion" that sustained urban life, from the immigrant man who went without a coat in February so that he could afford to keep his son in school to the women who maintained clean and well-stocked homes even as they worked long hours in sweatshops (*Spirit of Youth* 34).

Addams did not doubt immigrant parents' commitment to their children's well-being, nor did she dismiss the working-class family as "a social failure and a moral disaster" as so many urban crusaders had done (Boyer 40). In previous decades, the charity organization movement focused on what it saw as the failings of the poor, the "assumption that the urban poor had degenerated morally because the circumstances of city life had cut them off from the elevating influence of their moral betters" (Boyer 149). Addams saw poor parents differently, especially in the aftermath of the economic crisis of the mid-1890s, in which unemployment and underemployment were the rule rather than the exception, and tenement families had to struggle to maintain even a minimal standard of living. She testified to the "wonderful devotion to the child . . . in the midst of our stupid social and industrial relations, [and] all that keeps society human" (*Spirit of Youth* 33). The family as a social unit "blends the experience of generations into a continuous story," and close communication and even friendship between generations was the key to preventing the ruin of young women and the corruption of young men (*Spirit of Youth* 34). Teenage girls in the work world, particularly vulnerable to the predations of the city, were, in Addams's eyes, also particularly uplifted by connections to their mothers. As she argued: "The mothers who are of the most use to these . . . city working girls are the mothers who develop a sense of companionship with the changing experiences of their daughters. . . . Their vigorous family life allies itself by a dozen bonds to the educational, the industrial and the recreational organizations of the modern city" (*Spirit of Youth* 47).

But all the companionship in the world would be of no use if the daughters themselves were unable to see their mothers as models but rather as primitives and sources of embarrassment. Addams devised the Labor Museum as a way not just to reconnect mothers and daughters but also to make clear the links between handcraft—the old way that Addams believed young women derogated—and factory work. The story Addams tells of her inspiration to establish the museum embodies these issues and suggests a solution to them. Walking toward Hull-House one day, Addams saw "an old Italian woman, her distaff against her homesick face, patiently spinning a thread by the simple stick spindle so reminiscent of all Southern Europe." This image of the persistence of traditional crafts in the face of immense cultural disruption and isolation dovetailed with Addams's concern that older immigrants "so often lost their hold upon their Americanized children," who felt contempt for the "greenness" of their parents' limited mastery of English and alienation from U.S. culture (HH 172).

Addams imagined the Labor Museum as a living history of handicrafts, tracing their development from the most basic techniques to their transformation by mechanization. In its exhibits, the museum traced specific crafts such as spinning and put varieties of spindles "in historic sequence and order . . . to connect the whole with the present method of factory spinning." By establishing a generic link between artisanal crafts and their industrialized equivalents, Addams hoped to show the factory-working children of immigrants that their labor was not so different from the work their parents participated in that they despised for its "greenness." By exposing her neighbors to the museum, Addams also wanted to make possible interethnic harmony based in a belief in the commonality of human experience, since it "enabled even the most casual observer to see that . . . industry develops similarly and peacefully year by year among the workers of each nation, heedless of differences in language, religion, and political experiences" (HH 173).

Strongly affected by the pedagogical theories of John Dewey, particularly his declaration that "education is a process of living and not a preparation for future living" ("My Pedagogic Creed" 78), Addams designed the Labor Museum as a site of experiential learning. Young women in the needle trades could actively relate the physical processes of their own work to the craftwork their mothers were exhibiting, healing the rift between immigrant mothers who stayed close to home and their daughters who organized their lives around sweatshops and factories. As Addams argued: "If these young people could actually see that the complicated machinery of the factory had been evolved from simple tools, they might at least make a beginning toward that education which Dr. Dewey defines as 'a continuing reconstruction of experience'" (HH 172). In addition, Addams envisioned the museum as allowing immigrant parents, so often in the position of learning from their children about what it meant to be American or of using their children as intermediaries to interpret between them and the Anglo-American world, to reinvest in the parental role of teacher, guide, and transmitter of cultural knowledge (HH 174).

In Addams's narrative of intergenerational conflict, the teenage counterpart of the old woman at the distaff is "Angelina," who "did not wish to be too closely identified in the eyes of the rest of [her] cooking class [at Hull-House] with an Italian woman who wore a kerchief over her head, uncouth boots, and short petticoats." In a metaphor of generational distance that Addams must have found poignant, Angelina and her mother walked to Hull-House together but entered through separate doors so that others would not know that they were related. The Labor Museum changed all that, however.

One evening [visiting the museum], Angelina saw her mother surrounded by a group of visitors from the School of Education who much admired the spinning, and she concluded from their conversation that her mother was "the best stick-spindle spinner in America." When she inquired from me as to the truth of this deduction, I took occasion to describe the Italian village in which her mother had lived, something of her free life, and how, because of the opportunity she and the other women of the village had to drop their spindles over the edge of a precipice, they had developed a skill in spinning beyond that of the neighboring towns. I dilated somewhat on the freedom and beauty of that life—how hard it must be to exchange it all for a two-room tenement, and to give up a beautiful homespun kerchief for an ugly department store hat. I intimated it was most unfair to judge her by these things alone, and that while she must depend on her daughter to learn the new ways, she also had a right to expect her daughter to know something of the old ways. (HH 176)

As Addams tells it, the change in relationship between the two was immediate and tangible. Rather than rejecting her mother as a relic of the old world, Angelina "allowed her mother to pull out of the big box under the bed the beautiful homespun garments which had been previously hidden away as uncouth; and she openly came into the Labor Museum by the same door as did her mother, proud at least of the mastery of the craft which had been so much admired" (HH 177).

As is clear from Addams's story, the role of elites in reconciling immigrant mothers and their adolescent daughters is far from uncomplicated. Angelina values her mother because the visitors from the School of Education do. Addams reflects the values of the educated bourgeoisie in championing handcrafts over factory-made goods for the very reasons that Angelina herself might treasure the products of industrialization: mass-produced objects are uniform, cheaply made, inexpensive, disposable, ephemeral. Angelina is convinced of the worth of her mother's labor and the culture that she literally wears on her back because Jane Addams argues for the "beautiful homespun kerchief" over the "ugly department store hat" that was the staple of working girls.

Addams's defense of Angelina's mother has more than a touch of the imperialist aesthete who "dilates" upon the "freedom and beauty" of primitive lives while maintaining the sophisticated superiority of her own cultural practices. But her goals in the Labor Museum went far beyond a sort of ethnic tourism or snobbery against the vulgarities of factory girls. Like the Arts and Crafts innovators for whom the Labor Museum was a touchstone, Addams believed in the "restorative power in the exercise of a genuine craft" (HH 260). Her critique of industrialization was not that the goods it produced were cheap and worthless, but that factory labor itself was depersonalizing and monotonous—that young women had been convinced that tedious industrial work was somehow more glamorous than the emotionally rewarding labor of their mothers. It's no surprise that Hilda Satt found Hull-House "an oasis in a desert of boredom and monotony" (97).

Indeed, despite the ways in which involvement in the urban workplace defined adolescence for the children of immigrants, the experience of intellectually tedious but physically exhausting labor was one of the things that united immigrant parents, particularly fathers, and their American-born children. Addams's goal in the Labor Museum was not to convince the parents that their ways were superannuated, but to demonstrate to the children that work could be fulfilling in and of itself, not just as a means to gain spending power in a culture already drenched in commerce. Addams tells story after story of immigrants transformed by the opportunity to practice crafts or destroyed by the denial of that opportunity: the Bohemian goldsmith who succumbs to alcoholism and eventually suicide after working as a coal shoveler; the Russian women who, disappointed at missing a party at Hull-House, were shown the Labor Museum:

> Gradually the thirty sodden, tired women were transformed. They knew how to use the spindles and were delighted to find the Russian spinning frame. Many of them had never seen the spinning wheel, which has not penetrated to certain parts of Russia, and they regarded it as a new and wonderful invention. They turned up their dresses to show their homespun petticoats; they tried the looms; they explained the difficulty of the old patterns; in short, from having been stupidly entertained, they themselves did the entertaining. (HH 174)

Even more significant for Addams was the reestablishment of the traditional role of community elders. In contrast to their usual helplessness in the face of a hostile foreign culture whose hostility was often mirrored by that of their own children, the Russian spinners "were able for the moment to instruct their American hostesses in an old and honored craft, as was indeed becoming to their age and experience." In this narrative, the museum reempowered immigrant parents, reestablishing them, as Addams herself pointed out, "into the position of teachers, and we imagine that it affords them a pleasant change from the tutelage in which all Americans, including their own children, are so apt to hold them" (HH 174).[15]

The Labor Museum raises disquieting questions, though. After all, as Barbara Kirshenblatt-Gimblett argues, even in the best of circumstances, "when efforts are made to the contrary, live exhibits tend to make people into artifacts because the ethnographic gaze objectifies" (415). How much could Addams control the responses of the mostly elite, mostly Anglo museumgoers, whose agendas were very different from the working girls whose mothers were the museum's main exhibitors? This is particularly pressing given the timing of the museum, which opened the same year in the same city as the Chicago Columbian Exposition, and which has been widely discussed as a central site for the kind of objectifying ethnographic gaze Kirshenblatt-Gimblett describes.[16]

How much did the Labor Museum participate in what Svetlana Alpers has called "the museum effect—the tendency to isolate something from its world, to offer it up for attentive looking" (27)? How much did it "turn cultural materials into art objects" (Alpers 31), or transform immigrants into specimens? In some ways, the Labor Museum exemplifies what Kirshenblatt-Gimblett calls "*in situ*" ethnographic display, which is designed to "include more of what was left behind, even if only in replica, after the object was excised from its physical, social, and cultural settings" (389). In the Labor Museum, are immigrants themselves the objects, "confined to a pictorial, timeless ethnic space" (Haenni 511)? Undoubtedly, they have been removed from their original environments and cast into a new context.

At the same time, this analogy glosses over some significant differences between the Labor Museum and typical ethnographic display. Unlike the ethnographic exhibits of the World's Columbian Exposition, or the St. Louis World's Fair just over a decade later, the museum made no effort to recreate an authentic ethnic environment. Addams consciously mixed and matched craftspeople of different national backgrounds practicing similar crafts to show the similarities among them, rather than showcasing the irreducibility of ethnic and racial identity. In some ways, Addams was participating in the construction of the identity of the American immigrant, in which ethnic specificity takes second place to national domicile.

Second, ethnographic display makes clear distinctions between observers and observed, encouraging spectators to see themselves as essentially different from those on display while at the same time assuring them that they are watching authentic ethnic activity, as though the exhibitors have no idea that they are there. Kirshenblatt-Gimblett argues that "live displays, whether recreations of daily activities or staged as formal performances . . . , create the illusion that the activities one watches are being done rather than represented," itself a false image that allows viewers to believe that they are watching everyday life, rather than a performance (415). By contrast, the Labor Museum dissolved the line between audience and performers. On the one hand, the craftspeople in the museum were represented as experts, and the work they did as separate from their everyday lives as factory workers, homemakers, pushcart peddlers and so on. On the other hand, Addams's goal was to shrink the distance between immigrants and the American born, not calcify it. As Hilda Satt's experience shows, museumgoers were allowed to become craftspeople themselves, if only for the afternoon, and the immigrants' children were encouraged to see the links between their own factory labor and their parents' manual skills. Finally, the intended spectators of the museum were the children of the "exhibits," not the separate class of viewers constructed by other kinds of ethnographic display. The educational process of the Labor Museum was organized not around a kind of Anglo-paternalism but around the fantasy of the smoothing out of self-conscious difference between the women and men weaving, spinning, throwing pots, and so on, and the teenaged girls and boys who filed through the museum, forming connections between their work and the previously degraded work of their parents.

The Labor Museum also existed as a peculiar inversion of the status of the fine-art museums that came into existence after the Civil War. The Metropolitan Museum of Art in New York, the Philadelphia Museum of Art, the Boston Museum of Fine Arts, and the Art Institute of Chicago alone were founded between 1870 and 1874. As Alan Trachtenberg has demonstrated, the fine-art museum "established as a physical fact the notion that culture filtered downward from a distant past, from overseas, from the sacred founts of wealth and private power" (*Incorporation* 144–145). The kind of art worthy of display in these museums—old, European, removed from (while idealizing through representation) common people—was institutionalized in opposition to the everyday world of crafts. The Labor Museum turned these assumptions inside out. The folkways Addams's museum exhibited *were* from the past and from overseas, but rather than being separated from both their producer and their audience or reflecting the division implicit in fine-art display, the "works" (in both senses of the word) on display demonstrated the continuity between past and present.

However, like fine-art museums and the various world's fairs, the Labor Museum made a clear distinction between industrial and preindustrial cultures. The museum "placed performances in sequence, one national performer after another, to document a developmental history," from the most "primitive" to the most "developed," although still preindustrial (Jackson 254). Addams constructed a transcultural narrative of handcrafts that informed the exhibits in the museum: "It was possible to put these seven [different modes of spinning] into historic sequence and order and to connect the whole with the present method of factory spinning. . . . Within one room a Syrian woman, a Greek, an Italian, a Russian, and an Irishwoman enabled [museumgoers] to see that there is no break in orderly evolution if we look at history from the industrial standpoint" (HH 173).

Perhaps the most difficult critique of the Labor Museum, and of Hull-House in general, is the charge that Addams was participating in a kind of genteel sensationalism, exploiting immigrants for the benefit of bourgeois settlement workers and other reformers, who could garner a sense of self-satisfaction by transforming immigrant poverty and "backwardness" into spectacle. Ruth Crocker's claim that *Twenty Years at Hull-House* "aestheticized the poor" and represented them in enough detail only "to teach the residents different lessons about life" (179), is a penetrating criticism of much late-nineteenth-century poverty relief, and Addams was certainly formed by the philanthropic conventions of her era. For many of her contemporaries, after all, the ghetto was a place to go slumming, "a liminal site of commercial entertainment . . . , both potentially dangerous and safely classifiable within middle-class tourism" (Haenni 494).

I would argue, though, that Addams conceived of the Labor Museum *not* as a tourist attraction or a site of the objectification of "primitive" immigrant crafts. Indeed, looking back on her formative experiences with urban poverty in the East End of London, the mature Jane Addams felt deep ambivalence about what we might call the "tourism of degradation" that she witnessed as a young woman: "A small party of tourists were taken to the East End by a city missionary to witness the Saturday night sale of decaying vegetables and fruit" (HH 61). At the time, Addams was profoundly affected by this scene, and "while I was irresistibly drawn to the poorer quarters of each city [she visited on her two-year tour of Europe], nothing among the beggars of South Italy nor among the salt miners of Austria carried the same conviction of human wretchedness which was conveyed by this momentary glimpse of an East London street" (HH 62). On reflection, though, Addams recognized the manipulative and objectifying elements of her tour of the East End, which was "a most fragmentary and lurid view of the poverty of East London, and quite unfair," since it gave no sense of the reality of the lives of the inhabitants or the "gallantry" of poverty relief workers who lived side by side with East Enders. It's this very "fragmentary and lurid" representation of Hull-House's neighbors that the Labor Museum attempted to disrupt, in the eyes of both native-born spectators and the children of immigrant participants.

Addams's investment in the past was not a form of genteel Luddism. Industrialization was not in and of itself destructive, but the alienation from the products of one's labor on the one hand, and the commercialization of the culture on the other, certainly were. The transformation of both work and leisure into commodities deeply disturbed Addams. In terms of labor, she insisted that even in factories, workers "must be connected with the entire product—must include fellowship as well as the pleasures arising from skilled workmanship and a cultivated imagination" (*Spirit of Youth* 127). The rationalization of industrial labor robbed workers of a sense of skill and a sense of self. But the commercialization of recreation was even more destructive to a democratic culture, since it captured not just a person's work hours but her imaginative life as well. The spending power of thousands of young new Americans, Addams believed, constructed a new kind of city life in which adolescents had "only two possibilities, both of them commercial: first, a chance to utilize by day their new and tender labor power in its factories and shops, and then another chance in the evening to extract from them their petty wages by pandering to their love of pleasure" (*Spirit of Youth* 8). Consumer capitalism gave and consumer capitalism took away; just as it created the conditions by which children of immigrants had money to burn, it provided plenty of opportunities to burn it.

The Labor Museum provided an alternative model of production and consumption. First of all, for Addams, artisanal work could itself be recreational in the best sense of the word. Addams argued that "a long-established occupation may form the very foundations of the moral life" (HH 178), and she cited examples of immigrants who staved off despair by participating in traditional crafts. In contrast to the enervation of factory work, which in Addams's view "calls for an expenditure of nervous energy almost more than it demands muscular effort" (*Spirit of Youth* 108), craftwork engaged both body and mind.

Moreover, the museum itself became a site of industrial production. In the wake of successful exhibits, the museum "finally included a group of three or four women, Irish, Italian, and Danish, who have become a permanent working force in the textile department which has developed into a self-supporting industry" (HH 177). To this extent, then, the Labor Museum was more than a memorial of past skills or a monument to the "primitive." After all, most of the participants in the museum's exhibits participated in the industrial world and the marketplace in one way or another—they were hardly cut off from modern modes of production and consumption. At the same time, Addams believed, the museum could instruct the children of immigrants in the possibilities of labor beyond the experience of piecework:

> If a child goes into a sewing factory with a knowledge of the work she is doing in relation to the finished product; if she is informed concerning the material she is manipulating and the processes to which it is subjected; if she understands the design she is elaborating in its historic relation to art and decoration, her daily life is lifted from drudgery to one of self-conscious activity, and her pleasure and intelligence are registered in her product. (*Spirit of Youth* 122)

The Labor Museum was neither a nostalgic revisiting of the past nor a repudiation of modernity. Rather, for Addams, it was a palimpsest of labor in which each tool illuminated all the others. The factory loom was not a corruption of a hand tool, but rather the most recent development in the history of the work people do. The Labor Museum constructed a bridge between old and new, existing alongside contemporary industrial methods and offering a model of participation in the cash economy that did not insist on alienation from one's labor.

Ultimately, the Labor Museum was designed as a channel of communication between immigrants and their American-born children, using the vocabularies of labor as a common language. More than a "way to bond New World industry to Old World folk culture" (Dougherty 376), the museum was an instrument of family reunification beyond the pieties and threats of the mainstream. Addams recognized the immense changes that were altering not just the fabric of American life, but also the texture of that fabric: the years of adolescence were taking on new meaning, new associations, new sensations. Like her contemporaries, Addams saw the relations between immigrants and the dominant culture as metaphors for larger social structures, but she did not interpret this analogy through the language of primitivism or eugenics. From the conflicts and divided loyalties that told the story of the new separations between immigrant women and their American-born children, U.S. culture could recognize its own new class of adolescents; in the reconciliation that the shared heritage of labor afforded, America could see its own solutions.

Girls, Sex, and Calling in the Law

Jane Addams knew how to use the pleasures of meaningful work to disrupt the growing discourse of incommensurability between immigrant parents and their children; she and her immigrant neighbors had less luck with other kinds of pleasure. A mixed-sex workplace, access to money, a growing sense of independence that money fostered (as well as unchaperoned places in which to spend it), and a youth culture that developed outside the family circle all meant that parents were less and less able to supervise their children's romantic and sexual lives. While this was a less pressing issue for male children, who were given considerably more freedom than their female counterparts to roam unaccompanied by adults, this new "terrible American freedom" was, for young women, often understood as the kind of sexual liberty that was unavailable in their parents' home countries.[17]

Of course, this is not the whole story. As Natalie Zemon Davis has shown, rural and urban communities have for centuries both policed and made space for adolescent sexuality through a variety of courting and shaming rituals.[18] And sexual adventures before and outside marriage were hardly unknown to working-class women in American cities in the years before the great influx of immigrants in the 1880s and onward.[19] However, for this cohort of urban adolescents, sexual experimentation took place within a new context of commercial leisure and mixed-sex workplaces. Teenage children of immigrants invented what their Anglo-American counterparts would later call dating, a practice of courtship and romance that, as Beth Bailey has shown, "increasingly took place in public places removed, by distance and by anonymity, from the sheltering and controlling contexts of home and local community" (3). By the mid-1920s among the middle classes, dating had supplanted other forms of courting—calling on a girl, spending time with her family, going on mixed-age outings—much as it had among the children of immigrants in the decades before.

In its earlier incarnations, "dating" had multiple meanings. For many young working-class women, it was a way to experience the kind of luxuries they were unable to pay for themselves, given how much smaller women's wages were than men's. Dating was also an entrée into sexual activity, either in exchange for various treats—a trip to the beach or a movie, a night of dancing, dinner at a restaurant—or for its own sake.[20] At the same time, a date could connote not just the exchange of one kind of pleasure for another, but also informal or formal prostitution, a slippery slope for many young workingwomen. It was just this loosening of sexual mores that immigrant parents dreaded for their daughters, and against which they did almost everything they could think of, including summoning the power of the state to rein in their "incorrigible" offspring.

In her eloquent letters to her benefactor Fanny Quincy Howe, Maimie Pinzer chronicles her life as a young workingwoman and her struggles with her family over her sexuality, as well as her experiences with prostitution and its aftermath. As was true for many of the families historian Mary E. Odem describes, Pinzer's mother (her father had recently died) found that "regulating the sexuality of youth through family, community, and church were far less effective than they had been" in the villages and small towns from which they came ("Teenage Girls" 53). While industrialization had caused anxieties about the sexuality of young women from the early days of the mill girls in Lowell, Massachusetts, the intensification of urbanization and immigration in the late nineteenth century exacerbated these worries, not least among immigrant parents themselves.[21] Moreover, the rise of Progressivism meant that reformers, who had previously relied upon religious institutions to curb wayward girls, were looking to the state to intervene in what had earlier been thought of as uniquely moral issues, and new immigrants often turned to the police and the courts to enforce their authority over their daughters. A new narrative about the incorrigibility of adolescents and their impulsive sexuality dovetailed with governmental attempts to police teenage sexuality through legislation and incarceration.

As Odem shows, many parents used newly established age-of-consent laws to keep their daughters and other people's sons in line and out of each other's embraces. Their fears were not altogether misplaced: between 1880 and 1910, peak years of immigration to the United States, premarital pregnancy rates rose from 10 percent of all pregnancies to 23 percent (*Delinquent Daughters* 24). Reformers found that working girls' attitudes toward "instances of moral lapse" were "constantly less censorious" than they would have liked, in large part because they sympathized with young women and men who kept company with each other outside the gaze of parents and neighbors (Woods and Kennedy 87). However, unlike the thinking in the pre–Civil War period, when young sexually active women were imagined as lost souls to be saved by evangelical intervention, Progressive reformers blamed conflict between generations for a young woman's "fall into immorality," since she was probably "unhappy at home, out of sympathy with other members of the family, hungry for affection, and without any direct outlet for [her] emotional energies" (Woods and Kennedy 84).

Certainly, this interpretation of events made sense to Maimie Pinzer. After the death of her father, her comfortably middle-class family experienced a precipitous drop in fortunes. Resisting the increase in domestic work at home and short of money to pay library fines, the thirteen-year-old Pinzer took a job as a "saleslady" in a Philadelphia department store. Like many department stores, Pinzer's workplace was, as she put it, "quite the place to come during the afternoon hours to make 'dates' for the eve" (193). Pinzer's newfound liberty was in large part due to her power as a wage earner. Even at thirteen, she had enough freedom of movement, as she relates, that "I could stay away from dinner, and go along with some boys, and come home and tell some sort of story—and that it was accepted, due to the $5.00 I was bringing home!" (193).

Nonetheless, her mother soon began to exert her authority, "and when I threatened to leave home, my mother said she hoped it was soon" (Pinzer 193). This moment, a typical quarrel between a mother and her teenage daughter, had consequences neither could have anticipated. The young Maimie did run away from home, staying with a young man of her acquaintance for several days. But more striking than the rebelliousness of her actions is the way the now-adult Pinzer characterizes her decisive break from her parents and her seemingly radical choice, at barely fourteen years old, to live with a man, if only for a short while. "Of course," she says of the aftermath of the argument with her mother, "the inevitable thing happened. Some young chap took me to his room; and I stayed three or four days before I put in an appearance in the neighborhood of my home" (193).

Pinzer's insouciant "of course" brings the reader up short, as does her assertion that her actions were "the inevitable thing." Perhaps she is reconstructing the narrative from her later knowledge of her life as a prostitute—that this is a kind of *post hoc, ergo propter hoc* inevitability, the first predictable step on the road from "incorrigible girl" (the charge her mother brought her up on and under which she was remanded to the Magdalen Home, a reform school for sexually adventurous girls) to "disreputable woman." Or it may be that she is implicitly blaming her mother's lack of sympathy for her own slide from respectability; her running away and shacking up with a young man is the "inevitable" response to her mother's unconcern for her well-being.[22] Pinzer's account of her arrest as an incorrigible girl reveals the closeness between state policing of adolescents and the desire by immigrant parents to control their sexually active sons and daughters. In a "horribly filthy, vile-smelling" prison cell, she "cried and begged they should send for my mother," but "she refused to come," compounding Maimie's feeling of terror and abandonment. Ironically, given that the charges against her were for sexual immorality, it was only when she allowed one of the guards "to take all sorts of liberties with me" that Maimie was released from her cell into a larger room. The police also attempted to arrest Maimie Pinzer's "young chap" for statutory rape, since in order to place her in public charge, he had to be "produced" (Pinzer 193).[23] Ultimately, there was never a hearing at which he testified—whether because the police were unable to find him or because Maimie's mother and uncle were in a hurry to get rid of her and did not want to wait is never made clear—and rather than being returned to prison, Maimie was sent to the Magdalen Home, "a mild sort of reform school for girls who have gone astray" (Pinzer 196).[24]

In her letters Pinzer frequently mentions the divide between her mother and herself, caused in large part by her mother's eagerness to view her as a "disgraceful hussy," but also by what Pinzer saw as the generational divide between them. In an anecdote Pinzer tells that also functions as a fascinating echo of Mashah Smolinsky's desire for her own toothbrush and towel in *Bread Givers*, sixteen-year-old Maimie bought Listerine, a toothbrush, and tooth powder to preserve her teeth, which one of her mother's grocery customers had admired. Returning home one day, Maimie found that these things had disappeared and confronted her mother, who admitted to throwing them away for fear of the shame Maimie would bring on the family. Her mother had heard from a local Jewish shop owner that Maimie had been "doing unnatural things" with her mouth and that tooth powder and Listerine were used to "keep the mouth free from disease from such practices—and that explained why I didn't become pregnant" (Pinzer 274).

Pinzer's reaction to this attack reveals the ways in which she understood her status both in her community and in relation to her immigrant mother. Her first response was humiliation that "I had to live in that neighborhood and know for certain everyone who would listen had been told this" (274). Maimie's fear that her family's judgment of her would translate into community opprobrium was hardly misplaced. While many reformers saw overcrowded tenements, rather than the poverty that caused the overcrowding, as the "prolific source of sexual immorality," the opposite was often true (Committee of Fifteen 164).[25] Certainly the density of immigrant neighborhoods contributed to "ill health, nervous tension, and a desire to escape," but young people were just as eager to escape the prying eyes of parents and neighbors as they were to flee the tenements themselves (Woods and Kennedy 2). Commercial institutions such as dance halls and movie theaters provided some of the few spaces in which teenagers could spend time together without the surveillance of the community bearing down upon them (see chapter 4). But, as Pinzer commented in her letters to Fanny

Howe, when young women like her wanted "shelter or warmth of any kind," both literal and emotional, "I had only a fellow's apartment to go to" (322). Young workingmen living in rooms or boarding with families had more disposable income to spend on the kinds of luxuries they shared with women like Maimie, who "went often, to stay for two or three days [with one young man] just because he had all the magazines" (Pinzer 322). Community standards, however, demanded that a girl who had been out late with a man be "locked out," leaving her few options, as Pinzer observed, apart from staying with her date or going to a brothel.[26]

Pinzer's analysis of her mother's rush to judgment of her, though, extends beyond her fears of community disapproval. She sees in her mother's assumption that for a young woman integrated into a new set of social and sexual mores (loosely categorized as "American" but really created by the children of immigrants), the process by which an alien substance like Listerine becomes a harbinger of still greater sexual license is a "circumstance . . . repeated daily by thousands of mothers whose daughters, naturally, living in a new age and learning the newer things, want them, and are continually hounded because they want to live different" (Pinzer 274). Pinzer recasts a family conflict over sexuality, modernity, and commodity consumption—Maimie wants to use tooth powder and commercially produced mouthwash rather than scrub her teeth with a towel as she has always done—as another example of intergenerational struggle.

Maimie Pinzer's story, so typical in some ways, is extraordinary in others. She was taken up by a series of members of the Anglo-American elite and aspired toward mainstream American respectability, even as she founded and maintained a home for girls who had "gone astray" that eschewed the usual pious trappings of mission homes for the wayward. (She refused to call these girls "friendless," as one of her sponsors wanted, arguing: "Any 'self-respecting' errant girl—if such a term is permissible—might be willing to admit that she is friendless . . . yet she wouldn't want any other girlfriend to know she was going to a mission for 'friendless girls.' Isn't that admitting defeat?" [341].) Through persistent detective work, historian Ruth Rosen discovered that later in life Pinzer may have been a published writer, lived and traveled in California in the 1920s, and become part of the Hollywood social set, quite unlike most of her Jewish immigrant contemporaries in major cities up and down the East Coast, who for the most part climbed into the middle classes and moved out to nearby suburbs.

However, the generation gap Pinzer represents between herself and her mother, and the ways in which it crystallized around issues of sexuality, is echoed by the analyses by social workers and reformers writing in the years in which Maimie spent her time in reform school and lived in sin with various young men in her teens and early twenties. Sophonisba Breckenridge,

Ruth True, Jane Addams, David Blaustein—all saw the recasting of sexual mores not simply as a matter of Americanization, but as a symptom of the breakdown of sympathy between immigrant parents and their adolescent children. While many Italian parents tried "to guard their girls almost as closely as they did in Italy" (Breckenridge 177), and the twin disciplinarians of gossip and the police attempted to keep young tenement dwellers in line, the power of the adolescent cultures these young people created often overwhelmed the efforts of even the most vigilant parents.[27]

The Italian parents weeping at the play they saw at Hull-House; Angelina watching her mother spin in the Labor Museum; Maimie Pinzer, afraid to come home and be labeled a whore, but having nowhere else to go—all are manifestations of the discourse of the generation gap that were echoed in the mainstream in the decades to come. But the gap stretched not only from parents unable to understand the desires of their new American children, nor simply from the children who could only incompletely make those desires known and understood to their parents. The flappers and flaming youth of the 1920s and their descendants, the teenagers of the 1940s, 1950s, and 1960s, were constructed at a distance from the culture as a whole. Even as adolescents became the largest percentage of the population, the belief in a chasm between their values and those of the culture as a whole—a belief formed in the early years of the twentieth century as social commentators constructed and then struggled to understand a new class of young people so radically different from their Anglo-American peers—continued to define the language of adolescence.

In the discourse of the generation gap we see the profound influence that urban immigration at the beginning of the twentieth century has had on understandings of white adolescence. Ironically, what barely survived were Jane Addams's efforts to reintegrate the generations through the experience of productive work. As the meaning of adolescence shifted away from the workplace and into the marketplace, this final site of reconciliation shrank into cultural insignificance. The Labor Museum and its goal to "reveal the humble immigrant parents to their children" became artifacts of a different time, museum pieces themselves, and the gulf between generations was transformed from an obstacle to be overcome into a commonplace.

4   *"Youth Demands Amusement"*

DANCING, DANCE HALLS, AND THE
EXERCISE OF ADOLESCENT FREEDOM

On a warm summer night in 1892 on the Lower East Side, twelve-year-old Rose Cohen, barely a year in New York, wandered out of her tenement apartment and "caught a few strains of music coming from the roof. . . . I went up and found under the sky, blue and bright with the stars and the city lights twinkling all around, a group of Irish-American girls and boys waltzing to the music of a harmonica. I sat down in the shadow near one of the chimneys and watched the stars and the dancing and listened to the song of 'My Beautiful Irish Maid' " (89).

Twenty years later, on another summer night, this time in Atlantic City, New Jersey, in mid-June of 1912, Mrs. Agnes E. Day enjoyed a strenuous evening of dancing the turkey trot "with friends in her home," according to the *New York Times.* Mrs. Day, the *Times* reported, "was lively and gay." Suddenly, "she was taken with a severe pain in her right side, which quickly became so intense that it caused her to swoon." Although several doctors were called, none reached Mrs. Day soon enough, and before she could receive medical attention, she was dead. A later investigation revealed that she had ruptured a blood vessel and died of internal hemorrhage. But, as the *Times* observed in its pointed headline, "Dies after a Turkey Trot," the true cause could be located elsewhere. Agnes Day, barely twenty-two years old and married "only a short time," was the tragic victim of a modern scourge: ragtime dancing.

These two stories provide only a taste of the importance dancing had for young working-class people at the turn of the nineteenth into the twentieth century, and the intensity of reaction from the political, social, and cultural establishment (embodied here by the *Times,* but in other instances by state and municipal legislatures, reformers, schools, and intellectual elites). The children of immigrants were, as reformer Belle Lindner Israels commented, "dance mad"; in New York, where Israels lived and worked, "if you walk along Grand Street on any night in the week during the winter months, the glare of lights and the blare of music strike you on every side" (494).

Dancing appears again and again in immigrant stories, however briefly. The space of dancing is the space of adolescent independence, of fun and heterosociality, of flirting, of asserting a specific kind of urban American identity. The dances themselves are rarely named in these narratives. Indeed, the physical act of dancing is sometimes beside the point, however much social reformers wrung their hands over its immorality and vulgarity. It is the room itself, the place where dancing is made to happen by young·people finally released from department stores, factories, and sweatshops, that looms large in these stories.

Dance halls were crucial to the construction of an adolescent urban culture at the turn of the nineteenth into the twentieth century. They provided a public space away from the eyes of parents and their allies where young people could experiment with new social and sexual arrangements, where gender relations could be reorganized (although not without ambivalence for all involved). Moreover, since they were commercial rather than strictly communal institutions, dance halls popularized the idea of leisure as inextricable from capitalism, a trend that, as many social historians have noted, characterized the end of the nineteenth century, and that suffused working-class adolescence in major cities.[1] Dance halls did not create this phenomenon, but they were one of the central commercial establishments that the children of immigrants made their own. Similarly, urban adolescents did not invent many of the dances that they adopted: the turkey trot, the grizzly bear, the black bottom had their roots in vernacular black dance, and the waltz had a long history in Europe and North America. But they transformed these dances and the spaces in which they were performed into vehicles for self-expression and sexual intimacy.

In this chapter I explore the role and meanings of social dancing, dance halls, and dance academies for the adolescent children of immigrants. A significant proportion of the writing about urban dancing came, of course, from reformers and activists. They saw the dance hall as a place of sexual license and alcoholic excess (and they weren't far wrong in either instance), and wanted either to close commercial dance halls down or to render them respectable by taking away the sex and the booze and placing them under "responsible" adult supervision. However, as the novels, stories, and memoirs I discuss here show, dance halls were crucibles for the formation of a specifically urban, specifically adolescent, specifically American sense of self. The association between social dancing and young people, and the dance crazes that swept through Anglo-America from the 1910s to the 1960s, had their roots in the passion for dancing expressed by adolescent children of immigrants in the late nineteenth and early twentieth centuries.

Although dancing played a huge role in the lives of the children of immigrants, it is rarely the focus of literary texts about immigrant communities (the same cannot be said of social scientific and reform texts; social reform writing about dancing and dance halls takes up thousands of pages). Rather, dancing appears as a motif, much as in a piece of music or a dance step—appearing, moving into the foreground, playing out a few phrases, and then receding as the major themes of the text take over. This chapter on dancing and dance halls, by necessity and by choice, reproduces those rhythms. It is kaleidoscopic, reenacting the patterns of the dance hall itself, with partners moving and switching, taking breaks, going outside to drink or smoke, or sneaking upstairs for a moment of intimacy. Voices interweave to create a layered sense of what the dance hall meant to the people who spent their time and their money there, and of how they changed the cultural meanings of dancing itself.

The two decades between Rose Cohen's encounter with the Irish American tenement waltzers and Agnes Day's untimely demise limn the outline of a cultural phenomenon that consumed Americans of all classes even as it disturbed social reformers and civic leaders: a dance craze that filled the ballrooms of big cities and small towns alike, and that culminated in the dance madness of the Jazz Age. The arrival of ragtime in white America was a significant factor in the explosion of dancing at the turn of the nineteenth into the twentieth century, but the association of dance trends and crazes with adolescence found its roots in the popularity of dancing among young urban workingmen and particularly workingwomen. Indeed, the word "popularity" seems far too mild for the passion the daughters of immigrants felt for dancing and the commercial institutions that catered to that passion. More importantly, the dance hall became a staging ground for the enactment of a particular youth culture that radiated into the larger culture over the course of the early twentieth century.

The shift from the waltz to the turkey trot, from European-style round dances (so called because they both spun dancers around and propelled them in a circle around the room) like the waltz, the mazurka, the polka, and, toward the end of the century, the two-step, to the tough dances or barnyard dances of the ragtime era—the turkey trot, the grizzly bear, the shimmy was remarkable. But it was certainly not as extreme as the differences between Cohen's scene of almost pastoral recreation and the *Times* account of the deadly turkey trot suggest. First, the waltz did not disappear as a social dance, although ragtime dancing by far dominated the social scene in the first two decades of the twentieth century until it was supplanted by jazz and swing dances like the Charleston and the lindy hop in the 1920s. Moreover, despite its current respectability, the waltz itself had hardly been free of controversy since its popularization in the United States in the 1830s. In fact, it had generated a steady stream of antidance literature.[2] The majority of antidance treatises attacked social dancing as contrary to Christian principles of modesty and sexual chastity, and the close physical contact encouraged by the waltz and related round dances evoked appalled condemnation from social conservatives.

Second, at the end of the nineteenth century young working-class women and men had adopted the waltz as a youth-specific activity, either supplementing or supplanting the mixed-age social dancing traditions of their home countries, with the understanding that the waltz was an American form of recreation. While Cohen's dancers are all Irish American, they are not performing a traditional Irish dance. Rather they are waltzing to "My Beautiful Irish Maid," one of many Irish nostalgia songs written at the end of the nineteenth and beginning of the twentieth century by Irish American balladeer James Chancellor Olcott, who adopted the more Irish-sounding Chauncey Olcott for his professional songwriting name (his two most famous songs are "My Wild Irish Rose" and "When Irish Eyes Are Smiling").[3] The song is, like the Irish identities that were forged in urban areas like New York, Boston, Providence, and Chicago, an entirely American invention, calling upon memories of an Ireland never seen with a dance style that was as much an import to Ireland as it was to the United States.

It is worth noting that Olcott himself was native to the United States. Born between 1858 and 1860 in upstate New York (either Lockport or Buffalo—the records are contradictory about date and place of birth) to Irish-born parents, Olcott didn't invent the phenomenon of Irish nostalgia. He was, however, hugely influential in popularizing it for his own generation of U.S.-born children of the famine generation, as well as for third-generation Irish Americans like the young people dancing on Rose Cohen's roof. It is certainly ironic that the creations of an Irish American have become synonymous with authentic Irishness in both the United States *and* Ireland (although less ironic than that "Danny Boy," the most iconic Irish ballad then and now, was written by an Englishman, F. E. Weatherly, based on a traditional Irish air sent to him by his American sister-in-law). But it is more significant that Cohen bathes this scene in a wash of her own nostalgia for childhood that crosses ethnic lines and embraces dancing as an immigrant activity. Finally, it's impossible that the song Cohen heard was "My Beautiful Irish Maid," since this memory dates from 1892 and the song first appeared (at least in sheet music) in 1894. In other words, Cohen merges an actual event featuring Irish Americans with an anachronism that narrates "Irishness" for her and her readers, and that reinforces the nostalgia for traditional ethnic music and dance.[4]

With the emergence of ragtime, the level of anxiety about social dancing ratcheted up considerably. In part this was due to the racial origins of ragtime's dances. The waltz's provenance was European, and however decadent white Protestant Americans believed European culture to be, it at least had the virtue of whiteness. Ragtime and its dances had their roots in African American culture, most famously in the Storyville whorehouses of New Orleans and San Francisco's Barbary Coast. As David Nasaw has shown, sheet music accompanying popular rags and cakewalks were identified with and illustrated by images of black musicians and dancers in familiar minstrel poses, with exaggerated racialized faces and bodies.[5] Ragtime dancing was also associated with sailors, who spread the dances from port to port, a trajectory that was seen as an accessory to their spread of sexually transmitted diseases, their drunkenness, and their encouragement of prostitution in port cities.[6]

Nonetheless, even before the explosion of ragtime dance onto the ballroom floor and the intensification of public concern about it (which came to a head in around 1912), the children of immigrants had carved out a space for themselves in the varied dancing places in cities across the United States. Spaces for dancing took many forms, from settlement houses and social clubs organized by young people to commercial dance palaces, dancing academies, and dance halls bankrolled by and adjoining saloons. The number of dance halls and related institutions in major cities was impressive—in 1910, Cleveland, with a population of over 560,000, had 130 licensed commercial dance halls. New York during the same period had more than 500 registered dance halls, which did not include the unregistered, informal, or illegal spaces in which dancing took place (McBee 60).

Most dance halls were financed by saloons or saloon owners. This link between dancing and drinking was especially disturbing to reformers, but, while drinking was an important adjunct to an evening's dance, it was not as central as middle-class observers assumed. As we shall see, of prime importance were the scene of dancing itself and the social world it created.

Yekl Goes to Joe Peltner's Dancing Academy

Four years after Rose Cohen sat on her roof and watched a group of Irish American teens waltz away a summer night, Abraham Cahan's *Yekl: A Tale of the New York Ghetto* was chronicling another element of youth dance culture: the dancing academy. While large commercial dance halls were usually the focus of reformist zeal—not surprisingly, given their connections, both financial and architectural, to saloons—they were hardly the sole site of dancing available to young people in the working-class and immigrant neighborhoods of major cities. The children of Jewish immigrants in particular flocked to dancing academies, smaller institutions that offered dance lessons and receptions several times a week (it's entirely possible that the Irish American adolescents on Rose Cohen's roof also learned to waltz at a dancing academy, since it's unlikely they learned from their rural Irish parents). The classes were loss leaders designed to attract dancers for the receptions, which were, on the whole, not much different from public dances.

Dancing academies were commercial institutions but were usually more intimate than dance halls and, unlike saloon-based ballrooms, did not commonly serve alcohol. As Belle Lindner Israels observed, dancing academies were "frequently located in rooms not adapted for such purposes," often little more than glorified tenement apartments, factories, or warehouses, as

Cahan describes Joe Peltner's Dancing Academy, the favorite haunt of his immigrant protagonist Jake, né Yekl Podkovnik:

> The room was, judging by its untidy, once-whitewashed walls and the uncouth wooden pillars supporting its bare ceiling, more accustomed to the whir of sewing machines than to the noises which filled it at the present moment. It took up the whole of the first floor of a five-story house built for large sweat-shops, and until recently it had served its original purpose as faithfully as the four upper floors, which were still the daily scenes of feverish industry. At the further end of the room there was now a marble soda fountain in charge of an unkempt boy. (15)

Cahan provides this description immediately after an atmospheric discussion of Suffolk Street, in the heart of the Jewish district of the Lower East Side of New York. For him, the intensity of activity at the dancing school is a necessary product of Suffolk Street, itself "in the very thick of the battle for breath" (13). Building up layers of lists within lists, Cahan uses the very structure of his sentences to impress upon his readers the atmosphere of over-population and the welter of sounds, sights, and smells that the "Ghetto of the American metropolis" (12) offers up:

> Hardly a block but shelters Jews from every nook and corner of Russia, Poland, Galicia, Hungary, Roumania; Lithuanian Jews, Volhynian Jews, south Russian Jews, Bessarabian Jews; Jews crowded out of the "pale of Jewish settlement"; Russified Jews expelled from Moscow, St. Petersburg, Kieff, or Saratoff; Jewish runaways from justice; Jewish refugees from crying political and economical injustice; people torn from a hard-gained foothold in life and from deep-rooted attachments by the caprice of intolerance or the wiles of demagoguery—innocent scapegoats of a guilty Government for its outraged populace to misspend its blind fury upon; students shut out of Russian universities, and come to these shores in quest of learning; artisans, merchants, teachers, rabbis, artists, beggars—all come in search of fortune. (13–14)

The boundaries between the street and the dancing school are diaphanous; *Yekl*'s narrator notes the "children dancing on the pavement to the strident music hurled out into the tumultuous din from a row of the open and brightly illuminated windows of what appeared to be a new tenement house," the building that houses Joe Peltner's Dancing Academy. Just as the music is "hurled" out of the window down to the street below, the density and intensity of street life find their way into the dancing school. Cahan's characterization of Jake's walk along Suffolk Street, "through dense swarms of bedraggled half-naked humanity; past garbage barrels rearing their over-flowing contents in sickening piles . . . ; underneath tiers and tiers of fire escapes, barricaded and festooned with mattresses, pillows, and featherbeds not yet gathered in for the night" (Cahan 13) is echoed in his entrance into the dancing school in its assault on every sense:

> As the spectacle [of the children dancing] caught Jake's eye his heart gave a leap. He violently pushed his way through the waltzing swarm, and dived into the half-dark corridor of the house whence the music issued. Presently he found himself on the threshold and in the overpowering air of a spacious oblong chamber, alive with a damp-haired, disheveled, reeking crowd—an uproarious human vortex, whirling to the squeaky notes of a violin and the thumping of a piano. (15)

While Cahan makes clear links between the larger immigrant Jewish community that surrounds Joe's dancing school and the space of the academy itself, he also draws distinctions between the multigenerational world of the street and the much more age-limited semi-private, semi-public social scene at Joe's. The dancing children are explicitly outside the academy, making do with the music that issues from open windows. While younger adolescent girls manage to find their way into the room—a "dozen or two of undergrown lasses of fourteen or thirteen who had come surreptitiously" from school or their mothers' less-than-watchful eyes (16)—most of the participants in the dance are in their late teens or early twenties. Moreover, Joe's is implicitly a place for unmarried young women and men, and peer-group heterosocial dancing—an activity organized around their social needs. Spatially, the room is divided by gender, with separate benches for "ladies" and "gents." But this division is honored as much in the breach as in the observance. Several male customers "nonchalantly overstepped the boundary line, and, nothing daunted by the professor's 'Zents to de right an' ladess to de left!' unrestrainedly kept their girls chuckling" (17).

Dancing expertise is not a requirement for attendance at Joe Peltner's, but single status is. Since his arrival in New York, Jake has kept his wife and son a secret, although he has sent money to them regularly.[7] And the same evening that he makes his appearance at the dancing academy, he has "firmly determined to keep himself from visiting Joe Peltner's" and instead to devote himself to saving the money required to bring his family over to New York. Joe's seems to exert a preternatural power over him, however—although he initially takes a route home that is in the opposite direction to Suffolk Street, "his feet, contrary to his will, turned into a side street and thence into one leading to Suffolk" (Cahan 12).

On the pretext of returning unsold ball tickets, and suffused with ambivalence, Jake enters Joe's with "an afflicted expression of *ennui* overshadowing his face" (Cahan 16). A familiar face at the dancing academy, Jake "was immediately noticed and became the target for hellos, smiles, winks, and all manner of pleasantry. . . . Jake was the center of a growing bevy of both sexes. He refused to unbend and to enter into their facetious mood, and his morose air became the topic of their persiflage" (16–17). But he can sustain his ill temper for only so long. His role at the dancing academy is not just that of customer but also that of informal employee of a kind common to such establishments, a "spieler" whose job, as Israels characterized it, is "to attract and interest young girls. He dances with the wall flowers, and he is expected to keep everybody happy and everybody busy" (495). This Jake does with impressive energy, urging young women to dance and young men to " 'gu right aheat an' getch you partner!' " (17).

Jake's position as spieler shapes his relationship to the dancing academy. His are not simply two of the "two hundred pounding, gliding, or scraping feet" (Cahan 17). Rather, he plays the combined role of huckster, dancing instructor, matchmaker, Lothario, and standup comedian:

> Jake went on yelling right and left. "Don't be 'shamed, Mish Cohen. Dansh mit dot gentlemarn!" he said, as he unceremoniously encircled Miss Cohen's waist with "dot gentlemarn's" arm. "Cholly! vot's de madder mitch *you*? You do hop like a Cossack, as true as I am a Jew," he added, indulging into a momentary lapse into Yiddish. . . ."Dot'sh de vay, look!" With which Jake seized from Charley a lanky fourteen-year-old Miss Jacobs, and proceeded to set an example of correct waltzing, much to the unconcealed delight of the girl, who let her head rest on his breast with an air of reverential gratitude and bliss. (17–18)

It's striking that Cahan comments on Jake's "momentary lapse" into Yiddish. English, as Cahan notes, is the "official language of the academy, where it was broken and mispronounced in as many different ways as there were Yiddish dialects represented in that institution" (17). The overlay of Yiddish and English here point to the specifically immigrant, specifically American character of the dance academy. On the one hand, as Cahan makes clear, the English spoken at Joe's is primarily shaped by the Yiddish that is its speakers' first language, even conforming in accent and grammar to particular regional differences between Yiddish speakers. On the other hand, English is what the dancers speak, carving out a linguistic space in which English and Yiddish are in implicit and sometimes literal conversation with each other. Just as several Latino critics have claimed Spanglish as a distinctive mode of linguistic expression that is formed by and itself produces a specific cultural identity (for example, Nuyorican or Chicano), the English that emerges at Joe's, filtered through a sediment of Yiddish, is both hybrid and sui generis— mixing two linguistic structures and creating a new one with a rhythm and texture all its own.[8]

Indeed, what the habitués of the dancing academy do to English, they also do to dancing itself. The waltzing that takes place at Joe's is quite different from the formal round dance described in the dance manuals of the mid- and late nineteenth century.[9] In his guide to round dancing published in 1890, for example, Melvin Gilbert assures his readers that "a couple assuming the waltz position as illustrated . . . are acting in accordance with good judgement, propriety, delicacy, and refined taste" (33). Gilbert's model couple dances "removed from each other, a distance which will prevent the bodies from voluntarily coming into contact" (35), hardly the goal of young Miss Cohen and her fellow terpsichoreans at Peltner's. And when Jake takes a dance with Mamie, his soon-to-be paramour, "they swung along with all-forgetful gusto; every little while he lifted her on his powerful arm and gave her a 'mill,' he yelping and she squeaking for sheer ecstasy, as he did so; and throughout the performance his face and his whole figure seemed to be exclaiming, 'Dot'sh a kin' a man *I* am!'" (Cahan 20). This implicit declaration of identity (a catchphrase that, throughout the story, takes on a tone of increasing ambiguity) announces Jake's dancing as a creation of self, a yardstick for measuring who and what he is, in the context of the transient community formed by the dance.

This is not to say that Cahan represents the dancing academy as a place of pure pleasure. In fact, while the "general effect of the kaleidoscope [of the various dancers] was one of boisterous hilarity, many of the individual couples somehow had the air of being engaged in hard toil rather than as if they were dancing for amusement. The faces of some of these bore a wondering martyrlike expression, as who should say, 'What have we done to be knocked about in this manner?'"(16). For these dancers, attending Peltner's Dancing Academy is itself hard work—the work of participating in commercial leisure activities. That leisure and labor became on the surface indistinguishable did not diminish the power that the desire for "boisterous hilarity" had on the young men and women of immigrant neighborhoods. As Ruth True noted in *The Neglected Girl,* her 1914 overview of the daughters of immigrants on Manhattan's West Side, more than one young woman would "add to her long day at the factory several nights every week at dance halls where she stays until 1 or 2 o'clock"(6). Fun not only defined and enlivened the experience of these young workers, as I have argued earlier. Fun also became a part-time job for many adolescents, in which they worked on finding a place for themselves within the urban "kaleidoscope" (a word that appears repeatedly in discussions of immigrant communities) and reshaping commercialized leisure in their own images.

Out of the swirling dust they set into motion in the dance academies and other commercial centers of dancing, young immigrant sons and daughters sculpted the prototype of the American teenager: eager for fun, for the company of the opposite sex, for the "ecstasy" that Mamie feels spinning around in Jake's arms. As Randy McBee has meticulously shown, commercial leisure houses like dance halls "allowed young men and women to escape their parents' watchful eyes . . . [and] allowed for the development of a peer culture" (3). The flirting and canoodling laughingly countenanced at Peltner's Dance Academy was a common feature of dance halls of all kinds, extending from close dancing to furtive sexual intercourse in hallways and balconies of the larger establishments (Louise de Koven Bowen was less temperate about this phenomenon, complaining that in dance halls "young girls sit upon men's laps and allow all kinds of indignities" [*Dance Halls* 6]). Young people could experiment in any number of ways that were not available to them even on the street, conscious as they were of the networks of friendship and information sharing in which their parents participated; in dance halls, they could indulge in "alcohol or cigarettes, engage in sexually expressive dances, or even dabble in romance, all the while ignoring the manner in which their parents were trying to supervise intimacy and arrange marriages" (McBee 81).[10]

It's not surprising, then, that Jake's initial ill humor at Joe's is fueled by resentment toward the other dancers and articulated through the feelings of limitation and entrapment that he associates with his wife, Gitl, and son, Yosselé, who are still in his hometown of Povodye: "As he thus gazed at the dancers, a feeling of envy came over him. 'Look at them!' he said to himself begrudgingly. 'How merry they are! Such *shnoozes,* they can hardly set a foot well, and yet they are free, while I am a married man. But wait till you get married, too,' he prospectively avenged himself on Joe's pupils; 'we shall see how you will then dance and jump!'" (Cahan 17).

Jake's prophecy is realized, but not for his fellow dancers. Spurred by his father's death to finally send for Gitl and Yosselé, he must remake himself as the married man he has been all along. A significant part of this change is his surrender of the "fun" of the dance academy, something he has anticipated for years. Bringing his family to New York means one thing, in his estimation: "No more fun for me!" (Cahan 12). While this initial vow to forswear fun and embrace his former self is short-lived (in the narrative it precedes his visit to Joe Peltner's Dance Academy), the arrival of Gitl and Yosselé does seem to require a rejection of his membership in immigrant youth culture and a turning back to his responsibilities as a husband and father.

As I noted in the introduction, "fun" is reinvented in the world of urban amusement as a capacious, layered word. It does not mean only pleasure, exactly, since Jake thinks fondly (however infrequently) of his life with Gitl and the mistily recalled Yosselé. The pleasures of his life with Gitl are of a very different stamp from the "fun" he can have with girls like Fanny and Mamie: he remembers "the individual sweetness of her rustic face" (Cahan 31), and in a rush of guilty nostalgia declares to himself: "'I would not exchange her little finger for all the American *ladas*' . . . , comparing Gitl in his mind with the dancing-school girls of his acquaintance" (32). "Fun" is a

phenomenon of youth and urban single life, of the whirl of changing partners and swinging skirts. "Fun" is not "rustic sweetness" but "boisterous
hilarity" (15), and it is inextricable from the commercial institutions that
make it possible.

Jake's conflicted feelings about Gitl are interwoven with his longing for
renewed participation in youth culture. "He thought himself a martyr, an
innocent exile from a world to which he belonged by right . . . ; he would
bewail his lost youth and curse all Russia for his premature marriage" (Cahan
44). Russia is the place of early marriages, New York the locus of youthful
pleasures. Jake's sorrow over missed opportunities and anger at his wife and
son are not wholly unleavened by affection, however, and he "would gradually feel the qualms of pity and remorse, and make a vow to treat [Gitl]
kindly. 'Never min',' he would at such instances say in his heart, 'she will
oyshgreen herself and I shall get used to her. She is a _____ *shight* better than
all the dancing-school girls" (45).

At no point, though, does Jake imagine that his married life and the world
of the dancing school could ever merge. Accepting Gitl means abandoning
the social circles and activities he was a part of as a supposed bachelor, and
the terms in which he rehabilitates Gitl in his mind reinforce that dichotomy:
"he would inspire himself with respect for her spotless purity, and take com-
fort in the fact of her being a model housewife, undiverted from her duties by
any thoughts of balls or picnics." Finally, Jake acknowledges that dance halls
are way stations rather than destinations, places from which their denizens
graduate into adult life, "sooth[ing] himself with the additional consolation
that sooner or later the other fellows of Joe's academy will also be married"
(Cahan 45).

By the mid-1890s, then, dancing played a distinctive role in urban immigrant life. Even before the onslaught of ragtime and tough dancing, the commercial institutions that hosted waltzes, lancers, and polkas were also serving
as witnesses to the formation of an identifiable youth culture fostered by the
children of immigrants. Going to dance halls was not for married women
and men (except, perhaps, the married men who frequented taxi-dance halls,
which often doubled as centers for prostitution). The dance-fueled culture of
working-class leisure required ready cash and youth; it also brought into
being a new kind of American adolescent, liberated from parental oversight
and enmeshed in a heady world of (a kind of) sexual freedom, whose loyalties were to a forming American identity as much as to a home ethnic group.

Adolescent Representations of Dance Culture

Cahan's invocation in *Yekl* of a subculture organized around an urban adolescent peer group accurately represents the way both teenagers themselves
and the adults trying to control them saw the world of working-class social

dancing. The attribute of dance halls that reformist narratives of the late nineteenth and early twentieth century objected to the most was their resistance to surveillance by figures of authority, whether parents, social workers, or police.[11] Yet the freedoms dance halls afforded were not always represented negatively. While few texts of the era speak approvingly of the privacy and potential for sexual experimentation the dance halls provided, some do offer the space of dancing as a locus for the evolution of modern romance and a more fully articulated American identity filtered through immigrant experiences. Samuel Lewenkrohn's short story "Shadchen's Luck," published in the *Settlement Journal* (the official publication of the Henry Street Settlement) in 1905, sees dancing as a way for adolescent children of immigrants to assert their romantic desires in the absence simultaneously of their parents and of the accusation of sexual license.[12] Lewenkrohn's story both challenges parental authority over teenage children and reassures parents that, left to their own devices, those children will not stray very far from community standards.

"Shadchen's Luck" is, in texture, quite similar to the stories of Abraham Cahan, a story of conflict between generations, between the values of the Old World and the New. However, unlike Cahan's work, in which irony predominates and the happiness of the protagonists is often a matter of chance, Lewenkrohn's story vibrates with optimism and happy coincidence. The premise is simple: Baruch the *shadchen* (matchmaker) is called upon by the Feldman and Greenberg families to arrange a match between their children, Annie and Joe, respectively. However, in true "clash of the generations" style, Annie and Joe, independent of each other, refuse to enter into an arranged marriage. Although the parents of "both sides were willing . . . , the thing could not come to pass merely because the two youngsters objected" (2). Lewenkrohn's humor here is palpable—he clearly sides with the young Annie and Joe, and his dismissal of their objections is an ironic rehearsal of the attitudes of their parents.

All is not lost for the unfortunate Baruch, however, who depends financially upon the success of the match. Annie and Joe buy tickets for the annual Allandale Social Club dance and meet there by chance. As was typical of the combined hetero- and homosociality of such events, "Joe came without any lady friend, and Annie came with a bevy of other girls to represent her club." Annie quickly attracts Joe's attention, since "she was pretty, very pretty, and danced well." As Lewenkrohn points out, the dancers do not stand on ceremony: "according to the custom in this part of town, he asked her to dance. No need of such a thing as an introduction here; they calmly ignore such formalities on the Lower East Side"(2).[13]

In many ways, this dance encapsulates the worst characteristics of dance halls—hundreds of young women and men, many strangers to each other, dancing without the social protection of formal introduction and without any adult presence. In addition, Lewenkrohn argues, the attraction that grows between Annie and Joe is not just affected by but created by dancing. "So they danced," he says, "and because they both enjoyed it very much, they danced again. It was not the first time the feet instead of the head led to the heart" (2). Rather than embarking on a relationship brokered by their parents, Annie and Joe are drawn together by mutual sexual attraction, a feeling that is amplified by the physical closeness of dancing. The two start dating without their parents' knowledge, and eventually Joe proposes marriage, which Annie accepts, a development that could have major repercussions for their small community and for the relationships between the two families and between each young person and her or his parents.

But the romance ends happily for everyone. Baruch, the shadchen, learns about Annie and Joe's engagement and hastens to assure Joe's father, Abraham Greenberg, who had originally hired him, that the match was in fact his work. In the schema of the story, dancing allows everyone to get what he or she wants: the Greenberg and Feldman families make an advantageous match for their children, and Joe and Annie get to marry for love. The potential conflict between old ways and new is averted, and with some well-placed misinformation, Baruch can reassure Greenberg as to the continuity of the old ways while financially profiting from the new.

As the place of publication of this story suggests, dancing as a commercial leisure activity was not necessarily in conflict with reformist institutions like settlement houses. Although as Laura Hapke points out, "the lure of the dance hall surpassed that of the working girls' club or settlement house social," plenty of young men and women satisfied their urge to dance at the more respectable venue of the settlement house or social club dance.[14] Settlement houses were well aware of the appeal dancing had for young people and rather than fighting against the current, they determined to provide more pleasant environments in which their neighbors could slake their dance passion. The Henry Street Settlement or its various organizations sponsored dances almost monthly, selling tickets for fifty cents each with free hatcheck, and dancing academies like M. Heicklen's School for Dancing advertised in the pages of the *Settlement Journal*, offering "Classes every Monday, Wednesday, Thursday Evening and Saturday Afternoon. Receptions every Friday Evening and Sunday Afternoon."[15]

The centrality of social dancing, and its inextricability from the code of financial/sexual quid pro quo, was so much part of the social scene for the children of immigrants that it was under discussion even within the more respectable context of the settlement house. In "One Ballad of the Ball," a poem written by Henry Street Settlement member Solomon Linhart and published in the *Settlement Journal* in 1904, the unnamed male narrator riffs on the lengthy hours of the dance—"From nine to four, from nine to four"—and the trials of the mores of dance hall life. Intoxicated by the excitement of the dance, the speaker and his partner "danced as we had ne'er before. / The music played / As we both strayed / In Dreamland, O, from nine to four!" But not all is well. Early on in the ballad it is clear that the dreams of at least one of the dancers are firmly anchored in reality: "It seemed as if we happy were. / It *seemed*, I say / That both were gay / Were gay from nine to four." The speaker's partner might have been enjoying the evening, but the narrator's "heart was sad." His unhappiness is rooted in the financial strain treating his partner puts on him. At the beginning of the evening "My purse was full . . . ; and four / Found *me* quite full (of joy) no more; / For, in that plight, / My purse waxed light, / Waxed light from nine to four" (6).

The narrator's straits become humiliating when he attempts to take his date home. Arriving at the El station: "I took my purse to pay the fare; / Great Scott! There were but six cents there." Since the fare is five cents, he is forced to impose upon his date to provide the remaining four cents for her ride. Whatever sexual favors he had been expecting were clearly no longer on offer: "I got the four [cents] / And nothing more, / And nothing more, Oh, after four!" After pacing the streets from dawn to morning, the narrator finally returns home and sleeps "from nine to four." When he awakes "I vowed no more, / Though heart were light / And pocket tight, / To gyrate more from nine to four" (Linhart 6).

While this poem is something of a trifle, it opens up an element of the often unspoken social contract between young women and the dates who took them out dancing. While the narrator certainly doesn't like the way things are arranged—men pay with money, women pay with sexual attentions—he takes for granted the way the transaction operates. Seeing his money frittered away on an evening's amusement may make his heart sad, but he is far sadder when he is compelled to ask his date to pay her own way on the El. The possibility of any kind of sexual intimacy is foreclosed immediately; having asked for his date's money, he can expect "nothing more" (with the assumption that his readers would know what the "something" he was expecting might be). The social practice of "treating" dealt with by social reformers and later by historians takes on quite a different appearance here, in the context of a young man whose desires outstrip his means. His vow "no more . . . to gyrate more from nine to four," deals with the immediate cause and results of his penury—spending all his money on his date, becoming sexually excited, and being rebuffed—not on the gendered division of expenses.

A large part of the story of commercial leisure is, of course, having disposable income to spend on amusements. While women earned, on the whole, only about half what men made—in the early 1910s, 56 percent of women made under $8 a week (Peiss 52)—it was also true that many young women and men had more time for leisure and more to spend on it than at ever before.[16] For many young people, having the money to spend on the leisure activities of their choice was a defining element of a decent job. A 1913 editorial in the *Ladies Garment Worker,* the official organ of the International Ladies' Garment Worker Union, listed among its objections to the low pay received by many young women manufacturing "white goods" (that is, lingerie) not just subsistence issues such as being "forced to dwell in a dirty, dreary room of a crowded tenement house, in the heart of filthy slums; to eat the foulest food obtainable; to wear the shabbiest clothes," but also to be limited to attendance at "the cheapest amusement places," as though high-class leisure opportunities were a basic right of workingwomen (4.3:2).

If young women could not afford to finance their own pleasures, they counted upon their dates to do it for them. The narrator of "One Ballad of the Ball" takes that arrangement as a given. Whatever it is that he is spending his money on at the dance is not mentioned in the poem, but it is enough to leave him only six cents at the end of the evening. Moreover, pleasure itself is a unit of exchange: in exchange for the pleasure of dancing, the narrator's partner offers the promise of the pleasure of eventual sexual intimacy; in exchange for the pleasure of female company, the narrator pays for all the major and incidental expenses of the dance; in exchange for providing the pleasure of a place to dance, music to dance to, and something to drink while dancing, the dance hall charges accordingly.

This economy of pleasure underscores all three literary texts we have looked at so far. While the dances described in the two texts from the *Settlement Journal* seem quite modest and alcohol is not mentioned (most likely because they both appeared in an official publication of the Henry Street Settlement), both are quite explicit about the ways in which dancing and the free exercise of sexuality went hand in hand. The informality of the dance hall and the social club is part of their appeal—Joe Greenberg does not need a formal introduction to Annie Feldman to start dancing with her and their relationship develops completely outside the sphere of their parents' influence. Similarly, the narrator of "One Ballad of the Ball" and his dancing partner transact their pleasurable quid pro quo according to the mores of the ballroom, not of the immigrant culture of their parents. In both these texts, the young people themselves control the terms, intensity, and duration of their romantic involvements.

This may not seem so surprising to contemporary readers, but it might be instructive to contrast these scenes with another early twentieth-century representation of adolescent dancing, this one from Booth Tarkington's 1915 novel, *Seventeen.* The book is set in a white Anglo-Saxon middle-class community in an unnamed "middle-sized midland city"—which is to say, a very different environment from the Jewish working-class metropolis of "Shadchen's

Luck." The novel's plot (such as it is) revolves around a summerlong infatuation indulged in by seventeen-year-old William Sylvanus Baxter. William and his friends spend their copious free time sitting on each other's porches, eating at ice cream parlors, and competing with each other in paying court to their crush, Lola Pratt, an ingénue visitor to a local family.

The novel's climax comes in a dance thrown by Miss Pratt's hosts, the Parcher family, in honor of her trip home at the end of the summer. Once again, the dancing itself is only briefly described, although given the date, William and his friends are probably dancing very toned-down versions of the turkey trot (renamed the Long Boston) and the Castle Walk, a more genteel cakewalk invented by Vernon and Irene Castle, who brought ragtime dancing to the middle classes, sanitizing it in the process.[17] In many ways, the dance is a structural throwback to the nineteenth century: each dance is a defined unit, either a "regular" or an "extra," and the young women have dance cards on which they sign up their various partners. The party is supervised by Mr. and Mrs. Parcher, who also make sure that all the young women have partners to dance with. In an ironic twist, William initially has no dress suit to wear, because, being a middle-class boy, he has no income: he has to sell his books and clothes and ask his mother for money to buy appropriate clothes for the party. When he finally arrives, Miss Pratt's dance card is already full, and he is assigned to dance with the far less attractive Miss Boke, whose professed love of dancing is not matched by her skill.

There is no doubt that "dance madness" has found its way to this medium-sized midwestern city, but it has been almost completely transformed. Like most other elements of bourgeois adolescent life, particularly outside major metropolises, dancing is funded, organized, and supervised by adults. The teenagers need only to wear the right clothes (for which they are not expected to pay), to arrive at the right time, and to behave in the right way. The comedy in the novel is supposed to issue from William's inability to conform to these standards, mostly due to the intensity of his crush on Lola Pratt. Moreover, there is not even a hint of romance, let alone sexuality, in the scenes of the dance. Miss Pratt flirts with all her suitors, but it is unimaginable that she will have to reward any of them with any level of physical intimacy. After all, adults have provided for her benefit the orchestra, the refreshments, the space in which to dance, her clothes, and any other needs—the stakes of dancing are much smaller and much more subtle than for her working-class counterparts. Similarly for her dancing partners—dancing with Miss Pratt is a reward in and of itself for William and his friends, not a means to greater access as it is for Joe Greenberg and the narrator of "One Ballad of the Ball."

The financial semi-independence of teenage boys and, to a much more limited extent, teenage girls in immigrant communities meant that dancing took on a whole host of other meanings. Dancing became both an end in itself and a means to an end—freedom from adults, an entrée into sexual experience, a way to cement social ties, both homo- and heterosocial. In other words, for working-class children of immigrants, dancing as a cultural phenomenon resembled much more the teenage universe of swing clubs of the 1930s and 1940s and even discos of the 1970s and 1980s than it did the adult-dominated cabarets of the 1920s or the dance parties of middle-class teenagers of the same era.[18]

Dance Hall Reform and the Ragtime Backlash

By the 1910s, not only had the waltz, the polka, and the mazurka given way to ragtime dances like the turkey trot, the shimmy, the bunny hug, and the grizzly bear, but also these dances had spread to every echelon of dancing society, from northeastern elites who danced them in ballrooms to the middle-class couples taking classes with social dance entrepreneurs Vernon and Irene Castle, to the working-class dancers with whom they originated. They had spread over the Atlantic to Europe and south to Central and South America (something of an irony, since the tango had only recently made its way north to the United States). At the same time, Progressive reformers turned their attention in earnest to commercial dance palaces in hopes of reshaping the terms and conditions of social dance for the working people whose lives they wished to improve.

The groundswell of public interest in ragtime dancing coincided almost precisely with the upsurge of Progressive concern with the influence of dance halls on working people. Many of the headlines made explicit connections between the two. A 1912 *New York Times* story about the Committee on Amusement and Vacation Resources for Working Girls, led by the indefatigable Belle Lindner Israels, described a conference held by the committee at Delmonico's in which participants could "behold the 'Turkey Trot' as it ought to be danced, if at all, and then, as it often is danced" ("Social Workers See"). The aura of exoticism and the illicit that surrounded dance halls and their representation in the press was such a commonplace that Ruth True could comment that "the dance hall, with its air of license, its dark corners and balconies, its tough dancing, and its heavy drinking, is becoming familiar to every reader of the newspapers" (70).

At the same time, the media hysteria about ragtime dancing, both pro and con, had very different priorities from those of social reformers. The popular and elite media focused on the dances themselves—where they originated, what music accompanied them, how they were danced, and who the dancers were. Activists and settlement house workers were more concerned about the sites of dancing, particularly dance halls, which they believed (not inaccurately) to be corrupt and corrupting, interested only in profit, and breeding grounds for vice and disease. For them, ragtime dances were not pleasant, but hardly the greatest problem.

Although they saw commercial dance halls as "largely controlled by the brewery, saloon and vice interests," progressive reformers like Addams and Israels agreed with Bowen that prohibiting dance halls would do more harm than good (*Dance Halls* 3).[19] The adolescent desire for fun was paramount—as Belle Lindner Israels put it, "Youth demands amusement" (497)—and banning dance halls would just drive them underground, making them more difficult to observe and change. Rather, what young people needed were clean, safe, and supervised places to find that amusement, "a rationally conceived program of regulated and municipalized recreation resources" and, in a telling phrase that brings us back to Addams, access to the "general motherhood of the commonwealth" (Perry, "General Motherhood" 724–725).

Implicit in these critiques of modern amusement sites was nostalgia for older, less sexually explicit modes of recreation. G. Stanley Hall hearkened back to dancing's formerly "pristine power to express love, mourning, justice, penalty, fear, anger, consolation, divine service, symbolic and philosophical conceptions, and every industry or characteristic act of life in pantomime and gesture." Instead, the "dance of the modern ballroom" constituted "only a degenerate relict, with at best but a very insignificant culture value, and too often stained with bad associations" (214). Similarly, Addams contrasted "the public dance halls filled with frivolous and irresponsible young people in a feverish search for pleasure" with "the old dances on the village green in which all of the older people of the village participated" (*Spirit of Youth* 13).[20] And Gustav Stickley wrote fondly of the dances held at the *Craftsman* magazine, of which he was the editor, as a reenactment of earlier times, recreation that erased differences of class and age, and at which he saw

> bankers and painters and sculptors, business men and editors, art students and young men from their daily employment, schoolgirls and even children all dancing side by side; the elderly men largely with their elderly wives, looking younger and happier than I remember them a few years ago, lighter on their feet, chatting cheerfully between the dances, interested in what the young folks are doing, and the young folks in turn with the comradeship for their elders that has not been found in this country for a generation past. (243)

The authors of these accounts of dancing are most disturbed by what the young people attending dance halls most valued: the creation of a separate age-peer group that transformed dancing into a generation-specific activity.

A major objection reformers made to dance halls was the commercialization of leisure, and indeed of urban life more generally. Invocations of preindustrial times dovetailed with a critique of the imbrication of enjoyment and consumerism. In part, this was blamed on the inextricable relationship between wage labor and a commodity-driven culture, but for immigrants' advocates there was a more insidious pattern. The wage labor system gave and it also took away—in rent, food, and commercialized leisure. As Jane Addams charged: "The modern city sees in [working] girls only two possibilities, both of them commercial: first, a chance to utilize by day their new and tender labor power in its factories and shops, and then another chance in the evening to extract from them their petty wages by pandering to their love of pleasure" (*Spirit of Youth* 8).

The job of reformers, then, was to provide a space for dancing outside the corrupt and exploitive cash nexus.[21] If "industrial activity demand[ed] diversion" and the physical constraints of wage work "crie[d] out for rational recreation," it was up to dance hall reformers and settlement house workers to provide a meaningful alternative (Israels 486). In this context, the dances thrown by the Henry Street Settlement and social clubs take on new meaning. More than just alternatives to public dance halls, they were part of an organized resistance to the stranglehold that Progressives believed commercial institutions—from department stores to saloons to nickelodeons to amusement parks—had on working-class people more generally.[22] Dancing was not the problem, dance halls were.

Not all social reformers believed that dancing was a neutral activity. Certainly, there were conservative commentators, particularly those affiliated with evangelical Christianity, for whom dancing itself was a taint on American society, beyond salvaging for positive influence. As Dr. Revels A. Adams, a prolific author of social jeremiads, wrote in his 1921 screed *The Social Dance:* "In choosing the dance as one of his surest, truest, and most potent instruments of selection, the devil chose well" (3).[23] However, the extremism of *The Social Dance* is, on examination, one of degree rather than type. While Adams is undoubtedly at the far end of the scale in terms of his antidance sentiment, conservatives and progressives echoed his concerns. Hall himself posed the challenge to adolescents in similar terms, arguing that "the forces of sin and those of virtue never struggle so hotly for possession of the youthful soul" as they do when a young person is pursuing "a good time" (83).

For Adams, the threat of sin was ever present in the world of dancing, since dancing's "chief attraction is the intimate association of the sexes, the thing that fires the passions of young women and makes them easy prey to the lust of men" (R. Adams 15). Like Bowen and Israels, Adams was particularly worried about the virtue of young women and the challenges to their sexual and personal integrity that the atmosphere of social dancing posed. Adams saw the danger as more than the "indignities" Bowen complained about; for him, dance halls in particular were teeming with pimps (or "cadets," as they were known) and other "evil men" who, "with no thought or care for the shame which is to follow . . . allure women and even little girls to the dance; they allure them like the spider to the fly; they lead them farther and farther on the downward way till the girls themselves come to the place where they enjoy the sinful pleasure and thus drift on the tide to certain destruction" (16). The dance hall had become a contemporary island of the lotus-eaters, annihilating productive impulses and tempting its habitués deeper and deeper into their doom. Dancing was also a threat to the sacred bonds of marriage, since cities were filled with "thousands of young women who fear to get married and answer the purpose of the Creator, because they fear the duties of home and the care of children will deprive them of the pleasures of the dance" (11).[24]

As with his contemporaries, Adams's objections to social dancing were not just moral, but also physical. Dancing was injurious to young and old (assuming a dancer could make it to old age), and Adams had science on his side to prove his case, since "the most reliable statistics show not only that habitual dancers die young but that they suffer more from nervous diseases, and that women dancers have more operations, more diseases common to women as the result of the excessive exercises of the dance" (R. Adams 8).

Ultimately, though, cultural elites, from conservatives like G. Stanley Hall to reformers like Jane Addams, and a significant portion of bourgeois professionals like schoolteachers, social workers, youth club leaders, and municipal officials—all believed in the salutary effects of recreation. The challenge might be between "virtue and sin," as Hall claimed, but, as Addams implicitly rebutted, "recreation is stronger than vice . . . ; recreation alone can stifle the lust for vice" (*Spirit of Youth* 20).[25] Others were less enthusiastic but at the very least were resigned. An urban director of physical education interviewed in Ella Gardner's 1920 survey of dance hall regulations acknowledged that "it is impossible to suppress public dancing. The department of recreation is endeavoring to substitute clean wholesome neighborhood and community dances in the school buildings" instead of depending upon commercial dance halls (43). The mayor of Cleveland opened a municipal dance hall in 1912, and the superintendent of schools opened up school buildings for "three cent dances" in the wintertime "to put the school-houses in direct competition with the saloon dances" ("Municipal Dance-Halls").

The crucial question was how recreation could be organized to benefit both the dancing adolescents and society at large. "Organize" was the operative term here: reformers saw the rationalization and organization of leisure as inextricable from and essential to the kind of Taylorist work teenagers were doing in sweatshops and department stores. Forced to compartmentalize at work, young people let loose in their leisure hours with, according to reformers, disastrous results: drunkenness, sexual excess, and physical enfeeblement. Jane Addams voiced typical contempt for the lack of attention to the leisure practices of the adolescent working class in *The Spirit of Youth in the City Streets*, complaining:

> This stupid experiment of organizing work and failing to organize play has, of course, brought about a fine revenge. The love of pleasure will not be denied, and when it has turned into all sorts of malignant and vicious appetites, then we, the middle-aged, grow quite distracted and resort to all sorts of restrictive measures. We even try to dam up the sweet fountain itself because we are affrighted by these neglected streams. (6)

This careening between neglect and overregulation was bound to fail, as far as Addams and her counterparts in other cities were concerned. Indeed, it had failed and had put severe stress not only on the children of immigrants who frequented dance halls, but also on their communities. In her influential pamphlet *The Public Dance Halls of Chicago*—a report of the six-year investigation by the Juvenile Protective Association of Chicago, which she chaired—Louise de Koven Bowen traced the beginnings of the association's work in the dance halls to community concerns, not governmental or reformist impetus: the association "has always received so many complaints, regarding dance halls, from others whose children were attending these halls, or from neighbors who knew about the conditions existing there" that it decided to embark on a comprehensive study (3).[26] Rather than coming into a community to impose change from above, the association claimed that it was responding to demands from the community itself. Moreover, like Jane Addams in her thinking about the Labor Museum, Bowen saw the conflict between immigrant teenagers and their parents (or at least their parents' generation) as motivating her work, not the conflict between immigrants and Anglo-American reformers. No wonder, then, that dance hall reformers continually attempted to move dancing back into the community, hosting dances through schools and neighborhood groups, bringing adults back into the social lives of their teenage children.

Bowen was not wrong that dance halls were on the whole unappetizing places to be and did not "offer safe or wholesome recreation for young people" (*Dance Halls* 3). Poorly ventilated and overcrowded, the halls quickly filled with smoke, heat, and humidity, and the dust that was swirled up by women's substantial skirts "makes breathing both difficult and dangerous" (*Dance Halls* 7). Since dance halls were frequented most in the winter months (in the summer, dancers went to seaside and lakeside resorts, amusement parks, beer gardens, and other outdoor places), and owners were loath to pay to heat them, the windows were often boarded up to keep out the cold, worsening the problems with ventilation. The line between dance hall and whorehouse was sometimes thin, as well. Halls sometimes advertised cheap rooms for rent, and association investigators were occasionally approached by prostitutes.

For Bowen and the Juvenile Protective Association, though, the bedrock issue in the fight for dance hall reform was a problem dear to the hearts of many of their reformist colleagues: alcohol. Young people at dance halls had almost unfettered access to liquor, particularly at the halls owned by or adjoining saloons. The profit motive of commercial dance halls made the sale of liquor an obvious accompaniment to a night on the town, sometimes superseding the dancing itself. In many dance halls, dancing was actually kept to a minimum—perhaps ten minutes at a time, with thirty- to forty-five-minute "intermissions"—to encourage dancers to drink. Few halls had water fountains, so thirsty dancers had no recourse to any other refreshment than beer. Bowen listed various gimmicks that dance halls would resort to encourage drinking: contests, raffles in which the prizes were bottles of whisky, drinking games, and similar activities.

The link between dancing, drinking, and illicit sex was self-evident for Bowen, particularly given the lack of any meaningful adult supervision. In the absence of parents or other authority figures, "saloon-keepers and prostitutes are in many cases the only chaperones, and in many of the halls even young girls and boys fresh from school are plied with alcohol, and with the suggestion of vice, until dancing ceases to be recreation and becomes flagrant immorality" (Dance Halls 4).

Although Bowen condemns the "immorality" at dance halls, she rarely assigns responsibility for it to the dancers themselves. She blames the sexualization of dancing on alcohol and, by extension, the profit motive. The dancers are caught up in an atmosphere not of their own making and behave accordingly. She quotes one investigator as saying: "These young people did not appear vicious but rather like children who, with blood aroused by liquor, their animal spirits fanned to flame by the mad music, simply threw caution and restraint to the winds in a manner they would never do elsewhere. Rigorous supervision and no liquor would have made this dance almost an innocent party" (Dance Halls 5).

There is an appealing sense of utopianism here. According to this logic, these working-class adolescents would be perfectly happy at a dance without alcohol and with adult chaperonage. The corrupt saloons put temptation in their way, but, in the view of the association, drinking and sexual experimentation were not necessary parts of the dance hall experience for these children of immigrants. All that was needed was to provide "wholesome" alternatives to commercial dance halls, and young people would come running.

Of course, that was far from the case. As Belle Israels realized, young people often enjoyed, and at the very least usually did not object to, the disreputability of dance halls. Although most dance halls in New York were "thoroughly disreputable," dancers did not seem to mind. Young women "know the bad reputation of some of them, but the dancing floor is good, there are always plenty of men, and there are laughter and liberty galore" (Israels 488). Adolescents did not want "rational recreation"; they wanted fun and freedom. Given the creativity they employed in finding ways to drink after hours and experiment sexually in the "balconies and dark corners" Ruth True mentions, it is clear that there were more motives for maintaining the status quo at dance halls than the profit of the owners. Ironically, dance halls offered the most privacy young people could find; in contrast to the homoso-cial, ethnically bounded communities from which they came, dance halls allowed for mixing of all kinds: sexual, regional, ethnic (although *not* racial), and, to some extent, class.[27]

What of the dances themselves? If one believed the descriptions of reformers, one would think that ragtime dancing was an unfettered display of sexual expression. There is some truth to this; as Kathy Peiss argues: "Tough dancing not only permitted physical contact, it celebrated it" (102). Physical closeness was the sine qua non of ragtime dancing, and Louise de Koven Bowen's description of one evening's dance nicely encapsulates how central it was: the dancers "stand very close together, the girl with her hands around the man's neck, the man with both his arms around the girl or on her hips; their cheeks are pressed close together, their bodies touch each other; the liquor which has been consumed is like setting a match to a flame; they throw aside all restraint and give themselves over to unbridled license and indecency" (5). Even in the "respectable" ballrooms of bourgeois America, there was something so "clutchingly familiar in the manners of the girl's partners . . . that one could not help feeling that he was intruding on a scene that should have no witness" (Inglis 11).

According to *The Public Dance Halls of Chicago*, ragtime dancing hit the Chicago dance palaces at the end of the first decade of 1900. The Juvenile Protective Association began its investigations in 1910, by which point tough dancing was the rule for the working-class immigrant adolescents who flocked to the dance halls. About a year later, ragtime dancing exploded into the mainstream, analyzed in any number of newspapers and magazines, from the *New York Times* to the *Ladies' Home Journal* to *Harper's Weekly*, not to mention dime novels, the immigrant press, and antidance testimonials. The intensity of reportage about the dance craze is remarkable—the *Times* alone featured more than a dozen articles on the turkey trot and related dances between the beginning of 1911 and the end of 1912—but most interesting is how quickly the tide turned against the unmediated performance of ragtime dance. Only after the intervention of Vernon and Irene Castle, who rendered these dances acceptable for the middle classes, did ragtime dancing lodge comfortably in the parlors and ballrooms of the bourgeoisie.

The first mention of ragtime dancing in the *Times*, at least, appears in January 1911.[28] In a lengthy article entitled "Have You Tried the 'Long Boston'"

Dance?" the *Times* took on the persona of cultural tour guide, introducing its readership to the new varieties of dance making their way through high society. The dance itself was defined almost entirely in terms of social class: claiming that "society, unless it's middle-class, is at present amusing itself with a new dance," the article located the Long Boston at such society hotspots as Sherry's and Delmonico's, while distinguishing it from its "Coney Island" cousin, the turkey trot. Tracing the Long Boston's swift rise from obscurity to "a party Miss Helen Taft gave a few weeks ago at the White House," the article provides a brief description of its various incarnations (the Philadelphia Drop, the one step, the Boston Harvard, the Spanish Boston, and so on), and makes vague claims about its origins. Rather than acknowledging ragtime dance's roots in the U.S. urban environment, the *Times* traces the birth of the Long Boston to Europe; socialites from the "Summer colony at Old Orchard" discovered it in one of their numerous trips abroad and brought it home with them, full of "hops and turns." "New dances always begin in Summer resorts, by the way," the article confides. "Society is more concentrated in these places."

·Creating a narrative of trickle-down cultural transmission, the article traces the beginnings of the turkey trot, "the people's version of the new dance," to a desire by the habitués of Coney Island to imitate their social superiors:

> The people got glimpses of the Boston Trot and its successor the Long Boston. To try to dance as the Europeans did so as not to be embarrassed at one's social functions abroad did not strike them as important to any great extent. When they beheld the new dance they believed they were witnessing a would-be imitation of a turkey. They felt that they, too, could imitate turkeys. The next Coney Island social function introduced the "Turkey Trot." ("Have You Tried")

What's fascinating about this narrative, apart from its evidentiary status as near-total fiction, is the way that it deploys class as an explanatory mechanism for a popular culture phenomenon. The turkey trot, here denuded of its animality and imbued with a whiff of New England pedigree, is disarticulated from its working-class (let alone African American) origins. Its popularity is ascribed to the influence of both European and American high society, to New Women and proto-flappers who used ragtime dance as an exercise program, since "slenderness was just getting to be the style about two years ago" ("Have You Tried"). Moreover, represented as possessing minimal social ambitions and apparently limited powers of imagination, "Coney Island" (that is, immigrant and working-class) dancers here take on the role of naïve imitators, uninterested in emulating Europeans but eager to imitate turkeys. Similarly, in an article on the failings of immigrant girls, East Side House organizer Miss De G. Trenholm despaired of the mimetic impulses of the working classes, arguing that with "the 'bunny hug' and the 'turkey trot' in vogue along Fifth Avenue, what was First Avenue to do but follow suit and introduce them too?" ("New York's Biggest Problem").

Subsequent *Times* articles followed a similar script, commenting upon appearances of the turkey trot at any number of high society venues. At the end of 1911, the turkey trot and the grizzly bear surfaced in Newport, Rhode Island, as part of a new vogue for dinner dances ("'Turkey Trot' at Newport"). A couple of weeks later, Philadelphia society was reportedly embracing the turkey trot, which had "invaded Philadelphia's most exclusive dancing circles." Young people throughout the city were taking lessons, since "a debutante must know how if she expects to be a success." As was typical of reports of ragtime dancing, dancers described how strenuous the new steps were. Mrs. J. A. Drexel Biddle admitted: "I can do it a little now, but I get out of breath. It is a hard dance to do" ("Approve the Turkey Trot").[29]

With the arrival of Vernon and Irene Castle in New York in 1912, public opinion shifted away from the explicit physicality of tough dances and toward the more genteel reformulations of ragtime dance. There was a concomitant rash of condemnations of the turkey trot and other "barnyard dances," and a recuperation of ragtime by the middle classes through the periodical press. The *Times* reported a trend of turkey trot and grizzly bear bans up and down the East Coast from Philadelphia (only a year before a haven of the dance) to New Haven (both Yale and the city itself). Welfare inspectors were posted in dance halls and at debutante balls, on the Bowery and at Sherry's, to make sure that dancers were not indulging in indecency ("Welfare Inspector").

Despite the success of dance instructors in teaching ragtime dance, social critics were concerned that it was mostly learned informally, "passed," as George Kibbe Turner wrote in *McClure's*, "from one person to another, from the youths to the children with the thoroness [sic] of a great popular song. . . . Even little children dance the grotesque steps upon the sidewalk" (qtd. in "Turkey Trot and Tango" 187).

Getting to the crux of the matter, *Harper's Weekly* posed the question "Is Modern Dance Indecent?" accompanied by large photographs of an apparently middle-class, middle-aged couple dancing the turkey trot in their parlor, and one picture of a "thé dansant" at a New York restaurant. The writer, William Inglis, quoted the then New York mayor's diatribe against contemporary dancing, condemning the "lascivious orgies going on in so-called 'respectable' dance halls in this city" (11).[30] A *New York Times* editorial in January 1912 linked these banishments of animal dances to the narrative of social influence the paper had previously used to approve the dances. Given "the manner in which lax conduct in high social circles can influence the humbler to evil practices," the upper classes had a responsibility to working people to do away with animal dances. "The working girls," the editors of the paper of record declared, "get [the dances] from good society." Moreover, although these dances are already "grotesque" in their high-society manifestations, they are even more destructive when "imitated in the Saturday night dances of the poor girls, whose lives are not so well guarded and are ever subject to innumerable temptations." The responsibilities of noblesse oblige are the focus here, as well as the ways in which "the daintiest dalliance with evil by people of wealth and social influence frequently has pitifully degrading results among their less fortunate fellow beings" ("Influence of Social Follies").[31]

It was only when tough dancing emerged from urban immigrant dance halls and found its way onto the dance floors of the elite that the mainstream press took an interest in the kinds of dancing that were taking place in working-class neighborhoods. The story of the turkey trot combined several trajectories, all of which rehearsed a very specific class narrative. From the fleshpots of San Francisco's Barbary Coast to the ballrooms of Europe; from the parlors of Fifth Avenue to the dance halls of the Lower East Side; from vacation resorts in Newport to the seaside of Coney Island—ragtime dancing was invested with the power to corrupt the defenseless working girls who were in fact, as we have seen, its earliest and most enthusiastic participants. Rather than reflecting the actual progression of the dance—its East Coast and Midwestern roots in the Bowery and Chicago's West Side and (as I discuss in chapter 5) its dissemination through a variety of social networks connecting immigrants, bohemians, and intellectuals—popular accounts of the dance insisted on its transmission *down* the social ladder, and the mutual degradation of dancers and dance. By the time Belle Lindner Israels convened six hundred socialites, reformers, show business luminaries, and journalists in late January 1912 to "shudder at 'The Shiver,' gasp at 'the Bunny Hug' and then discuss reforms," ragtime dancing was no longer about breathless pleasures and had become a social problem. The questions Israels posed to her audience revealed the deep anxiety tough dancing now generated around the assumption that "there should be established some standard of decency in social dancing. What is good and what is bad? How are the supervisors to answer the working girl when she protests that every one is dancing the 'Turkey Trot'? Is it all a confusion in terms?" ("Social Workers See").

And yet, despite the similarity in music and steps, dances in working-class dance palaces and in bourgeois parlors and ballrooms were more different than they were alike. The scenes of ragtime dancing among the upper and middle classes most closely resembled the nostalgic intergenerational dances recalled by reformers than the riotous dance halls of the Bowery and Halsted Street. When William Inglis visited a dance in a southern resort hotel in 1913, he saw "scores of debutantes, a sprinkling of little brothers and sisters, a great many slender, downy youths who were identified as college 'men,' several dozens of preoccupied and gray-headed fathers . . . ; also flitting languidly here and there, various tall, slim, languid-eyed, hollow cheeked fellows of anywhere from twenty-five to forty years" (11). These, Inglis claimed, were "five hundred representative American people," a far cry from the age-specific crowds in immigrant dance halls in large cities across the country.

Even as these dances entered the recreational vocabulary of the middle and upper classes, they shed the specific social meanings that working-class adolescents attached to them. While the image of society matrons shimmying and hopping is more than a little incongruous, it is closer in content to the balls of the nineteenth century than to the dance academies of the Lower East Side. The leisured classes embraced ragtime dancing en masse, from children to pillars of the community; even in condemnations of ragtime dancing we do not see the kind of anxiety about intergenerational conflicts that suffused narratives about working-class dance. Not until the emergence of the flaming youth of the 1920s did that kind of split rise to the surface of bourgeois consciousness.

Ironically, by the time reformers had managed to pass enforceable legislation regulating working-class dance halls, the ethos of mixed-sex adolescent dancing, infused with sexual adventure and unbridled fun, had established a firm foothold in the middle classes. Ella Gardner's report on the regulation of public dance halls published in 1929 lists the hundreds of laws passed in the preceding years and coincided with the last gasps of the Jazz Age. The young people of Sinclair Lewis's *Babbitt* (1922) and Theodore Dreiser's *American Tragedy* (1925), speeding around in cars, assuming a level of autonomy and independence unimaginable to the teenagers of *Seventeen* only a decade earlier, had unknowingly inherited the freedoms that their working-class counterparts of the previous twenty years were now being denied in public dance halls. The bourgeois imprimatur on separation from the public sphere, which began the century as an obligation to remain under parental control, became a license for middle-class teenagers to carve out independent spaces in their cars, high schools, and college fraternities and sororities, to dance unimpeded by watchful adult eyes, a privilege hard-won by immigrant teenagers decades before.

5   *"Youth Is Always Turbulent"*

REINTERPRETATIONS OF
ADOLESCENCE FROM BOHEMIA
TO SAMOA

"The two generations misunderstand each other as they never did before,"
declared Randolph S. Bourne in his 1913 manifesto *Youth and Life* (34).[1]
"Youth"—a loosely defined period that for Bourne stretched from the midteens into the early twenties—had changed radically for the new generation
of young people. By the beginning of the second decade of the twentieth
century, youth had transformed into a "time of contradictions and anom-
alies. . . . The fiercest radicalisms, the most dogged conservatisms, irrepress-
ible gayety, bitter melancholy—all these moods are equally part of that
showery springtime of life" (3).

Bourne's analysis of youth, which is to say the period of adolescence and
early adulthood, sounds strikingly similar to the conventional wisdom both
about teenagers today and, as we have seen in the preceding chapters, about
the young working-class people living, laboring, and playing in the major
cities of the United States at the beginning of the twentieth century. In his
essays in *Youth and Life,* particularly in "Youth," "The Two Generations," and
"The Virtues and Seasons of Life," Bourne maps out the struggles and pleasures of the young people of his milieu. Implicitly, Bourne's "youth" shared his
demographic profile: middle class in origin, bohemian by inclination, highly
literate (and mostly college educated), rebellious if not radical, freethinking,
feminist (or at least antipatriarchal), determined to remake personal, sexual,
and ideological relations.[2] A full decade before the flaming youth of the 1920s
ignited, Bourne's bohemian peers were setting cultural fires in coffeehouses,
underground bars, and magazine offices, and, as Christine Stansell has docu-
mented, in hours and hours of intense conversation.

In this chapter I argue that the young bohemians of Randolph Bourne's
Youth and Life bear more than a passing resemblance to, faced many of the
same struggles as, and were represented in much the same language as their
working-class peers, and not merely by coincidence. Although bohemian
scenes flourished in Chicago and San Francisco, as well as in smaller cities
across the United States, the undulating center of American Bohemia bubbled
out of New York's Greenwich Village. And while the Village was bounded on

its eastern side by the old New York of Henry James's Washington Square, "in the bohemian geography of the imagination, Greenwich Village was proximate and permeable to the Jewish Lower East Side, twenty blocks to the south, crawling with its own bohemians and sizzling with its own ideas of modernity" (Stansell, *American Moderns* 6), as well as to the radical center of Union Square to the north, the site of intermingling between immigrant sweatshop and factory workers, progressive heiresses, incandescent anarchists, and the bohemians who drew from all these groups.

Moreover, I trace the pollination of these ideas across the country and over time from a variety of sources. Certainly, Bourne and the bohemians, living and working cheek by jowl with working-class young people, were one major source, particularly since artists, activists, and writers like Hutchins Hapgood, Jacob Epstein (born of the Lower East Side, but by identification and temperament an international artist), John Reed, Mabel Dodge Luhan, Max Eastman, Lincoln Steffens, and Susan Glaspell extended their reach beyond the enclaves of the Village into U.S. culture more widely over the course of the 1910s and 1920s. Along with bohemians, an active anarchist subculture, particularly as embodied by Emma Goldman, drew equally from working-class experience, high culture (one of Goldman's most popular lectures was on Henrik Ibsen and modern drama), radical politics, and the movements for free love and "family limitation." Goldman's wide-ranging early career—which took her from Russia to Rochester to New York City to every major labor and political controversy of the first quarter of the twentieth century, from mining towns to major cities—is a symbol for the ways in which new ideas about youth and generational difference spread through the country, unevenly and fitfully, but with surprising speed.

I end the chapter in the late 1920s, with the publication of Margaret Mead's *Coming of Age in Samoa*. During her time at Barnard and Columbia, Mead was involved in both the (by that point fading) bohemian scene and radical movements. Ruth Benedict, Mead's friend and lover, had strong ties with the downtown coteries, and Franz Boas, Benedict and Mead's mentor, was fascinated by the shifts in attitude toward adolescence from the 1910s to the 1920s. (To complete the circle, Benedict and Mead's senior colleague in anthropology at Columbia, Elsie Clews Parsons, was close with Randolph Bourne, by way of Bourne's years as an undergraduate at Columbia and his bohemian friend Alyse Gregory). *Coming of Age* explicitly takes on the attitudes toward female adolescence that were almost unknown at the beginning of the twentieth century but had become commonplace in the 1920s: that it was "characterized as the period in which idealism flowered and rebellion against authority waxed strong, a period during which difficulties and conflicts were absolutely inevitable" (2).[3] As we shall see, Mead represents the adolescent world in Samoa as, in some central ways, remarkably similar to the experience of the working-class children of immigrants she encountered in her earlier ethnographic work among Italian Americans in Pennsylvania and later in her adventures in radicalism downtown during her college years.

These networks among immigrants, radicals, bohemians, and academics were hardly the only channels through which new ideas about adolescence spread from working-class urban neighborhoods into the larger population. Indeed, the popularity of "working girl" serial movies in the 1910s chronicled by Nan Enstad, the representation of department store girls in films like the Clara Bow vehicle *It* (1927), the film adaptations of Anzia Yezierska's *Hungry Hearts* (1922) and *Salome of the Tenements* (1925), and the popularity of immigrant-themed movies more generally suggest that the movies were one important conduit through which images of the adolescent children of immigrants were disseminated throughout the country. Similarly, magazines, popular fiction, and (by the beginning of the third decade of the twentieth century) broadcast radio provided paths along which the new ethos of adolescence could travel. What follows is, therefore, more a case study than a comprehensive survey of the ways in which urban immigrant understandings of adolescent identity moved from working-class ghettos to a wider audience, one vector in a complex matrix of popular culture, immigrant communities, high society, and small-town American life.

Bourne, Goldman, Mead: as far as the historical record goes, none of them met, although they inhabited worlds that overlapped and intersected so much that it's remarkable that no two of them ever physically crossed paths.[4] Nonetheless, all three espoused some degree of radical politics, a belief in gender equality, and a commitment to sexual freedom. I see these three figures as punctuation marks in the narrative of adolescence that carries us from the sweatshops, department stores, and settlement houses of the 1890s, to the picket lines and little magazines of the 1910s, to the living rooms of intellectuals like Mead and of bourgeois parents in American small towns, equally concerned with the new phenomenon of adolescent rebellion.

Bourne, Goldman, and Mead were perspicacious theorists of adolescence and its relationship to the industrial, urban environments in which it was born. All three figures were relentlessly cosmopolitan in experience and outlook. They took a deep and personal interest in the political, cultural, and psychological development of young people. Most importantly, they were themselves conduits for the dissemination of ideas about adolescence from its origins in immigrant neighborhoods to larger American arenas. As I explore in the pages that follow, Goldman, Bourne, and Mead are products and germinators of changing concepts of adolescence, beginning with

Goldman's own radical teenage years, and ending with Mead's pointed contrast of the idyllic teen years of Samoan girls and the troubled adolescence of pubescent Americans.

A common thread that loops around Bourne, Goldman, and Mead is an investment in bohemianism, more an attitude than a political or cultural program. Bohemianism as a concept found its source in France (and perhaps etymologically in the French belief that gypsies, the original outrè artists, came from the Czech province of Bohemia). Henri Murger's 1845 collection of short stories, *Scènes de la Vie Bohème,* introduced the major themes of bohemianism to a mainstream audience: a righteous repudiation of bourgeois respectability, a commitment to (mostly high) art, louche living, and sexual liberation.[5] Bohemianism found its first major foothold in the United States in the late nineteenth century, but it did not fully flower until the second decade of the twentieth century, when it alighted upon the previously obscure New York neighborhood of Greenwich Village.

Coincidentally, Village bohemians shared a set of attitudes, a generational sense of self, and a geographic location with the children of immigrants living, working, and playing to the south of them. The alienation and autonomy of the modern subject found its voice among the young people flooding the dance halls and the almost equally young bohemians frequenting basement tearooms and garret studios.[6] In many ways, then, this chapter is an analysis of the history of the intertwining of bohemian energies and immigrant adolescent identities, both of which found their way—profoundly altered but still recognizable—into Mead's *Coming of Age in Samoa.*

Randolph Bourne's Anatomy of Adolescence

Although for the first half of the 1910s Randolph Bourne spent the majority of his time uptown at Columbia University where he was an undergraduate, and then in an extended tour of Europe, his social circle extended beyond the limitations of geography. One of his closest friends was Alyse Gregory, an active member of downtown bohemia and a participant in a women's salon that was, as Bourne wrote in 1913 to his frequent correspondent Prudence Winterrowd, "the most delightful group of young women . . . decidedly emancipated and advanced, and so thoroughly and healthfully zestful" (Bourne, *Letters* 82). Diametrically opposed to the relentlessly male atmosphere of Columbia, the Village represented a new kind of heterosociality (and heterosexuality) more like its working-class counterpart to the south than anything Bourne would have experienced either in his hometown of Bloomfield, New Jersey, or in his college classrooms. Indeed, bohemian New Yorkers reveled in mixed-gender sociability, whether in person or in the pages of their house organs, *The Masses* and Bourne's own *Seven Arts* magazines.

More than anything, bohemianism was a way of life and enacted what in the 1960s came to be called "prefigurative politics"—bohemians attempted to live their lives as though they had already defeated the stultifying forces of bourgeois ideology and morality. They "forged a politics that emphasize[d] style, energy, and pleasure," in direct counterpoint to a bourgeois existence that was, in their view, "conformist, money grubbing, moralistic, rationalistic, naively empiricist, and fearful of the body" (Borus 376–377). The bohemian world that Randolph Bourne catapulted himself into explicitly rejected the binarisms of the nineteenth century, and, as Casey Blake has argued, taking on the bohemian project of self- and social understanding entailed "overcoming the oppositions of masculine and feminine realms, of culture and society, of spirit and practice" (515).

For Bourne, the foot soldiers of this revolution were young people, who were uniquely able to evaluate and reject the piety and stodginess of their elders.[7] Youth was "a great, rich rush and flood of energy" (YL 3) brought into being by the specific historical moment, a time that was uniquely chaotic and cacophonous. A young person could not rely on the certainties of the previous century. Rather, youth, "suddenly born into a confusion of ideas and appeals and traditions responds in the most chaotic way to this new spiritual world, and only gradually learns to find his way about in it" (YL 4). Youth, Bourne maintained, "is always turbulent" (YL 5): the result of struggle, uproar, change. Sounding much like G. Stanley Hall writing a decade earlier, Bourne linked the dramatic changes that adolescence brought to the enormous shifts produced by industrialization, urbanization, and modernity more generally. Coeval with the twentieth century, young people were as percussive, as insistent, and as fragile as the age itself. But where Hall warned his readers, the parents and guardians of the enervated young men and neurasthenic young women who were the progeny of the modern age, of the dangers of the hothouse atmosphere of cities and the treacherous shoals of the adolescent years, Bourne celebrated the fragility and febrility of youth. While youth "is vulnerable at every point," Bourne argued, this vulnerability hardly generated a desire for prudence, "really a hateful thing in youth" (YL 10).

Instead, the young people Bourne envisaged were newborn into modernity. As Casey Blake argues, Bourne believed that the cultural upheavals of the era, "from the feminism of women in flight from 'feminine' gentility to the bohemian radicalism of students who reject the 'masculine' standards of commercial success, had roots in the industrial transformation of American life" (517). Whatever its drawbacks, and he recognized many, Bourne saw modernity as both protean and Promethean, capable of radical change and profound risk taking. In his essay "Youth," he encapsulated the mood of young people in the 1910s in a single word: "Dare!" "There is much to be done in the world," his young people said to themselves, "so much could be done if you would only dare!" (YL 17).

The modern era Bourne embraced was by definition an industrial era.[8] Industrialization had created this new generation, and the lineaments of young people of all classes were shaped by the patterns industrialization made, "the whole beauty and terror and cruelty of the world in its fresh and undiluted purity" (YL 12). And like many of his contemporaries, Bourne made connections between his own peers and his counterparts in what were called the "industrial classes."

For Greenwich Village bohemians, the adolescent children of immigrants provided an object lesson in what might happen when young people repudiated the world of their parents. Unlike Jane Addams, twenty years earlier in Chicago, who imagined the Hull-House Labor Museum as healing the rift between immigrant parents and their children, the bohemians of the 1910s celebrated the separation from their elders. To be sure, the terms in which Bourne diagnosed this state of affairs were reminiscent of the language of his predecessors. The older generation, he argued, "do not understand their children and their lack of understanding and of control over them means a lack of moral guidance," a sentence that could as easily have come from Twenty Years at Hull-House as from Youth and Life. In Bourne's view, however, young people should separate from their families: as he wrote to Prudence Winterrowd in 1913, just after the publication of Youth and Life: "Most of the modern restiveness of youth is a desire to get away from" their parents. "You see much of it among the immigrant families whose sons and daughters go to Columbia or City College and become inoculated with new ideas that produce a constant guerilla warfare with the irreconcilable tradition of the parents" (Letters 84–85).

Much like their immigrant counterparts, too, bohemians organized their lives around fun and self-expression. As Bourne acknowledged: "The charge that the rising generation betrays an extraordinary love of pleasure is true" (YL 35). The brief popularity of Dada, the endless parties, the focus on conversation as a liberating force—all were kin to the "random associations of immigrant free speech" and the miscellany of vaudeville that characterized Lower East Side life (Stansell, American Moderns 87). And many of the values that Bourne and his peers—Van Wyck Brooks, Hutchins Hapgood, Neith Boyce, John Reed, to name a few—held dear were part and parcel of the life experience of the children of immigrants. Bohemians rejected the providentialism of the nineteenth century and the social constructionism of progressivism, arguing that a true personality was "a self forged through a process of assimilating and refashioning one's cultural environment. . . . Personality was the realization of the self in tension—or in dialogue—with its environment" (Blake 520, 522). A self constructed through interaction with and assimilation and refashioning of the culture—this is as much a description of Jake Podovnik from *Yekl* as it is of Hapgood or Boyce.

Perhaps more so, in fact: while denizens of the Lower East Side like Robert Leslie—the child of immigrants who got involved with the Socialist Party at 1899 and by the age of fifteen was working with Eugene V. Debs and Emma Goldman—moved easily between Hester and Bleecker Streets, radical bohemians like Hippolyte Havel, with whom Leslie worked on Goldman's journal *Mother Earth,* or Max Eastman, editor of *The Masses,* were "more like Greenwich Village," far less able to shift according to their surroundings (Kisseloff 39). Leslie is an instructive example. Born on the Lower East Side, he remade himself several times: as radical, as college student (he graduated from City College in 1904), as journalist and journeyman printer, and eventually as small business owner.

These correspondences raise their own questions: How much interaction was there between bohemian and immigrant New York? Can we imagine some kind of cause-and-effect relationship between the explicit general divides that seemed to be ingrained in the lives of the children of immigrants, and the rejection of their elders among the bohemians? Certainly there were many points of contact between Anglo-American bohemians and the children of eastern and southern European immigrants. As Sabine Haenni shows, these connections were deeply rooted: already by the 1890s the "slums" had "become a site of strange fascination" for journalists and social commentators (494). The next generation reenacted the practice of slumming but also revisioned it through the scrim of class solidarity. This is not to say that there was not an element of slumming in bohemians' affection for and affectation toward their proletarian counterparts. Amid their attempts to identify with immigrant New Yorkers, these "self-styled sophisticates fanned across the poor neighborhoods to soak up 'experiences' construed as familiarity with plebeian life" (Stansell, *American Moderns* 16).

However, bohemians' interactions with their working-class neighbors went beyond mere tourism. The cosmopolitanism and egalitarianism of their cultural ethos and their explicit antibourgeois sentiments were mirrored by the spirit of the young people of the Lower East Side. Moreover, the socialism that infused the Greenwich Village of the 1910s resonated with the leftist (whether socialist, anarchist, or explicitly Bolshevik) chords being sounded further downtown. There were several points of contact between Village bohemians and East Side proletarians, of which the strongest were labor activism, café culture, and radical political projects such as Goldman's *Mother Earth* and the Modern School sponsored by the Francisco Ferrer Center (named after an influential Spanish anarchist and educational theorist).[9]

Bohemians looked to their working-class counterparts as models on many fronts. They certainly took inspiration from immigrants' political engagement. As Christine Stansell chronicles, while "political conviction—feminist, socialist, trade unionist—had never before been tied tightly to bohemianism . . . [in the 1910s] it became a distinguishing feature of the Village esprit" (*American Moderns* 60). In the preceding decade, the interests of strikers had been taken up mostly by society women—socialites Inez Milholand and Alva Smith Vanderbilt Belmont were frequent visitors to the picket lines for the shirtwaist workers' strike in 1909 (von Drehle 66–67). But in the teens, Village radicals immersed themselves in activist causes. Mary Heaton Vorse, a major figure downtown, along with her husband, Joe O'Brien, formed the Labor Defense Committee to support strikers financially and politically, and over the winter of 1913–1914 the committee demonstrated against rising unemployment and police brutality toward strikers (Stansell, *American Moderns* 112–115).

Another connection that bohemians perceived between their social experimentation and the proletarian values of the immigrant working class was a relaxation of gendered roles and sexual rules. Bourne believed (mostly incorrectly, but faithfully) that immigrant communities had at least partly achieved the gender and sexual liberation that he and his friends struggled for: "The line between the two 'spheres' has long disappeared in the industrial classes; it is now beginning to fade in the comfortable classes" (*YL* 36). Like his comrades, Bourne indulged in a certain degree of exoticism when it came to the sexual mores of immigrant communities, believing in "a link between proletarian assertion and sexual freedom. . . . Radicals thought working people were blessed with a sexual largesse that was scarcely imaginable to the middle class" (Stansell, *American Moderns* 281). At the same time, bohemians needed a figure who could translate their cultural resistance into a larger political project, who could speak the languages of Greenwich Village rebellion and working-class radicalism. They found that figure in Emma Goldman.

Emma Goldman's Acts of Translation

In Emma Goldman, Bourne certainly had a clear example of a woman who had freed herself from the political and sexual restraints of mainstream American mores.

Political radicalism, artistic and verbal self-expression, sexual freedom, gender equality: Emma Goldman stood at the crossroads of trends in all these arenas. Most importantly, however, Goldman represented the porousness of the boundaries between bohemianism, working-class radicalism, and new immigrant cultures, a porousness encouraged by all parties.[10] At any point in her long career, her social circle read like a who's who of prominent radicals, writers, artists, and performers (during a fallow period in the early twentieth century she was the theatrical manager for leading Russian actors Pavel Orlenev and Alla Nazimova, already a superstar in Russia and possibly

Goldman's lover). But her relationship with the expanding circles around bohemianism in New York and Chicago sustained a particularly fertile interchange among the various elements of her personal, political, and professional lives.

Her life combined a stereotypical immigrant story, a narrative of radicalization into anarchism by the Haymarket Massacre of 1887, a bohemian existence of free speech and free love, and a social calendar and circle of friends and acquaintances matched only by those of the indefatigable Mabel Dodge. Goldman moved easily among immigrant cafés, sweatshops, union halls, theaters, and elite social clubs. Coming to the United States in 1885 at the age of sixteen, she worked in garment factories, first in Rochester, then in New York City. Like her teenage immigrant coworkers, she was an enthusiastic dancer, counting herself as "one of the most untiring and the gayest" (*LML* 56).[11] And like them, she engaged in casual prostitution to make extra money (although with quite different results—her effort was a total failure—and for quite different motives: her foray onto the streets was to raise funds to outfit her lover Alexander Berkman's attempted assassination of Henry C. Frick over the violence at the Homestead steel strike).

Goldman attended Freud's early lectures in Vienna when she was studying midwifery in the 1890s. By becoming an immediate convert to his theories—having "grasped the full significance of sex repression. . . . His simplicity and earnestness and the brilliance of his mind combined to give one the feeling of being led out of a dark cellar into broad daylight"—she anticipated by decades her Anglo-American comrades who discovered psychoanalysis in the 1910s (*LML* 173). She was fairly skeptical of bohemianism when she first encountered it in St. Louis in 1909, judging its artistic scene as inhabited by "people to whom 'bohemianism' was a sort of narcotic to help them endure the boredom of their lives" (463). And even as she became more open to bohemianism over the course of the decade, she drew a distinction between these cultural rebels and the radicals of her youth in Europe. After a week with Margaret Anderson and her lover Harriet Dean in Chicago, she "saw that [they] were not actuated by any sense of social injustice, like the young Russian intelligentsia, for instance. Strongly individualized, they had broken the shackles of their middle-class homes to find release from family bondage and bourgeois tradition" (531). This ambivalence was not shared by Anderson, however—she described Goldman's speech "The Relationship of Anarchism to Literature" in 1914 as "one of the most stirring things I have ever sat through" (Glassgold 85).

In New York and Chicago, Goldman cultivated friendships with leading bohemians, including Hutchins Hapgood, who wrote the introduction to Berkman's 1912 *Prison Memoirs of an Anarchist,* which chronicled his fourteen years' incarceration after the Frick shooting. Through Hapgood and her own anarchist activities (including lecturing at the Ferrer Center, two blocks from her Harlem home), Goldman mixed with "poets, writers, rebels, and Bohemians of various attitude, behaviour, and habit" (*LML* 521). She attended Mabel Dodge's weekly salon, "a gathering place of Village dissidents, radicals, and artists, as well as the elite and the wealthy" (LeSueur xv).

Goldman was also related to bohemian circles by blood and by marriage: her nephew Saxe Commins worked with Eugene O'Neill, and her niece Stella Commins, to whom she was very close, married Teddy Ballantine, an actor associated with the Provincetown Players. In the summer of 1916, when the entire populace of Greenwich Village seemed to descend upon the tip of Cape Cod, Goldman visited the Ballantines in Provincetown: "Artists were everywhere, painting on the streets, wharves, shacks, or exhibiting in Town Hall and the new Provincetown Art Museum. Writers congregated on the beach and on the narrow sidewalks and talked about their assignments for popular magazines like *Scribner's* or revolutionary magazines like *The Masses*" (Egan 36). The Ballantine home was opened to *le tout monde bohemien*, "persons of outstanding individuality, such as Susan Glaspell, George Cram Cook, and my old friends Hutch Hapgood and Neith Boyce," Goldman wrote. "There were also John Reed and adventurous Louise Bryant, more sophisticated than she had been in Portland two years before" (*LML* 583).

Goldman counted among her lovers Hippolyte Havel, who himself intersected any number of identities: Czech anarchist, New York radical, Greenwich Village bohemian. Like the bohemians, Goldman wed her political beliefs to a highly developed aesthetic sense: for her, anarchism guaranteed "freedom, the right to self-expression, everybody's right to beautiful, radiant things" (*LML* 56). Indeed, "beautiful" was one of the highest compliments she could pay a person, a political program, a work of art, or an act of resistance. Goldman's commitment to free love and her arguments against marriage were legendary, bridging the gap between working-class experimentation, anarchist utopianism, and bohemian nonmonogamy.

Goldman powerfully affected bohemian thinkers with her intense passions—personal, political, sexual—and her eloquence, a quality they esteemed. In a 1914 essay in *Mother Earth*, Margaret Anderson spoke for many of her peers: "This is the function of Emma Goldman. She stirs and inspires and endows with new life" (Glassgold 86). Her home base for several years was on East Thirteenth Street, intersecting Greenwich Village, the factory district (the soon-to-be infamous Triangle Shirtwaist factory was less than ten blocks to the south), the Cooper Union (site of many a political meeting), and Union Square. *Mother Earth* combined political exhortation, cultural analysis, poetry, short fiction, and literary criticism—for example, Havel's review of Constance Garnett's 1912 translation of *The Brothers Karamazov* or George Brandes's appreciation of Ibsen—a stew that drew upon Goldman's heterodox interests.

In her critique of sexual hypocrisy, most notably in her essay "The White Slave Traffic" (later republished as "The Traffic in Women"), Goldman combined the muckraking tradition that attacked the stultifying working conditions that young women and men had to endure and with an anarchist approach that argued for sexual freedom for all. Sounding much like Louise de Koven Bowen, she painted a picture of "girls, mere children, work[ing] in crowded, overheated rooms ten to twelve hours daily at a machine." However, overwork was not the major problem here; rather the intensity of work "tends to keep them in a constant overexcited sex state." This excitation is exacerbated by the lack of "any home or comforts of any kind; therefore the street or some place of cheap amusement is the only means of forgetting their daily routine. This naturally brings them into close proximity with the other sex" ("White Slave Traffic" 117).

Goldman accurately described the social lives of many young working women and men, and the fact that the young women who were sexually active, either informally or for money, far from being imported directly for the purposes of prostitution, were often U.S. born: "Most of the girls speak excellent English, they are Americanized in habits and appearance—a thing absolutely impossible unless they have lived in this country for many years." Combining her defense of young working-class women with an attack on consumerism, Goldman speculated that the daughters of immigrants were "driven into prostitution by American conditions, by the thoroughly American custom for excessive display of finery and clothes, which, of course, necessitates money, money that can not be earned in shops or factories." Finally, Goldman turned the moralists' accusations back on themselves, arguing that they were not "disturbed by the respectable woman gratifying her [love of finery] by marrying for money; why are they so outraged if the poor girl sells herself for the same reason? The only difference lies in the amount received, and of course in the seal society either gives or withholds" ("White Slave Traffic" 118).

This rhetoric sounds familiar to contemporary ears—it was, after all, a staple of the radical wing of the second wave of feminism in the 1960s and 1970s.[12] Apart from her knack for shocking her bourgeois opponents, Goldman's skill here is in interweaving disparate elements of her own experience into a coherent anarchist argument. She brings to bear her sympathies with factory workers and her personal experience stuck behind a factory sewing machine for hours on end, but she sharpens that social commentary with a radical critique of commodity consumerism that few of her working-class factory mates would have shared. She leavens this with a free love defense of female sexual autonomy and an attack on conventional gender and sexual arrangements, winding up with a rhetorical flourish that puts the bourgeois wife in closer correspondence than the blameless factory girl with the streetwalker.

Goldman's approach here mirrors the interconnections she forged in her own political practice: discursively she brings together immigrant communities, radical analysis, and bohemian philosophy. Moreover, within an admittedly torrid representation of factory life, she reveals a sensitive understanding of the lives of the young people most often accused of sexual impropriety, the teenage girls whose "entire life and nature [are] thwarted and crippled" ("White Slave Traffic" 117). She takes for granted the inevitability of sexual desire during adolescence, those years the "sex nature asserts itself," as well as the conflicts adolescent girls experience in a social setting that both encourages and stifles sexual self-expression.

The layering of these multiple concerns did valuable political and cultural work for Goldman, creating common cause among her various constituencies. While bohemian leftists could tend toward the attitude of the "cosmopolitan flaneur," in Stansell's words, they also threw themselves into supporting working people, the majority of whom, like many of themselves, were under twenty-five.[13] The liberation of women, in particular, was a favorite cause, and "for the left intelligentsia, the emancipated woman stood at the center of a program for cultural regeneration" (Stansell, *American Moderns* 184, 225). Their interests were intensified and legitimated by the sexological studies coming out of Britain, in particular the work of Havelock Ellis and Edward Carpenter, as well as by Freudian psychoanalysis (a combination of forces that also came to bear upon the intellectual development of Ruth Benedict and Margaret Mead). And out of their passion for sexual liberation came what Bourne called "a wild disgust for everything that suggests artificial inequalities and distinctions" (*YL* 86).

Goldman facilitated these connections; as the 1910s progressed, she moved subtly away from the immigrant world of anarchism and toward Anglo-American bohemia (although, as Stansell points out, she maintained a close circle of Jewish immigrant anarchist friends). She saw the bohemians as a conduit to a larger audience beyond the Jewish and Italian communities for whom anarchism was simply part of the political fabric of working-class life. Moreover, she helped bring bohemian leftists into the major labor struggles of the day: Paterson, Lawrence, Wheatland. Goldman's skill was "to sense the ways in which progressive coalitions, feminism, and cultural democratization were opening up passages" that were previously unthought of (Stansell, *American Moderns* 142).

Through her speeches, writing, and personal interactions, Goldman infused the Anglo-American bohemian left with the values of immigrant anarchism (and vice versa—certainly, bohemianism's aestheticism, its focus on the grand gesture, and its commitment to high art found an eager interlocutor in Goldman). Moreover, as we can see from an essay like "The White Slave Traffic," her rhetoric effortlessly transferred the new reality of working-class urban life into a political program that Anglo activists could enthusiastically support, even as the children of immigrants were embracing an analogous cosmopolitanism that stepped beyond the social, religious, and political thresholds that they saw limiting their parents. With Randolph Bourne on the one hand and Emma Goldman on the other, new ideas of "youth" traveled across the United States—sexually adventurous; falling in love with every-thing, "whether it be art, a girl, socialism, [or] religion" (*YL* 75); politically fear-less; and willing to cross the chasms of class, gender, and respectability.

Margaret Mead and the New Anthropology of Adolescence

In Bourne and Goldman we can see the movement upward and outward of ideas about adolescence that had previously found expression only in working-class urban immigrant communities and the reports of settlement houses and social reformers. Unmoored from their geographic origins, untainted by the bourgeois patina of uplift, these new conceptions of adoles-cence could decouple themselves from the particularities of specific neigh-borhoods and ideologies, while maintaining the aura of rebellion and knowingness (if not exactly of sophistication).

By the 1920s, these once-horrifying (at least to respectable Americans) ideas had seeped into the consciousness of young people across the country. Most striking is the change in sexual values. The contrast between a charac-ter like Judy Jones in F. Scott Fitzgerald's short story "Winter Dreams" (1922) and Lola Pratt, the belle of Booth Tarkington's *Seventeen* (1913), is so sharp as to be almost ludicrous. As we have seen in chapter 3, Tarkington's novel car-ries no hint of physical intimacy between Lola and her brace of swains. In "Winter Dreams," however, Judy flirts with, kisses, and strings along dozens of men at a time. Fitzgerald's narrator coolly records every coquetry with studied nonchalance, remarking that "whatever Judy wanted, she went after with the full pressure of her charm. There was no divergence of method, no jockeying for position or premeditation of effects—there was a very little mental side to any of her affairs. She simply made men conscious to the high-est degree of her physical loveliness" (228). What was shocking to turn-of-the-century readers of *The Awakening* (1899) or *Sister Carrie* (1900) was commonplace to 1920s readers of, say, *An American Tragedy* (1925) or *Plum Bun* (1929) or, for that matter, farcical to readers of the comic bible of flapper-dom, Anita Loos's *Gentlemen Prefer Blondes* (1925).

I don't want to rehearse a history of the flapper or of the formation of adolescent identity in Anglo-America here—that work has been achieved admirably by Grace Palladino and Paula Fass. My interest is in how the suc-cessors to the bohemians of the previous decade, Margaret Mead and her circle being a prime example, melded leftist political consciousness and attach-ment to sexual liberation with an analysis of adolescence that borrowed from pre–World War I radicalism, psychoanalysis, free love movements, and bohemian lyricism, and equally from the cultural vernacular of the 1920s: Jazz Age angularity, New Negro adventurousness, and the lower-brow languages of movies and self-help movements.

Certainly, Mead's inclination as an anthropologist was to explain Americans to themselves rather than harangue, mock or ignore them for their bourgeois limitations (the usual strategy of the radicals and bohemians who preceded her). Indeed, in her memoir *Blackberry Winter,* Mead explains her anthropological bent as the reason for setting down her own life's experiences: "I have spent much of my life studying the lives of other peoples, faraway peoples, so that Americans might better understand themselves," she maintains, and now it is time for her to explain herself (*BW* 1). Her own mother had been a classic New Woman of the late nineteenth century, a woman for whom "life was real, life was earnest—it was too serious for trivial things." She was a committed suffragist and antiracist, a crusader of the old school who, like her contemporary Jane Addams, "felt it was important to continue her own intellectual life and to be a responsible citizen in a world in which there were so many wrongs . . . that had to be set right" (*BW* 22). Mead saw her own path quite differently—in the mold of her generation she pursued intellectual fulfillment through academic advancement and gender equality by way of personal liberation.

The New York that Margaret Mead discovered in 1920, particularly the world of Barnard College, was explosive and introspective, expanding and disintegrating. By then, much of bohemian Greenwich Village had diffused—Emma Goldman had been deported, Heterodoxy (the radical women's club that was one of the mainstays of the counterculture of the 1910s) had mostly disbanded, Mabel Dodge Luhan had moved to Taos, and the center of the American intelligentsia had migrated to the salons in Paris.

Nonetheless, Mead and her classmates found plenty to keep them occupied and inspired. There was a fair amount of mixing between uptown and downtown, and Barnard women were adventurous enough to venture often into Greenwich Village, to the extent that two students of Mead's acquaintance were expelled for spending the night downtown (with whom, Mead does not reveal) (*BW* 102). Mead and her circle "knew about Freud. Agnes Piel [one of her roommates] was being analyzed" (*BW* 103). They mixed self-knowledge with a measure of political activism: "All of us took part in a mass meeting for Sacco and Vanzetti during the period of their trial in the spring of 1921. . . . At different times we also made forays into radical activities, walking on a picket line or stuffing envelopes for the Amalgamated Clothing Workers" (*BW* 107). For most of Mead's circle, though, political activity was not a central part of their lives (even in Mead's fond reminiscences, it resembles the radical chic of the early 1970s more than the radical commitments of the bohemians of the prewar Village). Rather, it one aspect of a welter of experiences that comprised being young in the city, which could embrace lying on an analyst's couch, marching on a picket line, and carrying tributes of bouquets to Edna St. Vincent Millay, not yet relocated to New England.

Whereas free love carried markedly political freight for Emma Goldman and Louise Bryant, for Mead, "sex was a force that produced aesthetic and spiritual empowerment" (*BW* 218). Her friendship with Ruth Benedict connected her with the legacy of bohemianism that Benedict had experienced since her own arrival in New York at the height of the ferment downtown, in 1914. Benedict had numerous links to the bohemian world, both by design and by coincidence: she had gone to high school with Mabel Dodge (then Mabel Ganson) and to college with Inez Milholland, and had admired both. She attended several meetings of Heterodoxy, although she did not take to it, finding it too introspective and revelatory (Benedict was a deeply private woman). She was also immersed in immigrant life in New York as a worker at the Henry Street Settlement in 1919, an extension of her experiences as a social worker among Polish immigrants in Buffalo in the years before her marriage, even as she expanded her circle, taking classes first at the New School for Social Research and then uptown at Columbia with John Dewey and Elsie Clews Parsons (herself a member of Heterodoxy and of bohemian New York more generally).

But where Goldman, Bourne, and in part Parsons, immersed in the world of Greenwich Village and the Lower East Side, had looked to radical politics, artistic and sexual freedom, and pacifism as entry points to a dissenting, utopian worldview, Benedict and Mead set their sights farther uptown. They cast their lots not with radical bohemianism but with anthropology; not with opposing the mainstream but with seeing it as just another set of kinship structures and social hierarchies. Where Goldman, Bourne, Bryant, Havel, and their comrades divided their attention between self-actualization and political activism, Benedict and Mead, under the guidance of their mentor, Franz Boas, invested their energies in analyzing the self as a product of cultural practices. Both groups reimagined the values of their world, but while the radicals of the 1910s exulted in leaping outside those values, envisaging and performing a socius from which bourgeois moralism and capitalist heartlessness were finally ejected and forever banned, Boasian anthropologists of the 1920s theorized the origins, enactments, and meanings of the very concepts of insider and outsider.

In some ways, Benedict's shift from social work to anthropology (or even Mead's transition from political activism in college to cultural analysis in graduate school) embodies this shift. Ironically, the move from incursions against social norms to scientific analysis (and, one might even say, deconstruction) could imply a more intensive kind of radicalism; as Judith Butler has argued, resistance to a discursive regime can often be another way of acknowledging the legitimacy of its power; and the " 'I' who would oppose its construction is always in some sense drawing from that construction to articulate its opposition; further, the 'I' draws what is called its 'agency' in part through being implicated in the very relations of power that it seeks to oppose" (123).

By instead anatomizing discursive structures like kinship and social power, by revealing them to be relational, situational, and culturally specific, Benedict and Mead implicitly and explicitly argued that the social norms of the United States were no less constructed, no less arbitrary.[14] One might argue, for instance, that by showing the "natural" (that is, culturally conditioned) sexual freedoms of young women in *Coming of Age in Samoa*, Mead did more for sexual freedom in the United States than any of Emma Goldman's arrests for distributing birth control information or her lectures about free love and the oppressive power of heterosexual marriage. Indeed, when Mead was trying to choose between psychology and anthropology, Benedict convinced her by declaring: "Professor Boas and I have nothing to offer but the opportunity to do work that matters" (*BW* 114)—hyperbolic, perhaps, but deeply felt by both women.

On the other hand, Benedict's and Mead's turn from explicit social engagement to the world of anthropology can be seen as part of the rightward movement of the United States more generally in the 1920s. Their retreat into academia and to distant locations (the southwestern United States for Benedict, the South Pacific for Mead) was symptomatic of a more general withdrawal from the direct political action and noisy dissent of the 1910s.[15] Observing and recording a culture is, after all, markedly different from diving into it and taking up its battles, as the bohemians did for their immigrant neighbors and working-class people further afield. Moreover, Boasian anthropology, with its focus on identifying a culture synchronically, could flatten or even erase the role of history in shaping cultural expression. Reading *Coming of Age in Samoa*, one would have little sense of the effect of colonialism on the South Pacific communities that Mead visited, of the changes that missionaries had wrought on Samoan society, of the use of Samoa in the beginning of the twentieth century as a surrogate for disputes between various colonial powers (primarily Germany, Britain, and the United States), or of the role of the coconut plantation economy on the islands.

Whichever side one comes down on—1920s anthropology as a theoretically sophisticated improvement on the rawness of 1910s bohemianism, or as a crypto-conservative copout from political reality—it is clear that Mead, having been nourished by downtown radicalism and rebelliousness, in her commitment to the world of social science staked her claim permanently on uptown methodologies. Sitting in on Franz Boas's legendary lectures displaced hanging "a May basket, woven of willow withes and filled with wild flowers, on the door knob of Edna St. Vincent Millay's house in Greenwich Village" (BW 132–133).

Boas's influence over Mead led her to the research that gelled into *Coming of Age in Samoa*. As Lois Banner has shown, Mead had not immediately thought of teenage girls as a topic of investigation, but given the glamour surrounding the icon of the flapper, "the subject of adolescent sexuality was in the air, and Boas wanted someone to disprove the evolutionary theory of G. Stanley Hall," which still held sway more than twenty years after the publication of *Adolescence*, "that the emotionalism of adolescence was an inevitable evolutionary stage" (230). Much like Bourne in the previous decade, Boas maintained that the storms of adolescence were a product of urbanization, industrialization, and the pressures of the nuclear family. Boas believed that Mead could go further than Hall for one crucial reason: Mead's youth and gender would allow her to, as he said in the introduction to *Coming of Age* "identify herself so completely with Samoan youth that she gives us a lucid and clear picture of the joys and difficulties encountered by the young individual in a culture so entirely different from our own" (COA xv).

Certainly, Mead was closer to the front lines of the battle between the generations than Boas was or than Hall had been—like Bourne, she wrote her brief on youth when she was barely out of adolescence herself. But Boas's comment is worth lingering over, given the ways in which Mead repeatedly insists throughout the book how different Samoan adolescence was from the U.S. experience. Certainly, Mead was not the stereotypical schoolgirl in her early and midteens. Perhaps in part because of her parents' continual moves, which prevented her from staying in one school for more than a couple of years, she had never felt akin to her schoolmates; rather, she had always had a sense of herself "as if I were in some way taking part in a theatrical performance in which I had a role to play and had to find actors to take on the other parts." Familiar with the tropes of small-town youth (perhaps from the novels of Booth Tarkington himself!), Mead set out to embody all of them: "I wanted to live out every experience that went with schooling, and so I made a best friend out of the most likely candidate, fell sentimentally in love with one of the boys, attached myself to a teacher, and organized, as far as it possible to do so, every kind of game, play, performance, May Day dance, Valentine party," and the like (BW 80). Given that her parents were academics, not farmers or shopkeepers, and that her mother and grandmother had combined professional work with motherhood, "I always felt that I was special and different. . . . I felt that I had to work hard to become part of the life around me" (BW 81).[16]

Similarly, when Mead started college at her father's alma mater, DePauw University, she found herself an alien in an environment that seemed constructed (as she phrased it with uncharacteristic acerbity) "for fraternity life, for football games, and for establishing the kind of rapport with other people that would make them good Rotarians in future life and their wives good members of the garden club" (BW 90).[17] At Barnard, however, Mead was wholly at home, part of a group who saw themselves as belonging to a generational trend of "young women who felt extraordinarily free—free from the demand to marry unless we chose to do so, free to postpone marriage while we did other things, free from the need to bargain and hedge that had burdened and restricted women of earlier generations" (BW 108).

Given Boas's, and hence Mead's, bedrock belief that social roles are specific to the cultures that produce them, it is striking that Boas maintained that Mead's success was in large part due to her ability to identify herself with her adolescent subjects (particularly since he wrote to Elsie Clews Parsons while Mead was in Samoa that "she is getting a good deal that will clinch the point that fundamental individual natures depend upon cultural setting more than hereditary or innate characteristics" [qtd. in Lapsley 141]). Moreover, Mead herself argued in *Coming of Age* that "neither race nor common humanity can be held responsible for many of the forms which even such basic human emotions such as love and fear and anger take under different social conditions" (4). For much of her time in Samoa Mead despaired of adequately learning the language, let alone gaining the intimate confidences of her informers. Yet Boas constructs a narrative in which the continuum between Mead and her Samoans is almost seamless.

Perhaps Boas's assertion grew out of his discomfort with the sexual explicitness of Mead's text. *Coming of Age* was hugely successful in part because it landed on the American scene at a time in which sexual matters were in the forefront of the cultural imagination: the combined forces of the flapper, Freud, and the movies had taken care of that. By identifying Mead with her teenage subjects, Boas could both subtly distance himself from her more explosive findings and exculpate her as well: Mead and her sexuality are both inextricable from what she observed in Samoa and hence not Boas's responsibility; at the same time, as hardly removed from adolescence due to (or resulting in) her identification with the youthful Samoans, Mead cannot help her positive representation of them.

In fact, the Samoan attitude toward sex was quite different from Mead's near-spiritual attitude toward it. Unlike Mead, for whom sexual attraction and attachment were usually accompanied by considerable introspection, the Samoans understood "the essential impersonality of sex attraction which we may well envy them" (COA 222). Mead's phrasing is striking here, considering that during her writing of *Coming of Age* she was attempting to balance a marriage and two simultaneous love affairs (one with Benedict, the other with her soon-to-be husband, Reo Fortune). This insouciant envy toward the casualness of Samoan amours contrasts distinctly with Mead's Freudian-inflected sense of her own sexual involvements, and her assertion of the *"essential* impersonality of sex attraction" is a far cry from her belief that even the most basic human emotions are the product of cultural forces.

Mead set out her project in *Coming of Age in Samoa* by invoking themes of adolescence that were, by 1928 when the book was published, familiar to her readers, identifying "a younger generation diverging ever more widely from the standards and ideals of the past, cut adrift without the anchorage of respected home standards or group religious values" (1). For Mead, Samoa was a perfect control situation to test whether industrialized U.S. adolescents were acting out intrinsic biological imperatives or were simply playing out a script their culture had written for them. The simplicity and homogeneity of Samoan society, its smallness, and its comparatively static social relations made it a clear contrast to the complexity, overstimulation, diversity, and changeability of the United States.

Mead opens her book by evoking a kind of island paradise: "As the dawn begins to fall among the soft brown roofs and the slender palm trees stand out against a colorless, gleaming sea, lovers slip home from trysts beneath the palm trees or in the shadow of beached canoes" (*COA* 14). However, she makes clear over the course of her discussion that Samoa's is not a society of idyllic escape from social rules. The rules are simply different and take as their focus different kinds of hierarchies. While a fair amount of ink has been spilled debating the accuracy of Mead's findings, I am less concerned here with their verisimilitude than with the resonances between her descriptions of Samoan teenagers and the representation of urban immigrant teenagers in the preceding two decades.[18] Although Mead's analyses have been scrutinized in connection with her own sexual mores, there has been no discussion of the roots of her treatment of adolescent sexuality in relation to the ways in which these had been understood in the United States by the social workers, radicals, and bohemians who were her direct predecessors.

In many ways, Mead's characterization of Samoan sexual, gender, and kinship patterns echoes strongly commentary by observers of working-class teenagers during the years that Mead's mother was working with the children of Italian immigrants in Pennsylvania. While a Samoan girl's life was radically different from that of her bourgeois Anglo-American counterpart, it was quite similar in some ways to the lives of urban female children of immigrants. Younger Samoan girls were in charge of babies and toddlers, much as were girls of urban New York, Chicago, and similar sized cities (*COA* 24). As in immigrant communities, adolescent boys and girls in Samoa gained more freedom and responsibility by taking on adult work (although that work was strictly divided by gender). Mead herself pointed out this similarity, arguing that recent immigrants "still present a different tradition of education," expecting their older children to bridge the gap between childhood and adult life (which is to say, marriage and parenthood) by taking on modified adult responsibilities (*COA* 228).

In Mead's evocation of 1920s Samoa, young women and men (but particularly the women) love to dance, gossip, and carry on secret (and not so secret) love affairs. Samoan adolescence, for Mead, combined the best of all worlds—the sexual freedom, clear sense of self as a productive member of the group, and ability to engage both in hetero- and homosocial bonds that characterized working-class urban adolescence, along with freedom from the generational conflict that was endemic to immigrant communities and that had found its way into the American mainstream. Shrewdly, Mead saw that a major source of conflict between bourgeois teenagers and their parents was control over resources, both large and small. By removing their adolescent children from the world of paid labor, middle-class American parents did not just protect their sons and daughters, they also extended their hold on them:

> If Mary doesn't stop purchasing chiffon stockings, Mary shall have no money to buy stockings. Similarly, a taste for cigarettes and liquor can only be gratified through money; going to the movies, buying books and magazines of which her parents disapprove, are all dependent upon a girl's having the money as well as eluding more direct forms of control. (*COA* 239)

Where the children of immigrants used the streets and their networks of friends and commercial leisure to erode the authority their parents had over them, and then further weakened parental control through participating in paid work, Samoan children's family lives were decentralized by culture norms in which they were "schooled not by an individual but by an army of relatives into a general conformity upon which the personality of their parents has a very slight effect" (*COA* 228). But the results were strikingly similar—minor resistances to parental authority, and the determination of young people to construct their own friendship groups organized around age cohorts.

For both groups, adolescence represented a short but distinctive period between the chores of childhood (particularly for girls, who were charged with caring for new babies and toddlers) and the permanent responsibilities of marriage. Samoan teenagers recognized that to approach adult expertise too quickly was a risk not worth taking, since "proficiency [especially for girls] would mean more work, more confining work, and earlier marriage, and marriage is the inevitable to be deferred as long as possible" (*COA* 38). Like their age peers in urban working-class neighborhoods, Samoan adolescents used work as a way to distance themselves from childhood while maintaining the possibility of indulging their passions: while a girl must spend her time working in the household, "her interest is expended on clandestine sexual adventures" (*COA* 32).

Most striking is Mead's description of the young Samoan woman's aim for her youth: "To live as a girl with many lovers as long as possible and then to marry in one's own village, near one's relatives and to have many children, these were uniform and satisfying ambitions" (*COA* 157). Given that this was how a large number of young immigrant women imagined and ultimately realized the trajectory of their lives, we can see clearly the parallels between two otherwise diametrically opposed groups of young people.

Of course, it would be absurd to extend this analogy too far. Urbanized, industrial, overcrowded, profoundly unequal, heterogeneous immigrant life could not have been more different from the pastoral, slow-moving world of Samoa. While the children of immigrants experienced their lives as punctuated by spasms of both struggle and pleasure, the defining characteristic of Samoan adolescence was its ease. That ease existed in "the general casualness of the whole society. For Samoa is a place where no one plays for very high stakes, no one pays very heavy prices, no one suffers for his convictions, or fights to the death for special ends" (*COA* 195). Mead argued that the harmony intrinsic to Samoan culture was a result of its preindustrial, communal qualities: "For the explanation of the lack of conflict we must look principally to the difference between a simple, homogenous, primitive civilization, a civilization which changes so slowly that to each generation it seems static, and a motley, diverse, heterogeneous modern civilization" (*COA* 206).

Despite these major differences, we can see that what defines both Samoan and immigrant adolescence is their opposition to the Anglo-American model of youth that by the 1920s was dissolving into something quite altered. The slightly ludicrous adolescents of Booth Tarkington's *Seventeen* had given way to the knowing young people of Fitzgerald's stories (or at the very least the clueless kids of *Babbitt,* who knew that they should be alienated from their parents, even if they weren't sure why or how). No longer the preserve of immigrants, anarchists, or bohemians, adolescence had found its way into the mainstream. As Mead herself commented, her generation by the 1930s had begun to reproduce these new ways of understanding adolescence and "were already deeply concerned about young people. In their eyes young men and women appeared to be alienated, apathetic, and lacking in moral fiber—the very words they used are still familiar phrases today" (*BW* 4).

Coming of Age in Samoa was as much a book about female adolescence in the United States in the mid-to-late 1920s as it was about young people in Samoa. This is not to derogate or trivialize Mead's ambition as an ethnographer, or to cast aspersions on her goals in recording the social and sexual mores of the members of various Samoan communities. Rather, the United States needed Samoa in 1928 as it needed the turkey trot and the bunny hug in 1914: as placeholders for unarticulated (or even inarticulable) desires about youth, sexual exploration, social class, and physical self-expression that could be voiced only through ventriloquism.

Mead learned from the Samoans some of what she must also have witnessed in the immigrant communities she saw in her earlier ethnographic work and in her mother's experience: that adolescent self-determination was a mixture of bodily independence, sexual experimentation, and freedom from parental controls. For young Samoans, this freedom was tightly bounded by other social hierarchies of age and status; for the children of immigrants by financial need, patriarchal families of origin, and the strictures of the industrialized workplace.

Like Bourne and Goldman before her, Mead borrowed from a variety of sources to concoct a narrative about the meanings of youth and adulthood, of restraint and freedom, of social tyrannies and communal freedoms. Within the parameters of anthropology, though, her analyses found expression through immersion in the young people of Samoa, rather than in her own social circle (as with Bourne) or in the rhetoric of political radicalism (as with Bourne and Goldman). By the time *Coming of Age in Samoa* was making its splash, youth had lost its patina of political radicalism and its articulation to urban life. As much as Mead synthesized the ideas about American adolescence that came before her, she also disconnected them from a specific time, place, and class, imagining an "American adolescent" all her readers could identify. With *Coming of Age in Samoa* the modern idea of the adolescent had come of age too, and left the children of immigrants who brought it into being far behind.

Epilogue

SMELLS LIKE TEEN SPIRIT

By the end of the 1920s, the reorganization of adolescence was complete. While it was to go through various incarnations over the next fifty years, these differences were more in degree than in type: the threatening sexual freedom of the flappers, for example, was remapped onto subsequent generations of girls, from bobby soxers to Beatlemaniacs to hippies and so on. Similarly, the knowing sophistication George Babbitt noticed in his son Ted transformed via the merging of immigrant and African American styles into different kinds of cool (radical cool, rock and roll cool, hipster cool, back to radical cool). Over the succeeding decades parents learned to bemoan the distance and independence of their adolescent children, just as their parents had done and as their children would do for the next generation of teenagers.

The most striking departure from the immigrant working-class styles of adolescence that Anglo-American teenagers made was their adoption of black idioms. They combined the white urban toughness and fun that emerged at the turn of the century with African American coolness and good times popular from the 1920s onward. As I showed in chapter 4, although ragtime dances originated in black juke joints and with southern black musicians, by the time these styles reached the white children of immigrants in the northern, midwestern, and western cities, they had been largely stripped of their African American origins, whose vestiges appeared only in the minstrel-like images on ragtime songsheets. In the 1920s, and again in the 1940s and 1950s, the African American sources for jazz, swing, and rock and roll were explicitly recognized—by teenage enthusiasts and by their disapproving parents.

The model of adolescence offered by the children of immigrants dovetailed in the years after the First World War with a new kind of affect that Peter N. Stearns describes in his fascinating social history *American Cool: Constructing a Twentieth-Century Emotional Style*. The increasing urbanization of the United States in the twentieth century reoriented Victorian earnestness toward modern cool—an aloof, insouciant style that Stearns characterizes as developing alongside a focus on romantic love, an emphasis on emotional and physical discipline, and a deemphasis of communal ties, all of which are hallmarks of the experience of the children of immigrants.

One might argue that with the adoption of the emotional distance of "cool," post–World War I Americans were simply catching up with their working-class counterparts: living in greater proximity in urban areas, participating in a wage economy, socializing in mixed-sex environments that required more self-examination and self-control. The flirtatious nonchalance of the young woman in "A Ballad of the Ball" extended to her bourgeois sisters now that "young men and women spent more and more time in each other's company as coeducation gained ground and novel practices such as dating reconfigured the social activities of high school and college-age youth" (Stearns 195).

An equally crucial change in adolescent styles that Stearns does not take into account is the immense influence of African American aesthetics on young white people from the 1920s onward, an influence that was not possible before the demographic changes of the Great Migration. By the mid-1920s, middle-class white teenagers had at their disposal not only white immigrant working-class values of fun, sexual freedom, and financial independence but also African American urban cool, the self-restraint coupled with nihilism that was born of black displacement and white supremacy and that Gwendolyn Brooks encapsulated in her poem "We Real Cool":

We real cool. We
Left school. We

Lurk late. We
Strike straight. We

Sing sin. We
Thin gin. We

Jazz June. We
Die soon. (331)

Yet one of the most influential changes that move white bourgeois youth ever closer to the model of adolescence that their working-class predecessors had originated was the invention of the cash allowance. This phenomenon empowered previously homebound teenagers to experience mobility and freedom in ways that had previously been unavailable.

If access to income and the availability of age-specific places to spend it, away from the eyes of parents and other adults, was crucial to the formation of an adolescent subculture among working-class children of immigrants, the institution of allowances had a similar effect for middle-class kids from the 1920s. Consumerism had long been part of the bourgeois child's and adolescent's experience. In her classic sentimental novel *The Wide, Wide World* (1850), Susan Warner takes the reader on a tour of department stores and bookshops with her protagonist, Ellen Montgomery, in search of the perfect Bible or writing desk or black merino fabric. However, shopping is a pleasurable experience for Ellen only in the company of her mother, and the money with which to buy the precious items is hard-won: since Ellen's father will not part with money for her mother to spend on anything but "mere clothing," Mrs. Montgomery pawns a family heirloom to raise the funds (29).

In Warner's novel, Ellen must be educated as a consumer. Her mother provides the guidance for her to buy the perfect Bible; while Mrs. Montgomery tells her daughter that "you are old enough" to judge the right purchase, Ellen's decision comes after considerable discussion (30–31). Her mother picks out the right supplies for writing, remembering all the small items that Ellen might need to write, address, and seal letters. By contrast, when Ellen is forced to venture out by herself to buy fabric, the trip nearly ends in disaster—she has trouble choosing the right material and is terrorized by the clerk.

Clearly, for Warner, women's buying power is not the problem. Indeed, as Peter Stoneley has argued, throughout the second half of the nineteenth century, girls and young women were trained to be consumers, to "buy into womanhood," to the extent that by the end of the century, "the girl's development comes to include—and even to be centered around—the acquisition and management of spending power" (4).[1] However, the power of that money originated not with the girls themselves or with middle-class women, but with husbands and fathers, who doled it out at their discretion (or, as with Mrs. Montgomery, forced them to procure the money through emotionally trying means). This scenario differed from that in many urban working-class families at the end of the nineteenth century: as Viviana Zelizer points out, mothers received the pay packets, then parceled out spending money to husbands and children (*Meaning of Money* 57).

In the final years of the nineteenth century, the idea began to take hold that children might receive money from their parents by right as a weekly or monthly allowance. *Outlook* magazine noted in 1903 that "the poorest class are rich in comparison with many young people who are dependent for their pennies" (qtd in Zelizer, *Pricing* 103). Increasingly, parents were discouraged from financially rewarding their children for chores around the house— rather, the allowance should be an entitlement to teach an adolescent responsible spending.

Even as money that children earned was derogated, as august a body as the White House Conference on Child Health and Protection recognized and recommended the shift toward children's receiving regular allowances. As Viviana Zelizer argues, allowances were seen as preventative of juvenile delinquency, whereas children's earning money was a predictor of future delinquent behavior (*Pricing* 104). Moreover, the growing centrality of consumerism to the U.S. economy led to a focus on teaching young people to be effective and responsible spenders. An allowance was, in effect, wages for being a dependent, even as the amount of money teenagers required gave them access to more and more independence.[2]

Books about adolescence, which ranged from medical and psychological volumes (clearly inspired by G. Stanley Hall on the one hand or by Margaret Mead on the other) to manuals for parents and teachers, spent at least some time on what kind of money teenagers should have access to and how they might spend it. In *Our Teenage Boys and Girls: Suggestions for Parents, Teachers, and Other Youth Leaders* (1945), Lester D. Crow and Alice Crow advised parents to expect their teenage children to want their own money, and recommended that parents be as hands-off as possible. In terms of buying clothes, they suggested, "the young person should be given considerable freedom of selection. . . . As the boy or girl advances into the upper teen years, he or she should be encouraged to do most of his shopping alone" (56–57).

More to the point, the Crows strongly discouraged parents from voicing disapproval of their children's choices. An adolescent had to learn to develop her or his own style, and "an outstanding means of asserting one's developing maturity is through personal dress and grooming" (57). We are a long way from Booth Tarkington's small-town adolescents in *Seventeen*, who were unable to make any decisions without the oversight of their parents and other adults. By the 1940s, money to buy clothes and the ability to express oneself through clothing were a given for the middle-class children of the readers of *Our Teenage Boys and Girls*. We can look back here to Mashah Smolinsky of Anzia Yezierska's *Bread Givers* or the soigné Miss Beckie Fisher, girl picketer of Cleveland, for whom the power to select their own wardrobe was a significant element of their identities as new Americans.

By 1956, which marked the height of the new teen culture, guides to raising adolescents were giving detailed advice about allowances, year by year. In *Youth: The Years from Ten to Sixteen*, Arnold Gesell and his coauthors advised that fourteen-year-olds receive about two dollars in allowance, although "clothes-hungry girls need to have a clothes allowance, not for them to enjoy, but rather to control them within bounds" (190). These authors take for granted that a fourteen-year-old girl will be selecting and buying her own clothes—the issue is to control her desires and her spending power, not to be there when she exercises them. Ironically, where working-class parents had fought with their children over control of their pay packets, bourgeois parents were advised to give their teenage children an allowance to teach them the value of money.

Indeed, the parentally imposed poverty of middle-class teenagers had come to an end. Adolescents were not just a self-defined group but also a market, an audience of consumers with money that was theirs to spend.[3] The rash of teen rebel movies in the 1950s expressed a level of anxiety with the new powers of adolescents that the immigrant parents of the 1890s could certainly have identified with: here were young men and women who pushed their independence to the limits.[4]

This push-pull of freedom and control that has characterized adolescence for more than a hundred years now, particularly in terms of money and commodity consumerism, is going through a peculiar metamorphosis in the early twenty-first century, however. Over the past few years, news outlets have reported almost obsessively on the phenomenon of "helicopter parents" who "hover" over their children in school and then in college, and children who keep in contact with parents by cell phone and instant messaging.[5] The Fort Wayne, Indiana, *News-Sentinel* placed responsibility for this phenomenon as much with the adolescent children as with their overinvolved parents: according to University of Indiana psychologist Chris Meno: " 'It's not unusual for students to be calling and checking in with mom three or four times a day,' asking about making a purchase or whether to drop a class" (Boen).

It is too soon, I think, to argue that this represents a significant change in the way adolescents understand themselves in relation to the marketplace and their parents. After all, this may be just one trend among many. And the material realities of teen life have changed enormously since the mass adoption of the Internet: the separate space that teenagers sought in cars, ice cream parlors, dance halls, parking lots of 7–11 convenience stores, and city streets has been reconstituted in large part online in social networking sites like Facebook and MySpace. Adolescents can construct an entire world apart from their parents without ever leaving their homes—to paraphrase Beth Bailey, it is as though teenagers have traveled from front porch to backseat to family room computer in less than a hundred years.

However, I still hold out hope that rebellious, space-claiming, sexually curious teenagers will find each other the old-fashioned way. Much of my adolescence was spent trolling the streets of London and then New York, alone, with a friend, with a gang of other kids, looking for fun wherever it might be, dancing, making and breaking romances, hoping that my clothes were as hip as I thought they were. I wish for the adolescents of the future the same teenage pleasures and attendant parental hand-wringing that was my heritage and, if they're lucky, can be theirs too.

Notes

1. Many years later I saw this experience borne out in Dick Hebdige's classic of Birmingham School cultural studies, *Subculture: The Meaning of Style* (London: Methuen, 1979). Although Hebdige's argument deals almost exclusively with working-class youth cultures, there was a surprising amount of interplay between my own middle-class Jewish youth in the early 1980s and the urban youth subcultures Hebdige describes: my friends and I socialized with Nigerian immigrant rude boys, working-class mods in Fred Perry sweaters, Hampstead antinuke activists, South London habitués of 1950s nights at various clubs around town, and punk and metal kids of diverse kinds. Despite the rigidity of class boundaries, young Londoners combined, divided, and recombined with the speed and avidity of atomic particles.

2. Of course a more challenging, and arguably more realistic, version of the 1980s suburban teenage experience is Amy Heckerling's *Fast Times at Ridgemont High* (1982), which portrays the challenges of popularity, sexual (in)experience, and gossip with emotional depth. Moreover, rebel youth films did not disappear from Hollywood in the 1980s; rather, they more often dealt with adolescents of past generations. Francis Ford Coppola's *Rumblefish* (1983) and *The Outsiders* (1983), Philip Kaufman's *The Wanderers* (1979), and even the raunchy *Porky's* (1983, plus various sequels) all focus on teenagers in the 1950s and 1960s, the paradigmatic adolescent era that was replayed over the 1970s and 1980s.

3. For a recent discussion of the connection of youth rebellion with consumer capitalism, see Klein, *No Logo*.

4. Several striking examples: the disrespect Linda Brent's brother William shows for their father and later their grandmother in Harriet Jacobs's *Incidents in the Life of a Slave Girl* is explicitly linked to the depredations of slavery; Mrs. Johnson's abandonment of her "fallen" daughter Maggie in Stephen Crane's *Maggie, a Girl of the Streets* is a direct result of the drunkenness and poverty endemic to the tenements; in Paul Laurence Dunbar's *The Sport of the Gods* (1902), Kitty and Joe reject their mother's moral guidance because of the racist false imprisonment of their father and the corrupting influence of New York City.

5. See, for example, Bailey, *From Front Porch to Back Seat*.

6. My focus here is mainly on these regions since they were the locations of the largest most industrialized cities—New York, Chicago, Rochester, Cleveland,

Pittsburgh. While I do on occasion cite studies of West Coast cities, particularly San Francisco and Los Angeles, my central observation is that adolescence formed mostly among the children of European immigrants, in large part due to their dual status as white and "foreign." The racism directed at immigrants from Mexico, China, and Japan interfered significantly with the ability of their children to absorb and be absorbed into U.S. popular culture. For a full discussion of the obstacles arrayed against Asian and Latin American immigrants, see Takaki, *Iron Cages*.

7. The *Oxford English Dictionary* cites the first appearance of the term "teenager" in *Popular Science Monthly* in 1941; during the 1940s it became so popular that W. H. Auden used the word in his poem "The Age of Anxiety" in 1945.

8. Many Anglo-Americans in the first decades of the twentieth century, even in the face of significant evidence to the contrary, held fast to the belief that the typical American was rural, or at the very least lived in a small town. In her 1910 advice manual *Side Talks with Girls*, Ruth Ashmore imagines the "average girl" as "whole-hearted, happy, generous, pretty and pleasant to look upon, and very anxious to do what is right. She lives in a small country town, or maybe on a farm" (1). Insofar as Ashmore could envisage this girl in a city, it was as a migrant from her country home, looking for work. Her chapter "Girl Life in New York City" is replete with warnings to these whole-hearted bourgeois, revealing to them the horrors of the life of the New York working girl, in the hope of convincing her readers that no amount of financial independence is worth undergoing the depravities of city life.

9. For an in-depth discussion of different familial expectations, in this case for Jewish and Italian immigrants, and their conflict with the mostly evangelical Christian assumptions of Anglo-American culture, see Ewen, *Immigrant Women in the Land of Dollars*.

10. For a discussion of the conflicts between nineteenth-century middle-class reformers and their poor and working-class subjects, see Boyer, *Urban Masses and Moral Order in America*. For a discussion of the work of the Tract Visitors, see Tompkins, *Sensational Designs*.

CHAPTER 1 — "YOUTH MUST HAVE ITS FLING"

1. Age was not the only category that underwent significant change in the beginning of the twentieth century. As I show in *Technology and the Logic of American Racism: A Cultural History of the Body as Evidence*, the racial classifications the U.S. census employed changed several times. In the 1890 census, a person of African heritage could check off "Negro" or "mulatto" as a racial identifier, while in 1920 only "Negro" was available (3–4). Even in recent years, the census has been embroiled in controversy over the possibility of "multiracial" as an option.

2. In the two decades between 1880 and 1900, there were almost nine million immigrants to the United States (in six of the eleven years between 1905 and 1915, there were a million immigrants per year), and in the twenty years between 1900 and 1920 there were almost fifteen million. This compares to an entire population increase of just

under twelve million people in the forty years between 1800 and 1840 (although a smaller proportional increase—in the first four decades of the nineteenth century, the population more than tripled [Miller 106]). Of course, this does not take into account the attendant emigration, which was up to 30 percent of immigrants in the early decades of the twentieth century and reached over 50 percent in 1916, largely due to the pressures of World War I. However, the immigration figures are still remarkable: between 1900 and 1909, more than eight million people entered at New York ports alone (although New York was by far the densest port of entry for that period; the next busiest was Boston, which for the same years processed well under half a million, just over one-fifth of New York's arrivals [Carpenter 55]).

An ancillary figure is the proportion of adult men to women in the population in the same years. Between 1880 and 1920, men consistently outnumbered women in the population by at least 1,036 to 1,000 and, at the height of immigration in the first decade of the twentieth century, by 1,060 to 1,000. Bearing in mind that these numbers average in communities in which the numbers of women and men were roughly equal or, as is often the case, women slightly outnumbered men, the ratio of men to women in regions characterized by heavy immigration was noticeably disproportionate. For a powerfully argued, although not always credible, analysis of the causes and effects of disproportionately high male populations, see Courtwright, *Violent Land.*

3. Between 1890 and 1920, the average age for men at first marriage varied between about 24.6 and 26 years old; for women it was about 22. By contrast, in 1950, the average age of first marriage for women had dropped to just over 20 years old. In 1910, 98.3 percent of men and 87.9 percent of women between fifteen and nineteen years old were unmarried. In 1950, 96 percent of eighteen-year-old men and only 75 percent of eighteen-year-old women were unmarried, and only half of nineteen- and twenty-year-old women were still single (Taeuber and Taeuber 154–155).

4. A corollary to these shifts in the national origins of immigrants was the change in new Americans' religious affiliations, a demographic change that became clear in the next generation. Protestants had been the majority of the New York population at the end of the nineteenth century, but by 1935 they had been pushed into third place behind Catholics and Jews (Moore 5).

5. For a detailed discussion of Hall's theories of recapitulation and their relation to the development of U.S. masculinity, see Bederman, *Manliness and Civilization.*

6. Of course, Hall could not completely let go of his social Darwinist beliefs. For Hall, every failure to advance brought with it the threat of declension, every "failure to mount almost always means retrogression, degeneracy, or fall. . . . The consciousness of childhood is molted, and a new, larger, better consciousness must be developed, or increased exposure and vulnerability will bring deterioration" (2:72).

7. See, for example, Jacob Riis's *How the Other Half Lives,* published in 1890, particularly chapter 3, "The Mixed Crowd." Riis cites the estimate of "the agent of a notorious Fourth Ward alley" that "there was not a native-born individual" in the entire tenement

development (19). Riis's ironic characterization of the Lower East Side as "cosmopolitan" (19), and tenements by definition as housing for immigrants both recent and more established, is of a piece with Hall's discussions of "urbanization," and the perils to American society of "uncivilized" adolescent children of immigrants.

8. Of the 200 girls Bowen surveyed, 173 lived at home. Of those, 126 gave all their wages to their families. They made between $2.50 and $11 per week, mostly making between $4 and $8. The low pay often tied girls to their families—Bowen estimated that a girl could not live on her own or even with roommates for less than $8 a week.

9. Interestingly, Palladino and Kett both note that the new teenagers of the mid-twentieth century were not regarded with the trepidation occasioned by their earlier and later counterparts. In the 1940s, teenagers may have been seen as "fun-loving" but they were also anodyne, "wholesome high school students eager to try out adult freedoms, but willing to live by adult rules" (Palladino xv).

10. While the *Oxford English Dictionary* traces the use of "fun" as a noun back to the mid-eighteenth century, the idiom is a little different. None of the several examples the dictionary cites from before the twentieth century use "fun" as enjoyment for its own sake; rather, fun seems to constitute a diversion from more serious matters, or even something into which real wit can "degenerate." This idea of fun is very different from its 1920s incarnation in the popular song "Ain't We Got Fun," the 1960s Beach Boys heroine who has "fun, fun, fun till her daddy takes her T-Bird away," or Cyndi Lauper's girls who "just want to have fun."

11. In 1900 there were more than ten thousand saloons operating in the greater New York area. More importantly, the saloons, poolrooms, and social clubs that workingmen frequented encouraged male bonding and were either implicitly or openly hostile to women. Alcohol, prostitution, and "the sporting life" more generally (which could include gambling and boxing, as well as sports of various kinds) often folded into the world of the saloon.

12. Marianna Valverde, in "The Love of Finery: Fashion and the Fallen Woman in Nineteenth Century Social Discourse" (*Victorian Studies* 32, 2 [Winter 1989]: 168–188), analyzes the nineteenth-century bourgeois critique of young women's love of "finery" and the inevitable link between superficial love of beautiful things and moral downfall.

13. An excellent resource on the fight against child labor is the Web site of the Campaign to End Child Labor (www.boondocksnet.com/labor/), edited by Jim Zwick.

14. See, for example, Pauline Goldmark's "What Boston Has Done in Regulating the Street Trades for Children" (*Charities* 10 [February 14, 1903]), which traces the beginnings of regulation of child labor in Boston to the early 1890s. Cited in www.boondocksnet.com/labor/cl_030214_street_trades.html (accessed August 22, 2002).

15. The stakes of neglecting this philanthropic duty of surveillance were high for many reformers. The Chicago Vice Commission, created in 1910, argued that "the

immigrant woman furnishes a large supply [of prostitutes] to the demand. Generally virtuous when she comes to this country, she is ruined and exploited because there is no adequate protection and assistance given her after she reaches the United States" (40). Abandoned to the forces of a corrupting city, immigrant women were defenseless against the snares of "cadets" and unscrupulous lovers.

16. Farah Jasmine Griffith's masterful *Who Set You Flowin': The African-American Migration Narrative* (New York: Oxford University Press, 1995) makes a similar observation. There were migration narratives in the early years of the twentieth century, most notably Paul Laurence Dunbar's *The Sport of the Gods* (1902) and James Weldon Johnson's *Autobiography of an Ex-Colored Man* (1912), but neither exactly fits a typical story of black movement from South to North. In Dunbar's novel, the Hamilton family is forced up to New York not by systematic racism but by their rejection by both their white and black home communities in the wake of a false accusation of theft against paterfamilias Berry by the deceitful brother of his white employer. In the novel, the rural South represents a prelapsarian world, however corrupted by racism, and New York a dangerous and poisoned environment that systematically destroys Berry's wife and children through violence, drink, drugs, and sexual license. Similarly, while antiblack violence is the catalyst that propels the narrator of *Autobiography of an Ex-Colored Man* out of the South, his story, inflected by interclass socializing and cross-race homoerotic attraction, is a far cry from what we now think of as classic migration narratives: Jean Toomer's *Cane*, Richard Wright's *Uncle Tom's Children*, and Ann Petry's *The Street*.

17. Not within the purview of this study, but a potentially fascinating topic, would be how and why African American culture did become such a touchstone for the generations of teenagers after 1945, starting with the adolescents inspired by the Beats and moving through the influence of R&B and the blues for the teenagers of the 1950s and 1960s.

18. For example, Thomas Ferraro's *Feeling Italian: The Art of Ethnicity in America* explores how Italian Americans, rather than simply going through the process of assimilation and racialization as "white ethnics," at least in part reshaped and continue to reshape U.S. culture in their own image through such iconic figures as Joseph Stella, Frank Sinatra, and Madonna.

CHAPTER 2 — PICTURING LABOR

1. While both versions of the Italian Madonna were published in Hine's lifetime, his accompanying caption suggests that he originally intended only the cropped image to be published. Perhaps technical problems prevented that (thanks to Maren Stange for that suggestion), or perhaps, as he occasionally did, he presented different versions for different audiences.

2. The cropped version closely resembles Raphael's famous *Madonna della Sedia* or seated Madonna, which focuses on the connection between Mary and the Christ child.

3. There are multiple ironies here. As child labor historian Hugh D. Hindman argues, the same forces of industrialization that created the Romantic child also made possible the drafting of hundreds of thousands of children into the workforce (8). At the same time, technological advances created by increased mechanization pushed children out of work as the tasks they performed in workplaces like glass factories, department stores, and canneries became automated (Nasaw, *Children of the City,* 44).

4. See Tompkins, *Sensational Designs.* This is not to say that children's bodies were not represented—far from it. As we shall see, pictures of the Romantic child lingered over the juvenile body: the plump, soft arms, the red lips, the chubby cheeks, the round buttocks. But children's bodies were understood not just as nonerotic but as beyond the realm of the human: children's bodies were those of angels rather than of people, "there and yet not there" (Higonnet, 78).

The invocation of angels was a common trope in photographs of children in the mid-to-late nineteenth century. Julia Margaret Cameron often posed her child models in large constructed wings, and Pre-Raphaelite painter John Everett Millais first made his name with his painting *Non Angli sed Angeli* (Not Angles but Angels), a phrase purportedly spoken by St. Gregory upon seeing enslaved blond Angle children for sale in a Roman marketplace. This topos was a common subject for British child portraiture in both painting and photography: see, for example the portrait of St. Gregory in All Souls Chapel in St. Peter's Cathedral, Prince Edward Island; a William Blake drawing, *Non Angli . . .* , from 1802; Herbert Luther Smith's painting of the same title from 1834; George Scharf's engraving of the subject from 1844. The British section of the World Columbian Exposition of 1893 included a gallery of photographs of children, also entitled "Non Angli sed angeli" (Bancroft 275). The subject was such a cliché that it even makes an appearance in William Makepeace Thackeray's humorous short story "Our Street" (1857). Writing under the pseudonym Mr. M. A. Titmarsh, Thackeray lampoons "George Rumpold, a historical painter," who specializes in the enormous classical- and mediaeval-themed history paintings that were the rage with the newly rich merchant classes of the time. While in Rome, George painted " 'Caractacus' [a Roman warrior popular in the British imagination]; a picture of 'Non Angli Sed Angeli' of course; a picture of 'Alfred in the Neatherd's Cottage,' seventy-two feet by forty-eight . . . , and the deaths of Socrates, of Remus, and of the Christians under Nero respectively." Thackeray's insouciant "of course" is enough to show his readers that by midcentury, the association between (white, Anglo-Saxon) children and angels has become embedded in British popular culture (*www.gutenberg.net/etext01/chmsb10.txt*; accessed April 1, 2004).

5. This phenomenon has reached a level of reductio ad absurdum with digital technology via which one can watch oneself capturing a present moment that will, in an instant, be in the past, or record an event and then reexperience it almost immediately.

6. Several activists against child labor also supported reform of work conditions more generally for adult workers and agitated for labor unions, safety regulations, and

so on. Jane Addams was a firm supporter of unionization, and Felix Adler explicitly linked his activism against children's work to a larger agenda for workers' rights and dignity. If one was opposed to the mistreatment of children in the workplace, believed that the child "has a soul which must not be blighted for the prospect of mere gain . . . [then] the same essential reasoning will be found to apply also to the adult workers; they, too, will not be looked upon as mere commodities, as mere instruments for the accumulation of riches; to them also a certain sacredness will be seen to attach, and certain human rights to belong, which may not be infringed" (Adler, "Child Labor" 24–25).

7. Not all reformers were so keen on children's work in family farms, particularly those who had grown up in farming families. While many NCLC spokespeople described rural life in idealized terms, some were less romantic about it. Woods Hutchinson, writing in the *Annals of the American Academy*, recalled his own farm childhood as signally unpleasant, and countered the pastoral fantasies of many of his colleagues, remembering that "farmwork is the hardest and most disagreeable work there is, with the longest hours and the poorest pay" (112).

8. A series of photographs in the *Child Labor Bulletin* illustrated these concepts. A full-page montage announces "Every Child Should Work" but lays out the guidelines for that work, each supported by pictures: "But the work must develop not deaden/ *Encourage work*/If it trains the child to be a better citizen/*Stop it*/If it merely makes money for parent or employer/ *We must not grind the seed corn.*" *Child Labor Bulletin* 3 (1914): 41 (emphasis in original).

9. One of Jacob Riis's most affecting photographs in *How the Other Half Lives* bears witness to this assumption that children should be free from adult responsibilities. A small girl, no more than four or five, holds a dirty baby on her lap on the stoop of a tenement building. Riis called the picture "Little Girl with a Baby on Her Lap" but informally titled it "The Little Mother," and it encapsulated the premature responsibility young children were expected to take on, caring for younger siblings as soon as they were able to carry them. Similarly, Owen R. Lovejoy, himself a later chair of the NCLC, wrote that "the child is not a little man or woman, but a being in the process of physical formation—with features of that development so delicate that no less caution is required at the age of ten or twelve than was required in infancy" (43).

10. Demands to end child labor often went hand in hand with cries for universal compulsory education. For Dewey's analysis of Froebel's ideas, see chapter 5, "Froebel's Educational Principles," in *The School and Society*. Adler's analysis of the basics of child development—that "the child must develop physically and to do so it must play; the child must develop mentally and to do so it must be sent to school; the child must develop morally and to do so it must be kept within the guarded precincts of the home" ("Child Labor" 23)—owes a great deal to both Froebel and Dewey. Similarly, Woods Hutchinson maintained that "the most crying demand before the American Commonwealth to-day is to make our public schools *educate the whole child.* . . . Train him physically and emotionally. . . . Fit him for life and for action" (114, emphasis in

original). And James H. Kirkland saw education as a human right and a human necessity, since "every child must have the privilege or working out his own life, of developing the best that is in him" (87).

11. In 1908, the National Child Labor Committee hired Lewis W. Hine as its staff photographer. He was charged with investigating and documenting incidents of child labor, particularly when they violated existing restrictions on child work, and proving that child labor was a significant problem in twentieth-century America. Hine came to this work with exactly the right credentials: born in Oshkosh, Wisconsin, in 1874, he had himself gone to work at fifteen after the death of his father. After studying at the University of Chicago, he was recruited as a botany teacher at Felix Adler's Ethical Culture School under renowned education reformer Frank E. Manny. At the ECS Hine began to pursue photography as a pedagogical and aesthetic practice. In 1904 he embarked on his first large project, photographing new immigrants at Ellis Island, and by 1906 he was working for the NCLC as a freelance photographer.

By the time Hine joined the NCLC staff, he was well known within Progressive circles. His Ellis Island series had been followed by his involvement in the Pittsburgh Survey, which dovetailed with his increasing interest in work generally and child labor in particular. Initiated by the sociological journal *Charities and the Commons* (which later changed its name to *The Survey*) and funded by the Russell Sage Foundation, the survey was a comprehensive investigation of living and working conditions in industrial Pittsburgh, exposing the dangers of the steel mills, the poverty of urban immigrants, and the growing disparities between rich and poor. Hine's experiences on Ellis Island and in Pittsburgh, and his commitment to photography as a tool for social change, made him an ideal candidate for the NCLC when it was looking for a photographer to document the ravages of child labor across the United States.

12. Of course, Hine was not unique in taking photographs immersed in connotative meaning. As W.J.T. Mitchell argues: "Connotation goes all the way down to the roots of a photograph, to the motives for its production, to the selection of its subject matter, to the choice of angles and lighting" (284). But what's striking about Hine's pictures is that much of the material Mitchell identifies as connotative was for Hine denotative: his motives for production and selection of subject matter were in large part the raison d'être of his NCLC pictures. The denotative language of his photographs is, I would argue, subtler than the conditions of their production, located instead in the implicit narrative links among, between, and within the pictures.

13. Like several of Hine's photographs, this picture has more than one title. In the New York Public Library collection, it is entitled "Bootblacks fill up spare time pitching pennies." In the George Eastman Collection, the repository for all Hine's personal prints and negatives, it is called "Newsies and bootblacks shooting craps." The first title seems more accurate—all the boys are carrying or leaning on bootblacking boxes, and they are clearly pitching pennies, not throwing dice. In general, I use the captions from the New York Public Library collection of Hine photographs, which is where I had an opportunity to

look at Hine's captions close up, unless the captions from other collections such as the George Eastman House and the Library of Congress seem more compelling.

14. In the Library of Congress NCLC collection, Hine identifies this boy as Raoul Julien.

15. Hine took many pictures of groups and pairs of working children. His photograph of dozens of breaker boys (these boys worked at the entrances of mine shafts, monitoring the movement of coal) is famous, and for good reason—the sheer size of the group drives home the point that child labor in the mines was hardly a small-scale or isolated phenomenon. But it is striking that when he photographed individual children, Hine attempted to keep the picture as empty as possible of other people.

16. Hine observes that one of the children in the flower-making Darelli/Tarelli family was ill with tuberculosis and that soon after his visit, their operation was shut down until the boy recovered. The spread of disease was a central argument against tenement homework more generally, not just in terms of child labor, but Hine's voice in noting the boy's illness is not nearly as judgmental as the tone he uses in pointing out the "indescribably dirty children" of the nut-picking family.

17. In fact, there is another picture of Olga in Hine's collection, in a group shot of children of different ages inside the cannery. Olga is hardly ugly by traditional aesthetic standards of the attractive child: with her chubby hands and arms, round eyes, and delicate features she fits quite neatly into an image of cuteness, if not beauty.

18. Thanks to Katrina D. Foster for insight into this regional expression.

19. As Susan Sontag points out, however, this is not completely Hine's fault. Photography does objectify—that is its function, to turn people, places, things, into consumable objects that can be held in one's hand, reproduced, passed around. Sontag argues that the main effect of photography is "to convert the world into a department store or museum-without-walls in which every subject is depreciated into an article of consumption, promoted into an item for aesthetic appreciation" (110; it seems clear that Sontag's use of the word "promoted" is highly ironic).

20. In several captions and comments, Hine mentions how the child he is photographing initially refused to tell her or his real age for fear of being barred from the work that helped support their families; or he does not discuss the role of migrant labor in agricultural work; or he indicts "lazy" fathers without acknowledging that adult work, especially in cities, while better paying than children's labor, was often unreliable, seasonal, and dependent upon the unpredictable fluctuations of economic forces.

21. The story of child labor legislation is marked by the development of lobbying as an institution on the federal level, in this case by southern textile-manufacturing interests—not surprising, given that by 1905 children made up 23 percent of the workforce in southern mills, with only 30 percent of the entire southern mill workforce over age twenty-one (Hindman 153). By 1906, two years after the founding of the NCLC, the

movement against child labor was taken up by Congress. The first piece of federal leg-islation, sponsored by Senator Albert Beveridge (it was informally called the Beveridge bill), made it as far as the floor of the House, where it was blocked by congresspeople funded by the textile industry. In 1916 the Keating-Owen bill passed both houses but was ruled unconstitutional by the Supreme Court on the basis that it interfered with states' rights to legislate work restrictions. The Child Labor Tax Act of 1919 also passed Congress but was similarly struck down (analogies between antisegregation and anti–child labor legislation are instructive in terms of the reactionary uses to which arguments for states' rights were put).

Local child labor laws were much more successful, even before the creation of a national movement. By the beginning of the twentieth century most northern indus-trial states had passed regulations limiting children's work to ten-hour days and sixty-hour weeks, and in 1903, a year before the founding of the NCLC, Alabama and North and South Carolina restricted paid work to children over twelve (Hindman 59). By 1913, homework in tenements was banned for children under fourteen in New York (which, ironically, sent sweatshop labor over the river to New Jersey [Hindman 196]). In the 1910s, southern states began to pass, although not necessarily enforce, child labor regu-lations for children under fourteen, and by 1916, all southern states but North Carolina had established the minimum age for millwork at fourteen and placed restrictions on hours and night work (Hindman 183). Of course, the existence of laws does not neces-sarily mean their enforcement (and the agricultural sector was often explicitly excluded from such legislation), and much of the work of NCLC inspectors was as watchdogs ensuring compliance with legal limits on working children. But the passage of state laws against child labor at the beginning of the twentieth century does indicate that there was meaningful public and legislative opposition to the widespread use of chil-dren in the industrial workforce.

22. Perhaps the most famous example of department store "temptation to expendi-ture" in U.S. literature comes in Theodore Dreiser's *Sister Carrie*. Carrie Meeber's ears are highly attuned to the siren song of consumerism. In her first visit to Field's depart-ment store, Carrie is swept away by the variety and beauty of the available goods, stop-ping at each counter, her "woman's heart warm with desire for them. How would she look in this, how charming that would make her! She came upon the corset counter and paused in rich reverie as she noted the dainty concoctions of colour and lace there dis-played. . . . She lingered in the jewelry department. She saw the earrings, the bracelets, the pins, the chains. What would she not have given if she could have had them all!" (55). For Carrie, consumer items are more than possessions; they create their own real-ity and speak their own language. Dreiser literalizes Carrie's relationship with com-modities by ventriloquizing consumerism through the goods themselves, turning them into animate beings that can plead their own case:

Fine clothes to her were a vast persuasion; they spoke tenderly and Jesuitically for themselves. When she came within earshot of their pleading, desire in her bent a willing ear. The voice of the so-called inanimate! Who shall translate for us the language of the stones?

"My dear," said the lace collar she secured from Partridges, "I fit you beautifully; don't give me up."

"Ah, such little feet," said the leather of the soft new shoes; "how effectively I cover them. What a pity they should ever want my aid." (81)

Given most adolescent workers' low wages, especially those of young women, this siren song was difficult to resist *and* difficult to indulge. Of the 200 girls Bowen surveyed, 173 lived at home. Of those 126 gave all their wages to their families. They made between $2.50 and $11 per week, with most making between $4 and $8. The low pay often tied girls to their families, since Bowen estimated that a girl could not live on her own or even with roommates for less than $8 a week.

23. Hine also undertook a series of photographs that he released as a book entitled *Men at Work* (1938), but they are mostly from the 1930s, most famously of the construction of the Empire State Building. His photographs of workingwomen were never collected or published as a thematic whole during his lifetime, although a number of the photographs were published in *Women at Work* by the George Eastman House, repository of all Hine's prints and negatives, in 1981.

24. Shelton Looms commissioned the photographs (much as Hine was engaged to photograph the Empire State Building) to represent the modernity and beauty of the new weaving technologies. Although Hine is best known for his sociological photography, he was essentially a commercial photographer and even won a prize from the Art Directors Club. The modernist, abstract pictures he took at the looms were designed to make the company look good—to contrast this workplace with the negative images of textile labor (particularly the grim child labor in textile mills that Hine himself had photographed a couple of decades earlier). Thanks to Maren Stange for pointing this out to me.

25. The National Center for Education Statistics report of 1999 showed that in October 1999, approximately 3.8 million adolescents were not enrolled in a high school program and/or had not completed high school, comprising 11.2 percent of the 34.1 million sixteen- through twenty-four-year-olds in the United States in 1999. Of those students who did enroll in high school, about 5 percent did not graduate. More importantly, young people whose families were in the bottom 20 percent in income were five times more likely to drop out of high school than were their counterparts in the top 20 percent. (Race and ethnicity certainly play a role in these numbers, but the most significant predictor of the dropout rate is poverty.) While these numbers do not necessarily reflect how many Americans will go on to earn a high school degree in nontraditional ways, such as through the GED, they do suggest that the assumption that high school is a universal experience is still held by the more affluent sector of the United States, particularly the white middle classes (for more details on dropout rates, go to the National Center for Education Statistics Executive Summary on Dropout Rates at *http://nces.ed.gov/pubs2001/dropout/* [accessed August 16, 2004]).

CHAPTER 3 — "IRREVERENCE AND THE AMERICAN SPIRIT"

1. This theme is explicit, for example, in Anzia Yezierska's autobiographical novel *Bread Givers* (1925), which is subtitled "a struggle between a father of the Old World and a daughter of the New." I would hasten to add, though, that this binary is itself in part an invention, invoking any number of other equally constructed dichotomous relations: antiquity/modernity, primitive/civilized, rural/urban, ignorant/worldly, apolitical/ politicized. Yezierska herself implicitly admits that it is a fabrication, since she sets the "Old World" section of her novel not in Poland, the narrator's birthplace, but on Hester Street, an avatar of bustling, industrialized modernity if ever there was one.

2. Citations of Addams's *Twenty Years at Hull House* will be indicated by HH, followed by the page number.

3. Carroll Smith-Rosenberg, "The Female World of Love and Ritual: Relations between Women in Nineteenth-Century America," *Signs* 1 (Autumn 1975): 1–29.

4. There was a certain amount of tension between the young women workers in the textile mills and their country parents, as Thomas Dublin observes, quoting from a nineteenth-century historian whose own sisters worked in the mills: "They went in their plain, country-made clothes, and after working several months, would come home for a visit, or perhaps to be married, in their tasteful city dresses, and with more money in their pockets than they had ever owned before" (qtd. in *Women at Work: The Transformation of Work and Community in Lowell, Massachusett, 1826–1860* [New York: Columbia University Press, 1979] 55). These young women, however sophisticated mill life made them, still "identified with the pride and independence of their yeoman farmer parents," although their taste of city life eventually lured many of them away from the countryside and into the urban world (Dublin 56–57).

5. The first mention of "generation gap" in a news publication I could find was in the *New York Times* on March 2, 1964, in an article entitled "Merman's Magic Enchants Britain." In a glowing review of Ethel Merman's cabaret show in London, the article commented upon the phenomenon of audience members bringing their teenage children to the performance. Merman, the article gushed, "has done what no other entertainer has managed since the Beatles and the rock'n'roll groups came on the scene. She has bridged the generation gap." The term does not reappear in the *Times* until 1966, and then only once. In 1967, it is mentioned thirty-five times, and in 1968, firmly established in the American idiom, it appears in the paper in a variety of venues: advertising, classifieds, and more than two hundred articles.

6. What caused some observers chagrin delighted others. As we shall see in chapter 5, New York bohemians celebrated the alienation between youth and their elders as an expression of new ideas and aesthetics.

7. Blaustein uses almost exactly the same language as Mangano, lamenting: "Old customs, dear to him as they had been to his fathers before him are dropped more or less

contemptuously by the children . . . ; the children are imbued with the idea that all that is not American is something to be ashamed of" (61).

8. Another example of children of immigrants creating their own specific culture, particularly through fashion, is the Mexican American zoot suiters of the 1940s. While their choices in clothing, music, and social styles were alien to their parents, they were also totally foreign to the Anglo-Americans of midcentury Southern California. For a detailed discussion of the zoot-suit phenomenon, see Mazón, *Zoot Suit Riots.*

9. See, for example, Ewen, *Immigrant Women in the Land of Dollars.*

10. In fact, bourgeois and upper-class women explicitly distanced themselves from the materialism of young working-class women. Nan Enstad observes that "middle class people used notions of character and taste to make a distinction between commodities with values and those without values," and the assertive gaudiness of working-class fashion at the end of the nineteenth and beginning of the twentieth centuries fell squarely into the category "without values" (27).

11. In *From Front Porch to Back Seat*, Beth L. Bailey traces how small-town and suburban adolescents became increasingly socially and sexually free with the introduction of automobiles into the middle classes. Where they had previously been limited to socializing and courting within the confines of their homes, bourgeois Anglo adolescents gained the kind of literal and figurative mobility in terms of their social lives that until then had been unimaginable.

12. The greater independence of the children of immigrants extended into the urban workplace as well. Union organizers were puzzled and alarmed by the comparatively low rate of involvement in union activities by young "Americans," particularly given the radicalism of Jewish and Italian American workers. In the ILGWU organ *The Ladies Garment Worker,* organizer Pauline M. Newman attempted to convince her readers that there was "no reason why the American girls should not join this Union. . . . They are treated just as bad or as good as the foreign girls are . . . ; the American working girl, too, is slowly but surely waking up to the fact that nothing but a Union can improve her conditions" ("Our Women Workers" 33).

13. Of course, this concern about the integrity of the immigrant home depended heavily upon race. The passage of the Page Act in 1875, which (in the guise of arresting the traffic in Chinese prostitutes to the United States) effectively excluded male Chinese immigrants from bringing over their wives and daughters, followed by the Chinese Exclusion Act of 1882, permanently broke up Chinese American families and created an immigrant society of predominantly single men among Chinese migrants. Thanks to Ting-Man Tsai for making this connection for me.

14. In the "sincere tribute of imitation," the young Jane tried to flatten her right thumb to make it more closely resemble that of her father, which was worn down by his work as a miller (HH 26). Similarly, her feelings of awe toward him caused her (equally enjoyable?) paroxysms of shame at her lies and of pleasure at confessing to them, since he so strongly disapproved of falsehood.

15. That immigration to the United States reverses the power relations between parents and children is a truism of immigrant narratives. Hilda Satt Polacheck observed that "the idea that the mother knows less than the children very soon destroys respect" (5). Similarly, in her influential account of her own experience as an immigrant, Mary Antin noted that immigrant parents "must step down from their throne of parental authority, and take the law from their children's mouths," which led to the "sad process of disintegration of home life" (213).

16. For a sample of the analyses of the Columbian Exposition as objectifying ethnography par excellence, see Rydell, *All the World's a Fair;* J. Brown, *Contesting Images;* Burton, "Rituals of Representations"; Yengoyan, "Culture, Ideology, and World's Fairs"; Di Leonardo, *Exotics at Home.*

17. The comparative freedom allowed to young men has its counterpart in the records of prosecution for sexual misconduct. Of all the young men prosecuted for sexual misdeeds, only 8 percent were turned in by their own parents, as opposed to over 60 percent of the girls prosecuted.

18. See, for example, Davis, "Charivari."

19. See, for example, Stansell, *City of Women;* Horowitz, *Rereading Sex.*

20. For a discussion of the sexual economy of the dance hall, see chapter 4.

21. Thomas Dublin discusses the regulation of the sexuality of Massachusetts mill girls in *Women at Work.* The Waltham-Lowell textile companies provided housing for their female workers, boardinghouses for single women and small cottages for married operatives. Dublin quotes a Unitarian minister from Lowell who argued that the productivity of the factories depended upon "the existence of an industrious, sober, orderly, and moral class of operatives," and the millowners heavily regulated the behavior of boardinghouse tenants to achieve this (77–78). Single women were required to live in the boardinghouses, which kept a curfew of 10 PM, and, as Dublin shows, boardinghouse keepers "were regarded as surrogate parents and operatives as minor children. . . . [Moreover,] the punishment for failure to live up to the required moral standards was dismissal from the mills and possible blacklisting" (79).

22. A little later in the letter, Pinzer reveals that her mother's accomplice in her arrest was an uncle who "did me the first wrong, when I was a tiny girl, and any number of times since then" (193). As Florence Howe argues in her afterword to *The Maimie Papers,* the collection of Pinzer's letters, Pinzer could easily have seen her sexual activity as a teenager, her running away with a man and subsequent slide into prostitution, as an "inevitable" result of the sexual assaults by her uncle. In addition, the apparent lack of anything but punishment from her mother seems closely connected to Pinzer's experience of sexual assault as a young girl, from which her mother was either unable or unwilling to protect her—a mother whom, in Howe's words, "she constantly described as hollow and unforgiving" (436).

23. Mary Odem's research reveals that the majority of prosecutions of statutory rape at the beginning of the twentieth century in Southern California were indeed only about the statute, rather than acts of sexual assault. In an average of three-quarters of the statutory rape cases in Alameda and Los Angeles counties between 1910 and 1920, the young women involved testified that they had consented to sex with the defendants ("Teenage Girls" 56). Given that most of these cases were brought to the attention of the police by the girls' families, Odem argues, charges of statutory rape were very often vehicles by which working-class, and particularly immigrant, families could regulate and punish their daughters, or, as in Maimie Pinzer's case, were a prerequisite for remanding them to reform schools and prisons.

24. Pinzer's incarceration is an excellent example of the interaction between reform, police, and immigrant actors. Her family started the ball rolling by calling in the law, but the police and the courts ran with it. Maimie's consignment to the Magdalen Home is typical of the policies recommended by the antiprostitution organization the Committee of Fifteen, which advocated that young women who are "notoriously debauched shall be coercively confined in asylums or reformatories" (176).

25. The Committee of Fifteen was, not surprisingly, tone deaf to the texture of immigrant life. In their report on prostitution in New York, they opined that in a major city "one has no neighbors. No man knows the doings of even his close friends; few men care what the secret life of their friends may be" (9). While that might have been the case for middle-class men, who could take advantage of the privacy made available by affluence, it was far from true of working-class and immigrant people, who lived in uncomfortably close quarters. Narratives of tenement life comment upon the signal *lack* of privacy residents of tenements enjoyed, as sounds, smells, and voices traveled through walls and windows.

26. Living in Montreal in her late twenties, Pinzer founded a residence and drop-in center for young prostitutes in large part so that a young woman could "feel at home and come to me for the night, no matter how late and I would put her to bed somewhere. In the morning I would hope to effect a reconciliation between the girl and her parent" (337).

27. Particularly, but not exclusively, in Italian families, the struggle between parental control and adolescent freedom resulted in elopements and "hasty and ill-advised marriages" at very young ages (Breckenridge 178). See Randy McBee's discussion of the rush to early marriage in immigrant communities in the first chapter of *Dance Hall Days*.

CHAPTER 4 — "YOUTH DEMANDS AMUSEMENT"

1. On the trend, see, for example, Levine, *Highbrow*; Garvey, *Adman*.

2. The Library of Congress Web site on western social dance and dance instruction manuals, *http://memory.loc.gov/ammem/dihtml*, is an excellent resource for antidance literature, ranging from an early-seventeenth-century attack on social dancing to Progressive Era exposés of commercial dance halls.

3. For a biography of Olcott, see M. Olcott, *Song*.

4. For an excellent discussion of the roots of Irish nostalgia ballads, see the "More Songs about Ireland and the Irish" page on the Parlor Songs Association Web site, *www.parlorsongs.com*.

5. Nasaw's chapter in *Going Out* on the specter of blackness in white American popular culture at the beginning of the twentieth century provides some excellent examples of the ways in which African American cultural inventions like ragtime and the cakewalk were both adopted/appropriated and disavowed by white Americans. See Toni Morrison's *Playing in the Dark* for a larger discussion of "the Africanist presence" in the white American imaginary, and Zora Neale Hurston's discussion of the ways in which black cultural expression is "cleaned up" by white and black bourgeois society in *The Sanctified Church*.

6. See, for example, Al Jolson's discussion in the *Times* article "Social Workers See."

7. Unlike the characters in many immigrant narratives, Jake did not begin his American life in New York. He first arrived in Boston, where he spent two years. During that time, he "used to mention his Gitl and Yosselé so frequently and so enthusiastically, that some wags among the Hanover Street tailors would sing 'Yekl and wife and the baby' to the tune of 'Molly and I and the Baby.'" But over time, he talked less and less of his earlier life, and after moving to New York, "he carefully avoided all reference to his antecedents" (24). Another change in this move was a shift of interest from American sport, particularly baseball, to dancing: "his enthusiastic nature before long found vent in dancing and in a *general* life of gallantry" (24–25). While I don't want to make too much of this narrative detail, it is telling. According to Cahan, in Boston, with its smaller Jewish population, Jewish immigrants tended to interact with members of the English-speaking, non-Jewish working class and were more likely to absorb American-identified pastimes like attending boxing matches and baseball games. In the "Jewish quarter" of New York, "a vast and compact city within a city," Jews found "incomparably fewer chances of contact with the English-speaking portion of the population than [in] Boston" (24). The fact that Jake transfers his enthusiasm from sport to dancing within that context strongly suggests that Cahan saw attendance at commercial dance halls and participation in the world of social dancing as a particularly immigrant activity created within the "Jewish quarter," rather than a more generally "American" leisure practice. Jake's reinvention of self as single, "gallant," and a dancer signals his self-imagination as a creature of the Lower East Side, reinforced by his catchphrase, "Dot'sh a'kin' a man *I* am!"

8. On Spanglish as a distinctive cultural and artistic phenomenon, see Aparicio, "La Vida," 147–160; Keller, "Literary Strategems."

9. For examples of dance manuals, see Cellarius, *Drawing-Room Dances*; L. Carpenter, *Universal Dancing Master*; Gilbert, *Round Dancing*.

10. That's not to say that young people were always successful in resisting the efforts of their parents, or even that they necessarily wanted to. The mores surrounding

socializing outside the family and participation in commercial leisure varied from one national and ethnic group to another. In 1910, as McBee observes, 29 percent of young Italian Americans between fifteen and nineteen years old were already married, while the numbers were much lower for eastern, western, and northern European girls. In addition, early marriage within one's ethnic group, and particularly to a partner from the same region or village, often staved off the deep loneliness felt by many young immigrants, particularly those who came to the United States alone or with only their nuclear families: "separated from their families, friends, and even parents when they left for America," these young people found "that marriage was the easiest way to reestablish the family ties they had lost" (McBee 34).

11. In their comprehensive 1911 report on prostitution, *The Social Evil in Chicago,* the Committee of Fifteen noted that dance halls were so poorly policed that formal and informal prostitution and casual sexual activity all flourished there. Many of the young women who frequented dance halls, mostly between the ages of seventeen and twenty-five, did not explicitly charge for sexual services but exchanged sex for drinks, a night on the town, or simply for their own pleasure (159). More shocking to the committee was the collusion between dance hall proprietors and the police. Beat officers were paid off or bribed with sexual favors or simply did not care about the sexual activities, commercial and otherwise, that transpired in dance halls.

Similarly, Louise de Koven Bowen deplored the flouting of dance hall regulations by young people, dance hall proprietors, and police. Observance of these rules was so lax that "minors are not only admitted unaccompanied by their parents but liquor is sold to them openly" (*Dance Halls* 3).

12. Lewenkrohn was the editor-in-chief of the *Settlement Journal* in 1905, the year that "Shadchen's Luck" was published. He later went on to write pulp boys' fiction under the name Elmer Sherwood, most notably the Lucky and Ted Marsh series.

13. It's striking that Lewenkrohn comments on how Annie and Joe meet. Certainly he did not have to explain the social mores of the dance hall to his fellow settlement members. The absence of formal introduction and the ease with which young women and men switched partners from dance to dance would hardly have occasioned comment. In part, he is adopting a trope familiar to writers of ethnic fiction of the time—a tone that assumes an outsider reader, someone for whom the story is as much ethnography as it is literature.

14. For an excellent discussion of the role of adolescent social clubs in working-class immigrant communities, see McBee, *Dance Hall Days.*

15. See, for example, the Henry Street advertisement in *Settlement Journal* 1.4:5 or 1.6:3. See Heicklen's School ads in *Settlement Journal* 1.5:15.

16. The International Ladies' Garment Workers Union reported that the average wage of young women in the white goods trade was $5.50 per week, out of which workers had to pay for their own thread, needles, machine electricity and any parts (*Ladies*

Garment Worker 4.3:1). Also, young women were much more heavily pressured to turn their pay over to their parents. In 1888, one study showed that 72 percent of female factory workers handed over all their pay to their parents. In the 1910s, things had changed very little: between three-quarters and four-fifths of young women surrendered all their pay, whereas young men submitted no more than one-half to cover room and board, not much different from the male boarders who lodged in many working-class immigrant homes (McBee 203).

17. For a discussion of the role and influence of the Castles on early-twentieth-century dance, see Badger, *Life in Ragtime*; I. Castle, *Castles in the Air*. For the Castles' own guide to dancing and their critique of "vulgar" ragtime dance, see *Modern Dancing*.

18. On a personal note, the descriptions of settlement dances in the early twentieth century reminded me intensely of my own experience at Jewish youth club dances in London in the early 1980s—the same gendered division of finances, the same intertwining of gossip, sexual experimentation, and homo- and heterosocial mixing, the same obsession with popular music and female passion for dance. Kathy Peiss's observation that "what mattered in the dance hall—popularity, dancing ability, fashionable clothes, and male attention—was a modern style that promised independence, romance, and pleasure" was equally true in my middle-class Jewish social circle (Peiss 114).

19. Bowen was particularly concerned by the intersection of capitalism and vice in the dance halls. She argued that "hundreds of young girls are annually started on the road to ruin, for the saloonkeepers and dance hall owners have only one end in view and that is profit" (*Dance Halls* 3).

20. As we have seen, Addams was deeply concerned with the rift between the immigrant generation and their children, both at work and at play. Her attention to dance halls was another facet of her desire to reunite parents and children within a multigenerational community.

21. In fact, the *Craftsman* magazine, a journal of the Arts and Crafts movement produced by Gustav Stickley, ran an article "by the editor" in 1914 entitled "The Relation of Dancing to a Commercial Age." Stickley combined a critique of the "overcommercialized age" in which Americans lived with an analysis of the dance craze that had swept the nation. He argued that the passion for dance was nature's way of evening the balance that had been disrupted by the mechanization of the era. "What is really happening," he claimed, was that dance had spread from its traditional arena of adolescence, and "that very young people are dancing and that middle-aged and elderly people are getting together evenings and practicing difficult steps and becoming more graceful, more interested in life and more cheerful" (241). In the context of capitalism, "we labor in order to be idle, and when we have labored so long that we have the time and the money to be idle we have forgotten how to be joyous." Dancing provides "our young people" with the "mental and spiritual occupation" of which industrialization robbed them; nature understood that the young "needed just what the dance has brought them, otherwise they would not have accepted it" (242). While in tone this is quite

different from the dance reform strategies of the settlement houses and social work agencies, it is quite similar in its attitude toward dancing as both potentially reuniting the generations and providing a counterpoint to the dehumanizing, disembodying effects of industrial consumer capital.

22. Of course, these objections to commercial entertainment were not motivated solely by a desire to counter an expanding mass culture. There was, as several commentators have noted, a significant amount of judgment caught up in the desire to create a rational, noncommercial system of recreation for the children of immigrants— judgments based on contempt for popular tastes, on a nostalgia for WASP hegemony, on fear of the social mobility implicit in commercialization. These arguments are extremely convincing, and I would not want to seem utopian in my representation of reformers like Addams, Bowen, and Israels. However, for the purposes of my discussion here, it is not enough to dismiss the elitism of the settlements or organizations like them. I am more interested in looking at how the concerns of reformers interfaced with dance halls and the young people who attended them, and the kinds of narratives that reformers constructed to render dance halls and their habitués both intelligible and malleable to their larger cultural projects.

23. The title page of *The Social Dance* lists Adams as the author of a number of other works, including *Exalted Manhood, Fighting the Ragtime Devil, Syphilis—the Black Plague,* and *The Negro Girl.* A fascinating figure, Adams was a leader in the African Methodist Episcopal (AME) church. He was named after Hiram R. Revels and James Alcorn: Revels was one of the few black army chaplains ministering to free black troops during the Civil War, an influential figure in the AME hierarchy, and later the first black senator from Mississippi; James Alcorn was a governor of Mississippi and founder of Alcorn College, a historically black college, of which Hiram Revels was the first president. As well as screeds, Revels Adams wrote the *Cyclopedia of African Methodism in Mississippi* (1902). He was a remarkable evangelist, converting thousands of believers, from Boston to Natchez to Chicago to Kansas City, where *The Social Dance* was published. He was editor of *Home Purity* magazine but was not averse to a little recreation himself, if exclusively in the service of God: his brief biography in Richard R. Wright's *Centennial Encyclopedia of the African Methodist Episcopal Church* (Philadelphia: Book Concern of the AME Church, 1916) mentions that Adams composed several musical productions, sings, "plays the piano, organ, cornet and violin, and directs his own choirs in evangelistic campaigns" (19).

24. As we've seen in *Yekl,* Adams was not completely wrong, although he reversed the cause and effect. As young women and men married later and had money to spend on themselves, commercial institutions like dance halls multiplied to absorb their disposable income. So social dancing became increasingly identified with unmarried adolescents.

25. At the same time, Revels Adams's objection to ragtime dancing in particular is consonant with the more mainstream discussions of social dancing. The association

between the various dances (which he lists at length: turkey trot, foxtrot, horse trot, fish walk, bunny hug, grizzly bear, buzzard lope, tiger dance, camel walk, hoochie coochie, shimmy, jazzamarimbo, shuffle) and animal movements was not innocent; rather, "it is well known that these animal dances are imitations of animals in their sex relations and sex exercise, and that they are intended to arouse sexual desire and result in sex satisfaction" (24).

26. The association's study was very comprehensive indeed. Agents visited hundreds of dance halls (338 in 1910 alone), from huge dance palaces to smaller establishments attached to saloons. They kept records as to approximately how many minors attended each dance, how many police officers were there, how many halls sold liquor, how many had water fountains, at how many there was "indecent conduct" or "immoral dancing," and so on (Bowen, *Dance Halls* 11–12).

27. The heterosociality of dance halls is a feature that several historians have commented upon; for example, see Peiss, *Cheap Amusements,* and McBee, *Dance Hall Days*. Of course, heterosociality does not mean gender equality, as both Peiss and McBee discuss; at the same time, dance halls did afford young women a level of mastery over their sexual lives, a chance to move between homosocial and heterosocial mixing, and a source of pleasure at which they had some skill.

28. Dance halls do appear earlier, but usually in connection with an earlier moral panic, that of "white slavery." In January 1910, the *Times* published an article connecting "low dance halls and amusement resorts" with the "social evil" (that is, prostitution) and "white slavery." With the remarkable political acuity that she brought to later discussions of ragtime dancing, Belle Israels linked the perceived epidemic of prostitution to the need for model dance halls, two of which the Committee on Amusements and Vacation Resources for Working Girls had already established, and "where the dangers of the social evil have been practically eliminated" ("Plan to Wipe Out White Slave Evil").

29. Commentators occasionally linked the popularity of the turkey trot with the new fashion for thinness among women. A *Times* reporter opined that "most of [the women learning the new dances] wanted to get thin. Slenderness was just getting to be the style about two years ago" ("Have You Tried"). An article in *Collier's* quoted a doctor defending the turkey trot as "the most sensible indoor amusement we have had in my experience as a practitioner—and the jolliest. It's making fat people thin, old men young, and young people content with elderly partners. . . . Naturally I believe in turkey trotting. There is nothing so moral as good health" ("Turkey Trot and Tango" 187–188).

30. In fact, Inglis came to the conclusion that the turkey trot was not indecent at all. His description of the dance as performed by visitors to a southern resort is mildly scandalized but mostly comical: "The man took the girl's right hand in his left, and they held their arms up, down, or curved, as fancy prompted them. The man half encircled the girl's waist with his right arm and drew her as near to him—or as hard pressed against him—as he wished or she permitted. They ambled or shuffled alternately forward or

backward and then spun around together half a dozen times. In the ambling or shuffling progress (I don't know its technical name) there was a certain resemblance to the waddling trot of the red-wattled turkey-gobbler as he struts among his hens in the spicy days of spring. This, I suppose, gives the dance its name. At various intervals in the music there came an accented beat, at which the dancers bent their knees halfway to the floor, sprang erect again, and resumed their rhythmic whirling" (11).

31. Of course, not everyone condemned the new dances. *The Independent,* a well-respected weekly, lauded ragtime dancing and the tango for the same qualities for which more conservative publications condemned it, making the audacious claim that "the new dances are better than the old." The insistence and rhythm of ragtime dance was, for *The Independent,* its virtue, "a rhythm as fascinating as it is primitive. When the world feels that rhythm pounding thru the strains of 'Too Much Mustard,' or other tune of the moment, it cannot help but dance" ("On Dancing" 383).

CHAPTER 5 — "YOUTH IS ALWAYS TURBULENT"

1. Several of the essays in Bourne's *Youth and Life* had first been published in the *Atlantic Monthly* in 1911 and 1912. Hereafter, *Youth and Life* will be cited in the text as *YL*.

2. Regarding their dismissal of the patriarchy, bohemians created for themselves a space in which, in Stansell's words, "metaphorical brothers and sisters might carry on 'life without a father'" (*American Moderns* 7).

3. I cite Mead's *Coming of Age in Samoa* as *COA* and her autobiography, *Blackberry Winter,* as *BW,* with appropriate page numbers.

4. It is possible that Bourne and Goldman met, particularly since Goldman was living in Harlem during Bourne's time at Columbia, but neither ever commented on an encounter. Goldman's magazine *Mother Earth* reprinted Bourne's antiwar essay "War Is the Health of the State" at the height of her fight against mandatory conscription during the First World War, and they shared acquaintances and a number of political beliefs, particularly in terms of educational reform. Mead missed the possibility of meeting either Bourne or Goldman by a hair: she arrived in New York in the summer of 1920, a year and a half after Goldman's deportation to Russia and Bourne's death from influenza, both of which took place on the same Christmas weekend of 1918. However, Ruth Benedict had lived in New York for several years by the time she became close to Mead, and given her connections to bohemian institutions like Heterodoxy, of which Bourne's close friend Alyse Gregory was an active member, it is more likely that Benedict met either Bourne or Goldman or both.

5. For a thorough discussion of the etiology and expression of bohemianism, see Wilson, *Bohemians.*

6. Thanks to Joseph Entin for pointing out this connection to me.

7. It bears pointing out that the generation that Bourne and his contemporaries derogated had its own sense of revolutionary difference from *its* forebears. While the

bohemians painted their elders with a fairly broad brush, in fact much of the previous generation had itself participated in momentous social change: the rise of anarchism in the 1880s; the sweeping legal reforms of the Progressive Era; the emergence of college-educated, independent women, black and white, who staffed settlement houses and women's clubs and who agitated for the vote; and, of course, the birth of an organized labor movement. It is true that many of these movements were segregated by sex, and mostly characterized by a sexual propriety (not to say prudishness) that for later eras defined the nineteenth century. And, of course, the great dividing line of Freudian psychoanalysis was for the bohemians the cultural Rubicon that they had been the first to cross, a boundary that forever separated them from their parents' generation. One of the few major figures of the nineteenth century who managed to cross that divide was Emma Goldman, in part because of her stupendous powers of self-promotion, in part because of her focus on sexual frankness and sexual freedom, and in part, as we shall see, because she provided a link between bohemian Greenwich Village and the radical (and often Jewish) Lower East Side.

8. This embrace was not without ambivalence, however—as Bourne's later essay "War Is the Health of the State" argued, modernity's greatest invention, the nation state, is constructed and maintained through nationalist violence.

9. Founded in 1911, the Ferrer Center was a remarkable institution. A radical version of the settlement house or the Educational Alliance, the center was a cultural hub that housed the Modern School—a school organized around the principles that children learn by play and that reason is more important than discipline—as well as adult education programs, theater groups, art classes, sex education courses, and political activism. Combining anarchism, bohemianism, free-speech activism, European radicalism, and sexual libertarianism, the Ferrer Center brought together artists like Robert Henri and Man Ray, activists, and writers along with a variety of immigrants and their children, mostly Jewish, but also Italian and other Europeans.

10. Tellingly, one place that bohemians deliberately imitated their working-class counterparts was on the dance floor. At the Liberal Club, claimed by bohemians in 1912 and reconstituted on MacDougal Street, members held weekly dances—"not mannerly waltzes but the turkey trot and the shimmy, imported from 'low' working-class dance halls" (Stansell, *American Moderns* 81).

11. I cite Goldman's autobiography, *Living My Life,* as LML, with appropriate page numbers.

12. See, for example, Millett, *Sexual Politics* (1969), which argues that "contemporary patriarchies . . . [wives'] chattel status continues in their loss of name, their obligation to adopt the husband's domicile, and the general legal assumption that marriage involves an exchange of the female's domestic service and [sexual] consortium in return for financial support"(34–35); and Dworkin, "Feminism: An Agenda" (1983): "Like prostitution, marriage is an institution that is extremely oppressive and dangerous for women" (136).

13. See my analysis of the age and national origins of urban workforces in chapter 1. The preponderance of young people in the industrial workforce in New York is reinforced by David von Drehle's detective work in reconstructing the list of the workers who died in the Triangle Shirtwaist fire. Of the 140 victims he traced, 114 were twenty-four or under (four are labeled "age unknown," and another six "unidentified"; given the numbers, it's likely that the majority of them were also young women and men). Because most of the young victims were identified by parents, siblings, or "sweethearts," we can infer that the majority were unmarried.

14. When Ruth Benedict took a course with Elsie Clews Parsons, "Women and the Social Order," Parsons asked students why they were interested in the class. Benedict replied "that she hoped to learn ways of criticizing contemporary society through studying pre-state ones and of lessening her 'blindness about conventions'" (Banner 147–148).

15. This is not to trivialize Boas's deeply held antiracism, which Benedict and Mead echoed. It is, however, to make a distinction between beliefs and action, between scholarship and activism.

16. Of course, the teenager who feels "different from everyone else" or as if she or he is "playing a role" is a familiar trope of adolescence. We can pick out any number of outsiders, rebels, or losers, from Sara Smolinsky of Anzia Yezierska's *Bread Givers* or Clyde Griffiths of Theodore Dreiser's *An American Tragedy* to Caleb Trask of John Steinbeck's *East of Eden* and Holden Caulfield of J. D. Salinger's *The Catcher in the Rye*.

17. Hilary Lapsley speculates that Mead's sense of herself as an outsider at DePauw was linked to her growing recognition of her sexual desire for her friend Katherine Rothenberger and her "suppressed fear that I after all am primarily a homosexual person" (qtd in Lapsley 26).

18. New Zealand anthropologist Derek Freeman led the most public of the debates over *Coming of Age*. Freeman constructed much of his career around debunking Mead's findings, most comprehensively in his 1983 book *Margaret Mead and Samoa: The Making and Unmaking of an Anthropological Myth*, in which he claimed that Mead's informants had deliberately misled her, and that Mead herself had engaged in a sexual relationship with a male Samoan, giving her an incentive to represent the Samoans as sexually unfettered. More recently, Freeman participated in a roundtable on Mead in *Current Anthropology* in 2000.

EPILOGUE

1. Thanks to Sabrina Vellucci for this reference.

2. Zelizer points to the potential danger of payment for dependence. If parents linked allowances to domestic labor, they ran the risk of "commercializing the home" and endangering the sacred domesticity of the private sphere. But if children did not have to earn the money they received for allowances, commentators feared that they would develop the habit of expecting something for nothing as adults. The solution was

to see allowances as "educational," that is, teaching children the value of money and how to spend it (*Pricing* 107–108).

3. Grace Palladino talks about this in detail in *Teenagers: An American History*. She traces the development of advertising culture more generally in the 1950s and links the mainstreaming of teenage identity through marketing and teen-oriented magazines like *Seventeen*.

4. Leerom Medovoi's *Rebels: Youth and the Cold War Origins of Identity* takes on the image of the teen rebel in the 1950s. Provocatively, Medovoi argues that "the rebel," particularly "the bad boy," was a necessary part of 1950s popular culture as a corollary and corrective to the man in the gray flannel suit. In its new identity as the "leader of the Free World," the United States "required figures who could represent America's emancipatory character, whether in relation to the Soviet Union, the new nations of the third world, or even its own suburbs," Medovoi claims (1). In an interesting reworking of the origins of adolescence in the urban working class, Medovoi charts how rock 'n' roll grew out of musical commodities such as R&B and country music, and repurposed those genres for a new, largely white, suburban teenage audience, geared to their interests. Songs about punching out for the weekend and going to the local bar, for example, became songs about getting out of school on a Friday afternoon and driving around looking for fun. Most interesting is his thesis that the self-contained identity of "teenage rebel" made space for the identity politics of the 1970s and 1980s.

5. A brief LexisNexis search for "helicopter parent" yielded almost a hundred hits from sources as varied as the *Omaha World-Herald* to the London *Evening Standard* to *The Australian*.

Bibliography

Abbott, Berenice. "Photography at the Crossroads" (1951). In *Classic Essays in Photography*, ed. Trachtenberg, 177–185.

Adams, Myron E. "Children in the American Street Trades." *Annals of the American Academy* 25 (May 1905): 437–458. Rpt. in *Selected Articles on Child Labor*, ed. Bullock, 97–105.

Adams, Revels A. *The Social Dance*. Kansas City: Published by the author, 1921.

Addams, Jane. *The Spirit of Youth and the City Streets*. New York: Macmillan, 1909.

———. *Twenty Years at Hull-House* (1910). New York: Signet/NAL, 1981.

Adler, Felix. "Child Labor in the United States." *Annals of the American Academy* 25 (1905): 419–429. Rpt. in *Selected Articles on Child Labor*, ed. Bullock, 18–25.

Alexander, Ruth M. *The "Girl Problem": Female Sexual Delinquency in New York, 1900–1930*. Ithaca, N.Y.: Cornell University Press, 1995.

Alpers, Svetlana. "The Museum as a Way of Seeing." In *Exhibiting Cultures*, ed. Karp and Lavine, 27–42.

Antin, Mary. *The Promised Land* (1912). New York: Random House, 2001.

Aparicio, Frances R. "La Vida Es un Spanglish Disparatero: Bilingualism in Nuyorican Poetry." In *European Perspectives on Hispanic Literature of the United States*, ed. Genevieve Fabre, 147–160. Houston: Arte Publico Press, 1988.

"Approve the Turkey Trot: Philadelphia Society Leaders Are Taking Lessons in Latest Dance." *New York Times*, December 12, 1911.

Ashmore, Ruth. *Side Talks with Girls*. New York: Charles Scribner's Sons, 1895.

Austin, Joe, and Michael Nevin Willard, eds. *Generations of Youth: Youth Cultures and History in Twentieth Century America*. New York: New York University Press, 1998.

Badger, Reid. *A Life in Ragtime: A Biography of James Reese Europe*. New York: Oxford University Press, 1995.

Bailey, Beth L. *From Front Porch to Back Seat: Courtship in Twentieth Century America*. Baltimore: Johns Hopkins University Press, 1988.

Bancroft, Hubert. *The Book of the Fair*. Chicago: Bancroft, 1893.

Banner, Lois W. *Intertwined Lives: Margaret Mead, Ruth Benedict, and Their Circle*. New York: Alfred A. Knopf, 2003.

Baxendall, Michael. "Exhibiting Intention: Some Preconditions of the Visual Display of Culturally Purposeful Objects." In *Exhibiting Cultures*, ed. Karp and Lavine, 33–41.

Beck, Leonora. "Movement to Restrict Child Labor." *Arena* 28 (1902): 370–378. Rpt. in *Selected Articles on Child Labor*, ed. Bullock, 9–17.

"Beckie Fisher: A Russian-Jewish Girl." *Ladies' Garment Worker* 2.10 (1911): 12.

Bederman, Gail. *Manliness and Civilization: A Cultural History of Gender and Race in the United States, 1880–1917.* Chicago: University of Chicago Press, 1995.

Berger, John. "Appearances." In *Another Way of Telling*, by John Berger and Jean Mohr, 81–130. New York: Vintage, 1995.

Bernadin, Susan, Melody Graulich, Lisa Macfarlane, and Nicole Tonkovich. *Trading Gazes: Euro-American Women Photographers and Native North Americans, 1880–1940.* New Brunswick, N.J.: Rutgers University Press, 2003.

Blake, Casey. "The Young Intellectuals and the Culture of Personality." *ALH* 1.3 (1989): 510–534.

Blaustein, David. *Memoirs of David Blaustein, Educator and Communal Worker* (1913). Arranged by Miriam Blaustein. New York: Arno Press, 1975.

Boen, Jennifer "'Helicopter Parenting' Hurts More Than Helps." *Fort Wayne News-Sentinel*, January 15, 2007. http://web.lexis-nexis.com.proxy.wexler.hunter.cuN.Y. .edu/universe/document?_m=ae9fe6e77502d7f0ef06bd5470a56fb8&_docnum=71&wchp=dGLbVzb-zSkVA&_md5=d066034c5e5d1388812dd7c8f5807996. Accessed January 25, 2007.

Borus, David H. "The Strange Career of American Bohemianism." *ALH* 14.2 (2002): 376–388.

Bourne, Randolph S. *The Letters of Randolph Bourne.* Ed. Eric J. Sandeen. Troy, N.Y.: Whiteston, 1981.

———. *Youth and Life* (1913). Freeport, N.Y.: Books for Libraries Press, 1967.

Bowen, Louise de Koven. *The Department Store Girl: Based upon Interviews with 200 Girls.* Chicago: Juvenile Protection Agency of Chicago, 1911.

———. *The Public Dance Halls of Chicago.* Chicago: Juvenile Protection Agency of Chicago, 1917.

Boyer, Paul. *Urban Masses and Moral Order in America, 1820–1920.* Cambridge, Mass.: Harvard University Press, 1978.

Breckenridge, Sophonisba P. *New Homes for Old.* New York: Harper Brothers, 1921. Rpt. Montclair, N.J.: Patterson Smith, 1971.

Bremen, Carrie Tirado. "The Urban Picturesque and the Spectacle of Americanization." *American Quarterly* 52.3 (2000): 444–477.

Brooks, Gwendolyn. *Blacks.* Chicago: David, 1987.

Brown, Edward F. "Child Labor in New York Canning Factories." *Child Labor Bulletin* 1.3 (1912): 12–16.

Brown, Julie K. *Contesting Images: Photography and the World's Columbian Exposition.* Tucson: University of Arizona Press, 1994.

Brumberg, Joan Jacobs. *The Body Project: An Intimate History of American Girls*. New York: Random House, 1997.

Bullock, Edna, ed. *Selected Articles on Child Labor*. Minneapolis: H. W. Wilson, 1911.

Burton, Benedict. "Rituals of Representations: Ethnic Stereotypes and Colonized Peoples at World's Fairs." In *Fair Representations*, ed. Robert W. Rydell and Nancy Guinn, 28–61. Amsterdam: Amsterdam University Press, 1994.

Butler, Judith. *Gender Trouble: Feminism and the Subversion of Identity*. New York: Routledge, 1990.

Cahan, Abraham. *Yekl: A Tale of the New York Ghetto* (1896). In *Yekl and the Imported Bridegroom and Other Stories of Yiddish New York*. New York: Dover Publications, 1970.

Carpenter, Lucien. *J. W. Pepper's Universal Dancing Master, Prompter's Book and Violinist's Guide*. Philadelphia: J. W. Pepper, 1882.

Carpenter, Niles. *Immigrants and Their Children, 1920*. Washington, D.C.: U.S. Government Printing Office, 1924. Rpt. New York: Arno Press, 1969.

Castle, Irene. *Castles in the Air*. New York: Doubleday, 1958.

Castle, Irene, and Vernon Castle. *Modern Dancing*. New York: World Syndicate, 1914.

Cellarius, Henri. *The Drawing-Room Dances*. London: E. Churton, 1847.

Chesser, Elizabeth Sloan. "Half-Times in the Factories." *Westminster Review* 172 (October 1909): 406–409. Rpt. in *Selected Articles on Child Labor*, ed. Bullock, 83–86.

Chicago Vice Commission. *The Social Evil in Chicago: A Study of Existing Conditions with Recommendations by the Vice Commission of Chicago*. Chicago: Gunthorp-Warren Printing, 1911.

Chinn, Sarah E. *Technology and the Logic of American Racism: A Cultural History of the Body as Evidence*. New York: Continuum Books, 2000.

Clement, Priscilla Ferguson. *Growing Pains: Children in the Industrial Age, 1850–1890*. New York: Twayne, 1997.

Cohen, Lizabeth. *Making a New Deal: Industrial Workers in Chicago, 1919–1939*. New York: Cambridge University Press, 1991.

Cohen, Rose. *Out of the Shadow: A Russian Jewish Girlhood on the Lower East Side* (1918). Ithaca, N.Y.: Cornell University Press, 1995.

Committee of Fifteen. *The Social Evil, with Special Reference to Conditions Existing in the City of New York*. New York: G. P. Putnam's Sons, 1902.

Courtwright, David T. *Violent Land: Single Men and Social Disorder from the Frontier to the Inner City*. Cambridge, Mass.: Harvard University Press, 1996.

Covello, Leonard, with Guido D'Agostino. *The Heart Is the Teacher*. New York: McGraw-Hill, 1958.

Cox, Julian, and Colin Ford. *Julia Margaret Cameron: The Complete Photographs*. Los Angeles: Getty Publications, 2003.

Crane, Lydia Hale. "The Messenger Boy." *Child Labor Bulletin* 3.2 (1914): 23–26.

Crane, Stephen. *Maggie, a Girl of the Streets* (1894). New York: Modern Library, 2001.

Crew, Spencer R., and James E. Sims. "Locating Authenticity: Fragments of a Dialogue." In *Exhibiting Cultures*, ed. Karp and Levine, 159–175.

Crocker, Ruth. "Unsettling Perspectives: The Settlement Movement, the Rhetoric of Social History, and the Search for Synthesis." In *Contesting the Master Narrative: Essays in Social History*, ed. Jeffery Cox and Shelton Stromquist, 179–193. Iowa City: University of Iowa Press, 1998.

Crow, Lester D., and Alice Crow. *Our Teenage Boys and Girls: Suggestions for Parents, Teachers, and Other Youth Leaders*. New York: McGraw-Hill, 1945.

Davidov, Judith Fryer. *Women's Camera Work: Self/Body/Other in American Visual Culture*. Durham, N.C.: Duke University Press, 1998.

Davis, Natalie Zemon. "Charivari, Honor, and Community in Seventeenth-Century Lyon and Geneva." In *Rite, Drama, Festival, Spectacle: Rehearsals toward a Theory of Cultural Performance*, ed. John J. MacAloon, 42–57. Philadelphia: Institute for the Study of Human Issues, 1984.

Dennett, Andrea Stulman. *Weird and Wonderful: The Dime Museum in America*. New York: New York University Press, 1997.

Dewey, John. "My Pedagogic Creed." *School Journal* 54.3 (1897): 77–80.

———. *The School and Society*. Chicago: University of Chicago Press, 1915.

Di Leonardo, Micaela. *Exotics at Home: Anthropologies, Others, American Modernity*. Chicago: University of Chicago Press, 1998.

Dimock, George, ed. *Priceless Children: American Photographs, 1890–1925: Child Labor and the Pictorialist Ideal*. Seattle: University of Washington Press, 2001.

———. "Priceless Children: Child Labor and the Pictorialist Ideal." In *Priceless Children*, ed. Dimock, 7–23.

Divers, Vivia H. *The "Black Hole"; or, The Missionary Experience of a Girl in the Slums of Chicago, 1891–1892*. N.p., 1893.

Dougherty, James. "Jane Addams: Culture and Imagination." *Yale Review* 71 (1982): 363–379.

Dreiser, Theodore. *Sister Carrie* (1900). New York: Signet Classics, 1983.

Dunbar, Paul Laurence. *The Sport of the Gods* (1902). New York: Modern Library, 2005.

Dworkin, Andrea. "Feminism: An Agenda" (1983). *Letters from a War Zone*. Brooklyn, N.Y.: Lawrence Hill Books, 1993.

Editorial. *Ladies' Garment Worker* 4.3 (1913): 1–2.

Egan, Leona Rust. *Provincetown as a Stage: Provincetown, The Provincetown Players, and the Discovery of Eugene O'Neill*. Orleans, Mass.: Parnassus, 1994.

Enstad, Nan. *Ladies of Labor, Girls of Adventure: Working Women, Popular Culture, and Labor Politics at the Turn of the Twentieth Century*. New York: Columbia University Press, 1999.

Ewen, Elizabeth. *Immigrant Women in the Land of Dollars: Life and Culture on the Lower East Side, 1890–1925*. New York: Monthly Review Press, 1992.

Ferraro, Thomas. *Feeling Italian: The Art of Ethnicity in America*. New York: New York University Press, 2005.

Fitzgerald, F. Scott. "Winter Dreams." *The Short Stories of F. Scott Fitzgerald*. New York: Scribner, 1995.

Gardner, Ella. *Public Dance Halls: Their Regulation and Place in the Recreation of Adolescents*. Washington, D.C.: U.S. Government Printing Office, 1929.

Garvey, Ellen Gruber. *The Adman in the Parlor: Magazines and the Gendering of Consumer Culture, 1880s to 1910s*. New York: Oxford University Press, 1996.

Gessel, Arnold, Frances L. Ilg, and Louise Bates Ames. *Youth: The Years from Ten to Sixteen*. New York: Harper and Row, 1956.

Gettis, Victoria. "Experts and Juvenile Delinquency, 1900–1935." In *Generations of Youth*, ed. Austin and Willard, 21–35.

Gilbert, Melvin Ballou. *Round Dancing*. Portland, Maine: M. B. Gilbert, 1890.

Glassgold, Peter, ed. *Anarchy! An Anthology of Emma Goldman's Mother Earth*. Washington, D.C.: Counterpoint, 2001.

Goldman, Emma. *Living My Life: An Autobiography* (1931). Salt Lake City, Utah: Peregrine Smith, 1982.

———. "The White Slave Traffic." In Glassgold, *Anarchy!* 113–119.

Griffith, Farah Jasmine. *Who Set You Flowin': The African-American Migration Narrative*. New York: Oxford University Press, 1995.

Haenni, Sabine. "Visual and Theatrical Culture, Tenement Fiction, and the Immigrant Subject in Abraham Cahan's *Yekl*." *American Literature* 71.3 (1999): 493–527.

Hall, G. Stanley. *Adolescence: Its Psychology and Its Relations to Physiology, Anthropology, Sociology, Sex, Crime, Religion, and Education*. 2 vols. New York: D. Appleton, 1904. Rpt. New York: Arno Press and the New York Times, 1969.

Hapgood, Hutchins. *The Spirit of the Ghetto* (1902). Cambridge, Mass.: Belknap Press, 1967.

Hapke, Laura. *Tales of the Working Girl: Wage-Earning Women in American Literature, 1890–1925*. New York: Twayne, 1992.

Harrison, Simon. "Identity as a Scarce Resource." *Social Anthropology* 7.3 (1999): 239–251.

"Have You Tried the 'Long Boston' Dance?" *New York Times*, January 29, 1911.

Higonnet, Anne. *Pictures of Innocence: The History and Crisis of Ideal Childhood*. New York: Thames and Hudson, 1998.

Hindman, Hugh D. *Child Labor: An American History*. Armonk, N.Y.: M. E. Sharpe, 2002.

Hine, Lewis W. "Contrasts." *Child Labor Bulletin* 1.2 (1912): 36–38, 62–66.

———. "The High Cost of Child Labor." *Child Labor Bulletin* 3.4 (1914): 63–65.

———. *Men at Work* (1938). Mineola, N.Y.: Dover Publications, 1977.

———. "Social Photography" (1909). In *Classic Essays on Photography*, ed. Trachtenberg, 109–113.

———. *Women at Work*. Mineola, N.Y.: Dover Publications, 1981.

Horowitz, Helen Lefkowitz. *Rereading Sex: Battles over Sexual Knowledge and Suppression in Nineteenth-Century America*. New York: Alfred A. Knopf, 2002.

Hutchinson, Woods. "Overworked Children on the Farm and in the School." *Annals of the American Academy* 333 (March 1909): 116–121. Rpt. in *Selected Articles on Child Labor*, ed. Bullock, 112–116.

Hurston, Zora Neale. *The Sanctified Church: The Folklore Writings of Zora Neale Hurston*. New York: Avalon, 1998.

"Influence of Social Follies." *New York Times*, January 5, 1912.

Inglis, William. "Is Modern Dancing Indecent?" *Harper's Weekly* 57 (May 17, 1913), 11–12.

Israels, Belle Lindner. "The Way of the Girl." *Survey* 22 (1909): 486–497.

Jackson, Shannon. *Lines of Activity: Performance, Historiography, and Hull-House Domesticity*. Ann Arbor: University of Michigan Press, 2000.

Jacobs, Harriet. *Incidents in the Life of a Slave Girl, Written by Herself*. Cambridge, Mass.: Harvard University Press, 1987.

Jerome, Amalie Hofer. "The Playground as a Social Center." *Annals of the American Academy of Political and Social Science* 35 (1910): 129–133.

Johnson, James Weldon. *Autobiography of an Ex-Colored Man* (1912). New York: Penguin Books, 1990.

Joselit, Jenna Weissman. *The Wonders of America: Reinventing Jewish Culture, 1880–1950*. New York: Hill and Wang, 1994.

Karp, Ivan. "Cultures in Museum Perspective." In *Exhibiting Cultures*, ed. Karp and Lavine, 373–385.

Karp, Ivan, and Steven D. Lavine, eds. *Exhibiting Cultures: The Poetics and Politics of Museum Display*. Washington, D.C.: Smithsonian Institute Press, 1991.

Keller, Gary. "The Literary Strategems Available to Bilingual Chicano Writers." In *The Identification and Analysis of Chicano Literature*, ed. Francisco J'menez. New York: Bilingual Press, 1979.

Kelley, Florence. "The Sweating System." In Residents of Hull-House, *Hull-House Maps and Papers*, 25–45.

Kelley, Florence, and Alzina P. Stevens. "Wage Earning Children." In Residents of Hull-House. *Hull-House Maps and Papers*, 49–76.

Kett, Joseph F. *Rites of Passage: Adolescence in America, 1790 to the Present*. New York: Basic Books, 1977.

Kirkland, James H. "School as a Force Arrayed against Child Labor." *Annals of the American Academy* 25 (May 1905): 558–562. Rpt. in *Selected Articles on Child Labor*, ed. Bullock, 87–88.

Kirshenblatt-Gimblett, Barbara. "Objects of Ethnography." In *Exhibiting Cultures*, ed. Karp and Lavine, 386–443.

Kisseloff, Jeff. *You Must Remember This: An Oral History of Manhattan from the 1880s to World War II*. New York: Harcourt Brace Jovanovich, 1989.

Klein, Naomi. *No Logo: No Space, No Choice, No Jobs*. New York: Picador, 2002.

Lapsley, Hilary. *Margaret Mead and Ruth Benedict: The Kinship of Women*. Amherst: University of Massachusetts Press, 1999.

Lathrop, Julia C. *The Child, the Clinic, and the Court*. New York: New Republic, 1925.

LeSueur, Meridel. "A Remembrance." In Goldman, *Living My Life*, xiii–xvi.

Levine, Lawrence W. *Highbrow, Lowbrow: The Emergence of Cultural Hierarchy in America*. Cambridge, Mass.: Harvard University Press, 1988.

Lewenkrohn, Samuel. "Shadchen's Luck." *Settlement Journal* 2.2 (1905): 1–2.

Lewis, Sinclair. *Babbitt* (1922). New York: Signet Classics, 1997.

Lindstrom, J. A. "'Almost Worse Than the Restrictive Measures': Chicago Reformers and the Nickelodeons." *Cinema Journal* 39.1 (1999): 90–112.

Linhart, Solomon. "One Ballad of the Ball." *Settlement Journal* 1.4 (1904): 6.

Lloyd, Phoebe "Posthumous Mourning Portraiture." In *A Time to Mourn: Expressions of Grief in Nineteenth Century America*, ed. Martha V. Pike and Janice Gray Armstrong, 79–82. Stony Brook, N.Y.: Museums at Stony Brook, 1980.

Lovejoy, Owen R. "Unsettled Questions about Child Labor." *Annals of the American Academy* 33 (1909): 49–62. Rpt. in *Selected Articles on Child Labor*, ed. Bullock, 40–54.

Mangano, Antonio. *Sons of Italy: A Social and Religious Study of the Italians in America*. New York: Missionary Education Movement of the United States and Canada, 1917.

Mazón, Mauricio. *The Zoot-Suit Riots: The Psychology of Symbolic Annihilation*. Austin: University of Texas Press, 1984.

McBee, Randy. *Dance Hall Days: Intimacy and Leisure among Working-Class Immigrants in the United States*. New York: New York University Press, 2000.

McCandless, Barbara. "The Portrait Studio and the Celebrity: Promoting the Art." In *Photography in Nineteenth Century America*, ed. Sandweiss, 48–75.

Mead, Margaret. *Blackberry Winter: My Earlier Years*. New York: William Morrow, 1972.

———. *Coming of Age in Samoa: A Psychological Study of Primitive Youth for Western Civilization*. New York: Blue Ribbon Books, 1928.

Medovoi, Leerom. *Rebels: Youth and the Cold War Origins of Identity*. Durham, N.C.: Duke University Press, 2006.

Miller, Kerby A. "Class, Culture, and Immigrant Group Identity in the United States: The Case of Irish-American Ethnicity." In *Immigration Reconsidered*, ed. Yans-McLaughlin, 96–129.

Millett, Kate. *Sexual Politics*. New York: Avon Books, 1969.

Mitchell, W.J.T. *Picture Theory: Essays on Verbal and Visual Representation*. Chicago: University of Chicago Press, 1994.

Model, Suzanne W. "Work and Family: Blacks and Immigrants from South and Eastern Europe." In *Immigration Reconsidered*, ed. Yans-McLaughlin, 130–159.

Montgomery, Louise. *The American Girl in the Stockyards District: A Study of Chicago's Stockyards Community*. Vol. 2. Chicago: University of Chicago Press, 1913.

Moore, Deborah Dash. *At Home in America: Second Generation New York Jews*. New York: Columbia University Press, 1981.

Morrison, Toni. *Playing in the Dark: Blackness and the White Imagination*. New York: Vintage Books, 1993.

"Municipal Dance-Halls." *The Outlook* 101 (1912): 902–903.

Nasaw, David. *Children of the City: At Work, at Play*. New York: Oxford University Press, 1985.

———. *Going Out: The Rise and Fall of Public Amusements*. New York: Basic Books, 1993.

Newman, Pauline. "Child Labor—A Menace." *Child Labor Bulletin* 3.1 (1914): 42–45.

———. "Impression of the Recent Convention of the Women's Trade Union League at Boston." *Ladies' Garment Worker* 2.8 (1911): 11–12.

———. "Our Women Workers." *Ladies' Garment Worker* 4.6 (1915): 31–34.

"New York's Biggest Problem Not Police but Girls." *New York Times*, August 14, 1912.

Nichols, Francis H. "Children of the Coal Shadow." *McClure's* 20 (February 1903): 435–444. Rpt. in *Selected Articles on Child Labor*, ed. Bullock, 133–141.

Odem, Mary E. *Delinquent Daughters: Protecting and Policing Adolescent Female Sexuality in the United States, 1880–1920*. Chapel Hill: University of North Carolina Press, 1995.

———. "Teenage Girls, Sexuality, and Working Class Parents in Early Twentieth-Century California." In *Generations of Youth*, ed. Austin and Willard, 50–64.

Olcott, Margaret (Rita) O'Donovan. *Song in His Heart*. New York: House of Field, 1939.

"On Dancing and Some New Dances." *The Independent* 77 (1913): 383.

Palladino, Grace. *Teenagers: An American History*. New York: Basic Books, 1996.

Paradise, Viola. "The Jewish Girl in Chicago." *Survey* 30 (1913): 700–703.

Parlor Songs Association. *Parlor Songs.* www.parlorsongs.com. Accessed March 20, 2004.

Peffer, George Anthony. *If They Don't Bring Their Women Here: Chinese Female Immigration before Exclusion.* Urbana and Chicago: University of Illinois Press, 1999.

Peiss, Kathy. *Cheap Amusements: Working Women and Leisure in Turn-of-the-Century New York.* Philadelphia: Temple University Press, 1986.

Perry, Elisabeth Israels. *Belle Moskowitz: Feminine Politics and the Exercise of Power in the Age of Alfred E. Smith.* New York: Oxford University Press, 1987.

———. " 'The General Motherhood of the Commonwealth': Dance Hall Reform in the Progressive Era." *American Quarterly* 37 (1985): 719–733.

Petry, Ann. *The Street* (1946). New York: Mariner Books, 1998.

Pinzer, Maimie. *The Maimie Papers: Letters from an Ex-Prostitute.* Ed. Ruth Rosen and Sue Davidson. New York: Feminist Press of CUNY, 1997.

"Plan to Wipe Out White Slave Evil." *New York Times,* January 25, 1910.

Polacheck, Hilda Satt. *I Came a Stranger: The Story of a Hull-House Girl.* Edited by Dena J. Polacheck Epstein. Urbana and Chicago: University of Illinois Press, 1989.

Residents of Hull-House. *Hull-House Maps and Papers: A Presentation of Nationalities and Wages in a Congested District of Chicago.* New York and Boston: Thomas Y. Cromwell, 1895. Rpt. New York: Arno Press, 1970.

Rich, Jessie P. "Ideal Child Labor in the Home." *Child Labor Bulletin* 3.1 (1914): 98–102.

Riis, Jacob. *How the Other Half Lives* (1890). Mineola, N.Y.: Dover Publications, 1971.

Rosen, Ruth. *The Lost Sisterhood: Prostitution in America, 1900–1918.* Baltimore: Johns Hopkins University Press, 1982.

Rotundo, E. Anthony. *American Manhood: Transformation in Masculinity from the Revolution to the Modern Era.* New York: Basic Books, 1993.

Rousmaniere, John P. "Cultural Hybrid in the Slums: The College Woman and the Settlement House, 1889–1894." *American Quarterly* 22 (1970): 45–66.

Rydell, Robert W. *All the World's a Fair: Visions of Empire at American International Expositions, 1876–1916.* Chicago: University of Chicago Press, 1984.

Sanchez, George J. *Becoming Mexican American: Ethnicity, Culture, and Identity in Chicano Los Angeles, 1900–1945.* New York: Oxford University Press, 1993.

Sánchez-Eppler, Karen. *Dependent States: The Child's Part in Nineteenth-Century American Culture.* Chicago: University of Chicago Press, 2005.

Sandeen, Eric J. "Bourne Again: The Correspondence between Randolph Bourne and Elsie Clews Parsons." *ALH* 1.3 (1989): 489–509.

Sandweiss, Martha A. "Photography in Nineteenth-Century America: The Faithful Image of Our Time." In *Photography in Nineteenth Century America,* ed. Sandweiss, xiiii–xv.

———. "Undecisive Moments: The Narrative Tradition in Western Photography." In *Photography in Nineteenth Century America*, ed. Sandweiss, 98–129.

———, ed. *Photography in Nineteenth Century America*. New York: Harry N. Abrams, 1991.

Satt, Hilda. "The Old Woman and the New World." *The Butterfly* 3 (1909): 4–5.

Sawaya, Francesca. "Domesticity, Cultivation, and Vocation in Jane Addams and Sarah Orne Jewett." *Nineteenth Century Literature* 48 (1994): 507–528.

"Social Workers See Real 'Turkey Trots.'" *New York Times* January 27, 1912.

Solomon-Godeau, Abigail. *Photography at the Dock: Essays on Photographic History, Institutions, and Practices*. Minneapolis: University of Minnesota Press, 1991.

Sontag, Susan. *On Photography*. New York: Dell, 1973.

Stange, Maren. *Symbols of Ideal Life: Social Documentary Photography, 1890–1950*. New York: Cambridge University Press, 1989.

Stansell, Christine. *American Moderns: Bohemian New York and the Creation of a New Century*. New York: Henry Holt, 2000.

———. *City of Women: Sex and Class in New York, 1789–1860*. Urbana and Chicago: University of Illinois Press, 1986.

Stearns, Peter N. *American Cool: Constructing a Twentieth-Century Emotional Style*. New York: New York University Press, 1994.

Stickley, Gustav. "The Relation of Dancing to the Commercial Age." *Craftsman* (1914): 241–243.

Stoneley, Peter. *Consumerism and American Girls' Literature, 1860–1940*. New York: Cambridge University Press, 2003.

Taeuber, Conrad, and Irene B. Taeuber. *The Changing Population of the United States*. New York: John Wiley and Sons, 1958.

Takaki, Ronald. *Iron Cages: Race and Culture in 19th Century America*. New York: Oxford University Press, 1990.

Tarkington, Booth. *Seventeen*. New York: Grosset and Dunlap, 1915.

Tilly, Charles. "Transplanted Networks." In *Immigration Reconsidered*, ed. Yans-McLaughlin, 79–95.

Tompkins, Jane. *Sensational Designs: The Cultural Work of American Fiction, 1790–1860*. New York: Oxford University Press, 1985.

Toomer, Jean. *Cane* (1923). New York: Liveright, 1993.

Trachtenberg, Alan. *The Incorporation of America: Culture and Society in the Gilded Age*. New York: Farrar, Straus and Giroux, 1982.

———. "Photography: The Emergence of a Keyword." In *Photography in Nineteenth Century America*, ed. Sandweiss, 17–47.

———. *Reading American Photographs: Images as History, Mathew Brady to Walker Evans.* New York: Hill and Wang, 1989.

———, ed. *Classic Essays on Photography.* New Haven: Leete's Island Books, 1980.

True, Ruth. *The Neglected Girl.* In *West Side Studies.* New York: Trow Press, 1914.

"Turkey Trot and Tango—A Disease or a Remedy?" *Current Opinion* 55 (1913): 187–188.

"'Turkey Trot' at Newport: Society Also Dances 'The Grizzly' between Dinner Courses." *New York Times*, November 4, 1911.

Van Kleeck, Mary. "Child Labor in New York City Tenements." *Charities and the Commons* 19 (1908): 1405–1420. Rpt. in *Selected Articles on Child Labor*, ed. Bullock, 123–133.

Veblen, Thorstein. *The Theory of the Leisure Class* (1899). New York: Augustus M. Kelley, 1975.

Vice Commission of Chicago. *The Social Evil in Chicago.* Chicago: Gunthorp-Warren, 1911.

Von Drehle, David. *Triangle: The Fire That Changed America.* New York: Grove Press, 2004.

Walker, Francis A. "Restriction on Immigration." *Atlantic Monthly* 77 (1896): 822–830.

Warner, Susan. *The Wide, Wide World* (1850). New York: Feminist Press, 1987.

"Welfare Inspector at Society Dance." *New York Times*, January 4, 1912.

Wexler, Laura. *Tender Violence: Domestic Visions in an Age of U.S. Imperialism.* Chapel Hill: University of North Carolina Press, 2000.

Wilson, Elizabeth. *Bohemians: The Glamorous Outcasts.* New Brunswick, N.J.: Rutgers University Press, 2001.

Woods, Robert A., and Albert J. Kennedy. *Young Working Girls: A Summary of Evidence from Two Thousand Social Workers.* Boston and New York: Houghton Mifflin, 1913.

Wright, Richard. *Uncle Tom's Children* (1938). New York: Vintage Perennials, 2003.

Wright, Richard R. *Centennial Encyclopedia of the African Methodist Episcopal Church.* Philadelphia: Book Concern of the AME Church, 1916.

Yans-McLaughlin, Virginia, ed. *Immigration Reconsidered: History, Sociology, and Politics.* New York: Oxford University Press, 1990.

Yengoyan, Aram A. "Culture, Ideology, and World's Fairs: Colonizer and Colonized in Comparative Perspectives." In *Fair Representations*, ed. Robert W. Rydell and Nancy Guinn, 62–83. Amsterdam: Amsterdam University Press, 1994.

Zelizer, Viviana A. *Pricing the Priceless Child: The Changing Social Value of Children.* New York: Basic Books, 1985.

———. *The Social Meaning of Money.* New York: Basic Books, 1995.

Zwick, Jim. "The Campaign to End Child Labor." http://www.boondocksnet.com/labor. Accessed August 22, 2002.

Index

Adams, Myron, 80

Adams, Revels A., 121–122, 175n23–25; *The Social Dance*, 121

Addams, Jane, 4, 10, 19, 65, 77, 80, 87, 88–92, 102, 120, 135, 143: and adolescent recreation, 19, 22, 122–123, 175n22; attitudes toward consumer capitalism, 95–96, 121; attitudes toward industrialization, 91, 95; attitudes toward work, 96, 97; and idealization of immigrant parents, 89; and the Labor Museum, 77–78; and leftist politics, 163n6; reconciling immigrant parents and children, 91, 97, 174n20; *Twenty Years at Hull-House*, 4, 135; visit to London, 94

Adler, Felix, 38, 39, 163n6, 163n10

adolescence: author's own, 1, 156, 157n1, 174n18; and bourgeois conformity, 27, 87; and commercialized leisure, 24; comparisons between nineteenth- and twentieth-century ideas of, 4, 80; consistencies in representations of over time, 12, 27; and consumerism, 2; current assumptions about, 6; dangers of, 17; definitions of, 1, 4, 8; dissemination of ideas about, 132, 151; early nineteenth-century representations of, 2; emergence of, 6, 7, 13, 23, 24, 78; equated with generational conflict, 2, 4; fashion and, 2; historians of, 3; and industrialization, 7; and masculinity, 12; as mainstream phenomenon, 150, 151, 152; as "neo-atavistic," 16; as phenomenon of modernity, 80; representation in popular culture, 1; in Samoa, 145; and the sapping of "vital forces" by urban life, 18; as separate from adulthood, 6, 33, 149; as separate from childhood, 6, 33, 149; as separate from "youth," 5, 8; and sexuality, 24, 152;

as state of (partial) independence, 33; theories of emergence, 3; and urbanization, 7

Adolescence. See under Hall, G. Stanley

adolescent boys and men, 12, 18; and independence, 97, 118; middle-class, 26–27; as "overcivilized," 18; and sex segregation, 26–27

adolescent girls and women, 5, 11; and access to commercialized leisure, 11; under adult surveillance, 79; as consumers, 88, 154, 155, 166n22; and dance halls, 124–125; and dating, 98; as department store workers, 19; as earning less than their male counterparts, 116–117, 167n22, 173n16; and enthusiasm for dancing, 105, 128; and fashion, 24, 25, 70, 72, 85, 155, 174n18; and glamour, 23, 85; and heterosociality, 24; as "incorrigible," 98, 99; and independence, 97, 118; leisure activities, 24; and premarital pregnancy, 98; seeking fun, 21; and sexual freedom, 97, 98; as unmarried, 24; vulnerability of, 89; as wage-earners, 24, 99; as working-class, 12

adolescents: as an age cohort, 1, 3, 7, 9, 153, 169n8; age range of, 8; and allowances, 153, 154–155; Anglo-American, 65, 75, 78, 117, 142; and assimilation, 10, 170n15; and bohemians, 11, 27, 135; as bridge between U.S. culture and immigrant parents, 78; as children of immigrants, 5, 12, 14, 32, 78, 87; class differences among, 26, 152, 154–155; and commercialized leisure, 4, 5, 8, 10, 64; concerns about, 22; as consumers, 5, 7, 33, 64, 75, 153, 155; creating a new identity, 78, 79, 81–82, 113; as damaged by modernity, 18; and dancing, 10, 104, 113, 120;

About the Author

Sarah E. Chinn is an associate professor in the English Department of Hunter College, CUNY, and the executive director of the Center for Lesbian Gay Studies at the CUNY Graduate Center.